Women Analyze Women

Women Analyze Women

In France, England, and the United States

Elaine Hoffman Baruch and Lucienne J. Serrano

New York University Press

NEW YORK AND LONDON

Library of Congress Cataloging-in-Publication Data
Baruch, Elaine Hoffman.
Women analyze women : in France, England, and the United States /
p. cm.
Includes index.
ISBN 0–8147–1098–0 (alk. paper)
ISBN 0–8147–1170–7 pbk.
1. Women psychoanalysts—Interviews.   2. Psychoanalysis—Cross-
cultural studies.   3. Women—Psychology.   I. Serrano, Lucienne J.
II. Title.
RC440.82B37   1988   88–4581
150.19'5'088042—dc19   CIP

New York University Press books are Smyth-sewn
and printed on permanent and durable acid-free paper.

p 10 9 8 7 6 5 4 3 2 1

Book design by Ken Venezio

*To all the analysts and writers who are
restoring women's voices to culture*

Contents

Preface

There are many people we would like to thank for their help in this book. First, the analysts themselves for graciously revising material and checking our translations where possible. Holmes and Meier Publisher (30 Irving Place, N.Y., N.Y.) for granting us permission to reprint the interview with Luce Irigaray, which originally appeared in *Women Writers Talking* (1983). *Partisan Review,* in which a short form of the Julia Kristeva interview appeared under the name of E.H.B. (1984/1). Jill Duncan, librarian at the British Psychoanalytic Institute, for her helpful suggestions, and Brom Anderson, who translated the Kristeva interview.

With the exception of the Julia Kristeva interview and the Joyce McDougall interview, which was done in English, all of the interviews of the French analysts were translated by us. In our editing, we have tried to retain the quality of the speaking voice and the style of the analyst in all of the interviews, whether originally in English or French.

In the bibliography which accompanies each interview, we have listed books chronologically according to the original date of publication. In cases where an English translation was available, we listed only the reference for the English translation and not the original title.

We would like to thank our editor, Kitty Moore, at NYU Press, for her warmth and comforting presence, Despina Gimbel, our manuscript editor, for her painstaking work, and Grace Hernandez and Jitka Salaguarda for their efficiency.

We are also indebted to those who helped us contribute *our* voices to culture. E.H.B. would like to thank Dr. J. A. Mazzeo and Dr. Alice Stahl for their generous encouragement; her parents, who believed that a woman should have a career of her own; and Greg, her son and astute critic. L.J.S. would especially like to thank Professor Germaine Brée, who introduced her to psychoanalysis and feminism, and Dr. Ruth Velikovsky Sharon for her constant support.

Both authors are grateful to Brenda Newman for her understanding and the PSC-CUNY Research Foundation for helping to fund our research. We would also like to thank the NEH for its support in the past.

Elaine Hoffman Baruch
Lucienne J. Serrano

Introduction

This book grew out of our conviction that there is a new form of psychoanalysis causing a quiet revolution, an analysis that is centered on women as seen by women. This, however, does not mean that a single point of view is represented here. Rather, there are multiple subjects and multiple voices in France, England, and the United States. In traveling from one side of the Atlantic to the other, we focused our interviews on the questioning of basic principles of psychoanalytic thought with the very people who are in the process of changing that thought.

Because women's voices are multiple (and combine different registers) and because psychoanalysis has so often been enriched by different disciplines, we have often turned to psychoanalysts who are also experts in other fields. For example, one of our English psychoanalysts, Dinora Pines, was originally a dermatologist. The American analyst Muriel Dimen is also an anthropologist. The French analyst Janine Chasseguet-Smirgel was a political scientist. Several, such as Monique David-Ménard and Monique Schneider, were trained as philosophers. Here too are literary critics such as Julia Kristeva and Luce Irigaray. We have turned also to analysts in different fields whose strong interest in psychoanalysis has informed their writing, such as the cultural critic Diana Trilling and the psychologist Dorothy Dinnerstein. All of them wish to give women a voice of their own freed of male parameters.

The reader might ask why we have chosen the interview format. After all, we might have reprinted essays, asked for new ones, or written our own about the work of these germinal authors. Yet the immediacy of the interview situation in some way replicates the analytic hour in that it can bridge conscious and unconscious and make manifest what is latent. The interview is a genre that is intermediary between thinking and writing. It catches thought on the wing. Like some modernist and postmodernist literature, it makes the process of creation itself part of its content.

The term *interview* comes from the French term *entrevoir*, meaning to see, to catch a glimpse of, in the sense of both to understand and to perceive. We feel that seeing the analyst in her environment is very important. That is why we describe where the initial interview took place, which is often also the analytic space or the analyst's workplace. (These places ranged from palazzi to monastic cells.) We also sometimes describe how the analyst looks, for we feel that to ignore appearance for fear of being charged with reducing women to objects is to deny an aspect of women in their particularity as subjects. (We feel the same way about men.) We also think that the interviewers should be heard as well as the respondents, for we believe that one may indirectly influence the formation of theory by asking the appropriate questions. The interview represents both thought and voice, many voices, what Mikhail Bakhtin calls *heteroglossia,* but it does so in an informal way. Process, fluidity, reconciliation of opposites, open-endedness, uncovering, sharing such is the interview, at least as we have conducted it. We were not interested in cross-examination but rather in interpersonal discovery, what Jean Baker Miller calls the "self-in-relation." As we envisage the interview, it is in fact a new form, that of the conversational essay.

Interviews can also be part of a support system, more important to some analysts than others. Some of the more marginal and original figures in France and the United States often feel isolated, and have told us that they sometimes feel as if they are working in a vacuum. Much of their most exciting work is done in solitude, and sometimes they feel unheard by their colleagues. Though many of our analysts are internationally known, some brilliant theoreticians are not. They were excited to find that women in foreign countries are interested in their work.

Still, at the same time that the interview can be a support, it is also a challenge that may be seen as a threat. Although the analysts welcomed our questions, they said they had never thought of some of them before. They may thus be engaged in the process of formulating new theory, which may also involve self-discovery. There is no question that biography influences theory and the interview helps to disclose this connection, which is sometimes seen as too revealing. Some respondents demand the power to edit and change their words. Once said, however, the words in some sense are indelible and will affect the analyst's future thinking even if they are erased from the transcription before publication. The first interview was only the beginning of a process that often included other meetings, lengthy transcriptions, authors' additions and revisions, by way of transatlantic phone calls and correspondence, and our translating and editing.

We see these interviews as a transatlantic bridge, a way of bringing ideas from one country to another as they are being formulated. But we also hope that these interviews will be of interest to a general as well as specialized audience. The interview format is a way of democratizing theory, not through simplification but through a different mode of presentation from the usual professional paper with its heavy apparatus. Personal and intimate, the interview cuts across barriers and boundaries and desacralizes the text, in many cases allowing us to hear the speaking voice of the analyst.

Happy as we are with the people represented here, unfortunately we were not able to see everyone we wanted to. Sometimes the analyst's own life story took her away: there were children to care for, conferences to attend, book deadlines to meet, the uncertain situation of old bodies if not minds, opposition to interviews themselves—or to the "feminist" scene. Try as we could, we were not able to convince some that we were not writing the radical feminist bible. More often than not, however, we met with kindness and generosity.

We may not have wanted to cross-examine the analysts, but during the preinterview sessions, we read their works as if we were about to take examinations ourselves. From early morning to night, we sat in the Bibliothèque Nationale, our refuge for more reasons than one. It is the only place in France, seemingly, where one must smoke outside. (We had been smoked out of a psychoanalytic conference in the elegant Trocadero section where we very much wanted to remain; brilliant analyst Monique Schneider was surrounded by so many fumes that she looked like Joan of Arc at the stake, a fitting image, considering her controversial position.) At the Bibliothèque we surrendered our identity cards at the narrow entranceway in exchange for a numbered plaque. We then proceeded with our book slips to the control desk, a high and forbidding fortress, where we surrendered our plaque with our slips. Then we went stealthily to our numbered and unchangeable seats, where we were surrounded by rows of French and foreign researchers—many of them Americans, all with piles of books in the close rows. In contrast to the confinement of our narrow spaces was the grandeur of the murals on the walls and ceilings in the two huge reading rooms, one with a large dome.

In some ways, the contrast here at the BN between narrow work space and visual grandeur is similar to that of New York's Forty-second Street Library (where we did some of our work on the American analysts), with its magnificent windows, enormous ceilings, and crowded desks. But since the Forty-second Street is a library of equality where all may enter, unlike the BN where one pays and is subject to screening, one finds the homeless, the onanists, the newspaper flippers, the sleepers in danger of being awakened abruptly by a guard, as well as the scholars who try to create and hide in a little corner of their own.

Like the BN, the British Museum is a beautiful enclave of elitism. And the British Psychoanalytic, a model of decorum and peace, is far lovelier in its Georgian house than the New York Psychoanalytic, for example. Freud's home in the London suburb of Hampstead, where he came for asylum with Anna Freud before the war, was opened in the summer of 1986 as a museum and library for scholars. His psychoanalytic couch from Vienna is here, a massive Victorian piece with thick pillows and lavish rugs on it. One can hardly control oneself from sinking into it. It is an invitation to fantasy, unlike some of the spare, skinny, monochrome Spartan cots that we see in many psychoanalytic offices today.

SOME NATIONAL DIFFERENCES

It is Jacques Lacan, with his emphasis on the phallus and the Oedipal, who has been the central influence in France, even for those who attack him. In contrast, it is Melanie Klein, with her emphasis on the pre-Oedipal and object relations, who is central in England. Her follower D. W. Winnicott has also been remarkably influential in his theory of the good-enough mother. In the United States, Freud is still the central figure in the major psychoanalytic circles, but Kohut, Kernberg, and Spotnitz, with their emphasis on the pre-Oedipal and narcissism, are recognized in court also, although some women thinkers find them too concerned with fragmentation and splitting. Whereas object-relations analysts on both sides of the Atlantic are optimistic about people achieving both a sense of self and a gratifying relationship, Lacan and his followers speak of a decentered self and a state of desire.

We might raise the question why Lacan in his rereading of Freud has had such great appeal for psychoanalysts in France and for literary critics here. His immense culture and knowledge of literature, linguistics, mathematics, and philosophy made him a figure of great intellectual charisma. But why, we might add, has he appealed to women when his analysis is so rigorously phallocentric? Perhaps it is because he made a distinction between the symbolic phallus, which represents power, and the factual penis. Nobody has the phallus, according to Lacan. (The problem as we see it, however, is that since the phallus as metaphor is related to the penis, it privileges that organ.)

Though it sometimes turns to Klein and Winnicott, in general, French analysis does not look to American psychoanalysis for inspiration. However, American analysts of the more subversive variety and even more so American literary critics are looking across the ocean to what they often see as their intellectual mothers and fathers. Nonetheless, Americans still think of themselves as pioneers and engage in new ideas without a conscious sense of rebellion. Though there are cultural bonds, there are important differences in psychoanalysis that we witnessed on both sides of the Atlantic in: (1) the representations of the pre-Oedipal mother, (2) perspectives on gender and sexual difference, (3) attitudes toward and conceptions of feminism, (4) the problematics of language, (5) phallic symbolism and its alternatives.

In our interviews, we found ourselves facing a central difference between the highly theoretical "avant garde" psychoanalysts in France and the more pragmatic, empirical English ones, known for their clinical expertise. We call "avant garde" that brilliant and revolutionary group, most of them women, all of them writers, such as Luce Irigaray, Julia Kristeva, and Monique Schneider, all of them influenced by Jacques Lacan, whether in support or rebellion against him, all having a grounding in literature and philosophy. Juliet Mitchell has similarities with this group even though she is based in England and is considered a member of the Independent School there. Of the other English analysts represented here, the great Kleinian is Hanna Segal. Dinora Pines belongs to the B group, the Anna Freudians, and Enid Balint to the Independents.

Equally striking in different ways are our other French analysts: Janine Chasseguet-Smirgel (a pronounced anti-Lacanian) and Joyce McDougall (who was originally in training with Anna Freud) are well known in this country. Of the others, Monique David-Ménard, Dominique Guyomard, Catherine Millot, and Françoise Petitot range from moderate to extreme Lacanians.

The American psychoanalysts we interviewed range from Karen Horney's daughter Marianne Eckardt, who was much influenced by the interpersonal school, to the feminist psychoanalysts Donna Bassin, Jessica Benjamin, and Muriel Dimen, who are in the forefront of creating new theory, as indeed has been psychologist Dorothy Dinnerstein, author of the highly influential *Mermaid and the Minotaur,* an examination of our destructive gender arrangements.

THE PRE-OEDIPAL MOTHER: POWER AND GENDER

Both Anglo-American object-relations analysts and the French theorists emphasize the pre-Oedipal mother (neglected by Freud and by Lacan also). However, we are struck by the attention to the so-called archaic, dangerous mother, that overwhelming abyss that threatens us in some (although not all) of the French analysts, a concept that goes far beyond Melanie Klein's concept of the good and bad mother in its possibilities for terror. For too many feminists, this will sound uncomfortably close to the devouring female creatures so familiar to us in Western mythology, such as Medusa and the Furies. The American analysts we interviewed— and even the English—see the mother in much more realistic terms.

One of our objectives was to question whether the decoding of traditional psychoanalysis in France through a new emphasis on the pre-Oedipal mother doesn't lead us in fact to a neomisogyny, in which the new subtext confirms the old misogynous text. One of our central questions to the analysts was how they work their way through this apparent confirmation of the patriarchy to a further decoding. Janine Chasseguet-Smirgel has pointed out that though myth may negate reality, it often expresses desire, something we cannot deny, however much we might wish to. (Merely recognizing it, however, may help change behavior, we feel.) Monique Schneider speaks of the multiple representations of the mother in both the conscious and the unconscious. She denounces the reductionism of the official views of culture and advocates a greater place for all the facets of the repressed.

While object-relations theorists in this country, such as Nancy Chodorow in her highly influential book *The Reproduction of Mothering*, pasteurize the unconscious and speak of the need for individuation in reasonable terms as the cause for both the little girl and the little boy's turning away from the mother to the father, some French theorists (such as Chasseguet-Smirgel, Irigaray, Kristeva, and Schneider) have a much more dramatic account of sexual difference. In their scenario, the father symbolizes all legitimate power while the mother represents either an engulfing abyss or a soft, smooth, visceral paradise.

While object-relations theorists imply that changing social structure would redistribute the allocation of power between the sexes, many of the French feel that the elimination of gender differences would lead to psychosis. As Muriel Dimen points out, this may be because the French conflate self/other differences, which everyone agrees must be recognized in order not to fall into psychosis, with gender differences. It may be also that since the French term for gender and genre (distinct form) is the same, they are more likely to recognize and to perpetuate differences. In addition, the French have a long tradition of intellectual women in spite of or perhaps because of strong gender differentiation. No matter how brilliant the woman, she was not seen as a threat, provided she had charm and elegance. American women do not have such a history of *vive la différence*. On the whole, the Americans we interviewed were much more optimistic about changing gender roles. The pioneer mentality is still alive and well on the Eastern seaboard, and no doubt on the Western one as well.

FEMINISM AND PSYCHOANALYSIS

But despite their attention to women's psychological status, their denouncing of women's reification through male domination, and their wanting to give women the position of subjects, not all of the analysts we interviewed call themselves feminists. We were surprised at the level of negation, the opposition to the term, especially in Europe, but to some extent here also.

For some writers, like Luce Irigaray in France, feminism is simply another "ism," a term modeled on "the other great words of the culture that oppress us." For others, the word carries an antimale connotation, even a hatred of men, and always a rejection of them to which they object. Some analysts, such as Enid Balint in England, worry about the capacity of feminism to oppress men. A view less directed toward men, such as that of Diana Trilling in this country, holds that feminism is sometimes objectionable because it is an ideology and like all ideology sacrifices truth to a cause. Even some who are comfortable with the term here understand the opposition, claiming that society has co-opted some of the principles of feminism and has therefore deradicalized it. Interestingly enough, there are those who reject the term, such as Marianne Eckardt in this country, whom we would classify as having affinities with radical feminists in that they are open to all kinds of new parenting and family arrangements.

It may be that the term *feminism* is both too limited and too large a term. Certainly it arouses all kinds of passions, both negative and positive. However, for want of a more exact word, we find ourselves using it as a kind of shorthand. To Freud's question, "What do women want?"—which has perhaps earned him more abuse than any of his formulations except that of penis envy—the analysts here might answer: "an equal place in culture," something that goes well beyond the principle of equal pay for equal work. This is, to us, certainly a type of feminism.

There are, of course, many forms of feminism, and they must be distinguished. We are here concerned with three major directions and their connections with psychoanalysis. Although terms vary, these are sometimes referred to as liberal, cultural, and metaphysical feminism. Simone de Beauvoir may be called the chief exemplar of liberal feminism, which holds that the male view of the world is the human view and that women should subscribe to it as much as possible. Though Beauvoir ostensibly rejected psychoanalysis, this form of feminism perpetuates the binary system supported by traditional analysis, which holds that the essential difference is the sexual one. Traditional analysis gives primacy to the Oedipal stage, the moment at which sexual difference is recognized by the little girl and boy, and so, seemingly, does liberal feminism. For in privileging the male side of a binary system, liberal feminists are not giving a place to an essential dimension of the human being, which may be called the archaic, primitive, preverbal, pre-Oedipal, and which relates to a period in which sexual difference is not recognized by the infant. This very terminology, however, is drawn from traditional psycho-analysis, and is sexist, for it privileges a later phallic stage of development and therefore falsifies and distorts, if it doesn't ignore the very early human experience. (One problem faced by any new theory or movement is how to work with or supplant a terminology that has become entrenched.) In this early period, the first distinction made is that between self and other (boundaries here are still indistinct). This will yield to the recognition of a more clear-cut difference, that between the sexes, a differentiation that inherits the same feelings of necessity and passion with which we try to separate and individuate.

It is not just traditional analysis and liberal feminism that are imprisoning us in the dualism of sexual difference. The so-called cultural feminists, with their transvaluation of women's traditional feelings and activities, are perpetuating the binary system also, this time by dwelling on the superiority of women. This group prizes the traditionally stereotyped feminine virtues of feeling and caring over the "masculine" ones of logical thinking and aggression. Whatever one may think of its view of the sexes, this group may be producing a necessary corrective to "phallic" language, in its attempt to create an *écriture féminine,* a feminine writing from the body, about which we will say more later.

There is yet a third major form of feminism that is exerting an important influence, one that seeks to overcome dualism altogether. It is a decoding system that wants to overthrow the patriarchal order and eliminate the hierarchical opposition between male and female. It desires a fusion or at least a continuum between such terms as mind and body, feeling and thought, subject and object, culture and nature. The term *metaphysical* perhaps captures the essence of this form of feminism, if we understand metaphysical to refer to the attempt to fuse thought and feeling, passion and reason, in which the metaphysical poets, for example, John Donne, engaged.

What is needed and what we think we have the beginnings of here is an analysis that puts into question the androcentric views of culture and women, an analysis that is free of oppression of women *and* men, that does not privilege the body parts of either sex, that sees the mother as a creature of reality who *helps* the child to individuate, and that restores the male to his pre-Oedipal inheritance. Possibly *feminist psychoanalysis* in the third sense in which we have used the term *feminism* is a good interim term. Still we must point out again that many of the analysts in this book do not wish to be associated with the term *feminism* at all, a position that is itself worthy of analysis. Opposition to feminism may reveal a fear of overthrowing the father or of rebelling against the traditional mother, a fear of submerging the individual in the group or of going against the state and losing its protection. Opposition may also reveal a clarity of thought, a desire to be free of entangling allegiances or dominating structures.

Nonetheless, some of our contributors are happy to be called psychoanalytic feminists, if not feminist psychoanalysts, which brings us to the question of why, after its early attacks on Freud for his theories of penis envy, female narcissism, passivity, and women's deficient superego, feminism is turning increasingly to psychoanalysis, even of the traditional variety, to explain the oppression of women.

Theories of the social construction of reality, though very popular at first, were found to be insufficient to explain why even with increased opportunities in the public world, women were not gaining equality. Feminism has come to the realization that the oppression of women does not lie solely in the institutions of the society, the social and economic structure. It now recognizes that something hidden fuels this structure, the unseen and often unspoken but powerful feelings of the unconscious, the entire apparatus of what is called the symbolic order, that is, the language, values, myths, images, and stereotypes that influence and are influenced by our psychological life.

Let us take the treatment of stereotypes as an example of the new thinking. Feminists formerly denounced stereotypes because they were seen to victimize women on a political level. However, it is now recognized that their formation on the psychological level cannot be ignored. A stereotype is an emotional not a rational response to a problem that endangers the individual. For example, the stereotype that women are passive is less a logical analysis than a wish fulfillment, which installs men in a dominant position. Stereotypes are hard to change because they support emotional needs. We might ask whether women have supported these stereotypes. And the answer surprisingly is yes, not simply because the culture conditions them to do so, but because we are all, women and men, unconsciously overwhelmed by the omnipotent, pre-Oedipal mother, still trying to separate from her and afraid of eliminating the boundaries between self and other (however much we may desire fusion at some moments).

What psychoanalysis, particularly of the revisionist type, reveals, is that the reasons for women's inferior position are overdetermined. The mother in the pre-Oedipal or preverbal period is a highly ambiguous figure. The child sees her as either the magical nurturer or as the denying witch. Both seem omnipotent in the child's perception. Therefore a split into the good and the bad mother will occur, according to Melanie Klein. We wonder if this early cleavage between the idealized and denigrated mother may have contributed not only to the splitting of the woman into goddess and whore but also to our entire binary system. This archaic dichotomy, which is not yet sexually differentiated, could be the cradle of all later hierarchical oppositions, including those between the sexes.

What happens to the unlimited power that the primitive mother is invested with? It will be transmitted to a highly idealized father. In the case of the absent father, it may become impossible for the child to separate from a very ambiguous mother who is seen as bringing death at the same time that she brings life.

In a patriarchal society, the child will also become aware of the status of the mother as a dependent, subordinate being, and this debased representation of her may contribute to the child's feeling unmothered. This debasement may also make the child believe that women are unfit for cultural achievements.

Traditional psychoanalysis is monist. It accounts for the behavior of only one sex, but even there it is deficient, for it has not looked sufficiently at why men are afraid of women. Why is it that traditional psychoanalysis has not applied the principles of psychoanalytic thought to itself? Why has it so seldom been suggested by establishment analysts that penis envy can be a projection or a reaction formation, a denial of womb envy?

The new psychoanalysis reveals that men's denigration of women is both a matter of cognition, learned prejudice, and a response to the biological: a defensive reaction to the recognition of women's superiority in the reproductive sphere and their capacity for sexual pleasure, what Lacan called supplementary *jouissance*. In the face of women's insatiable sexual demands, men have fears about their problematic erection. Furthermore, like Oedipus (and this *is* recognized by traditional analysis), they fear being united with the mother though they unconsciously desire it.

The new psychoanalysis sees women's anatomy not as a wound to be sutured, as Monique Schneider puts it, a lack, but rather as an opening. In deconstructing the old psychoanalysis, the new one often reverses its terms. For example, we would say that the baby is less a substitute for a phallus than that the phallus is a substitute for a baby.

TRADITIONAL PSYCHOANALYSIS AND HER/STORY

Despite the limitations of traditional psychoanalysis—its insistence on women's penis envy with no parallel for men and on the baby as a substitute phallus—the history of psychoanalysis has in some sense been a story of women, a her/story, even if told from the male point of view. The earliest case studies, of course, were of women.

Unlike history, which has excluded women almost entirely from its pages until recently, psychoanalysis has always dealt with inner space, with interiorization, with what has been traditionally associated with women. In giving a place to desire, traditional psychoanalysis has helped to create a completely different view of history, allowing a return of the repressed. A large part of what was repressed is her/story. In addition, psychoanalysis allowed women the voice they never had in history, even if the language was in some cases dictated by the male and the voice limited to the body, as was the case with hysteria.

Though traditional psychoanalysis has given a place to the unseen, the unspoken, the repressed, and has seemingly dethroned the scopic economy—the visual—problems remain. We might object that it continues to privilege the visual in its emphasis on the penis. We might further ask, Why, if it privileges the visual, does it ignore the breasts and the pregnant belly? Because, of course, it is phallocentric. Furthermore, there is no female mythological figure who stands in the center of Freud's work the way that Oedipus does. Women in Freud's psychology, in general, are at best players in the wings. It is only the male who is center stage. (Freud would admit this readily, claiming that he left it to poets and writers to tell us more about women. It was the feminists of the 1970s who insisted on ignoring his disclaimer.)

But the matricide of traditional psychoanalysis may not be due to patriarchal culture alone. Each little girl in her individual development dethrones the mother and therefore herself. Only in this way can she separate from the mother and turn to the father. At least, such has been his/story, the story of the female Oedipal stage in traditional psychoanalysis. We think that there is another story that has barely been told, that of Jocasta and her daughter Antigone, to say nothing of the sphinx.

In the restoration of woman's her/story that is taking place in the new psychoanalysis, it is prehistory or the preverbal that is crucial. It is in the early pre-her/story (his/story) that our apprenticeship for life begins. Our membership in the guild of emotions and feelings starts in the pre-Oedipal (even in the prenatal, as Schneider says). It is the male child who will not be able to retain his membership in this union, who will be thrown out because of the signifier of the phallus. This is one form of male castration, to be cut off from the mother, the primary caretaker.

Contrary to Freud, who (in Ernest Jones's words) felt that the little girl was an *homme manqué,* what current revisionary theory holds is that the little boy is in fact a little woman, what we might call *une femme manquée,* who, in patriarchy at least, must divorce himself from the first couple of mother/child to become a man. The big question, perhaps, is not what does a woman want, but what does a man want? In traditional psychoanalysis, what he wants is the phallus. In the new psychoanalysis, the answer might be, to be a woman.

From Persephone, the voiceless mythological character, to Freud's Dora, the hysteric, women's her/story has been the story of a displacement of women's speech and power. Although women were excluded from the symbolic, they were allowed a body language, that of hysteria. Not permitted to communicate their sexual desire verbally in Victorian society, women managed to speak through the body, not in a direct expression of desire but in re-placements of it. But the audience for the hysteric, for this burlesque of the psyche, was men only, the doctors within the walls of La Salpétrière, the famous Paris hospital, where Freud attended Charcot's case presentations.

Hysteria represents lack, not anatomical lack as traditional psychoanalysis would have it, but the deprivation of subject status within the symbolic order. Hysteria is a silent affront against the patriarchy, in which women's bodies lived out the commandments of the culture: "Thou shalt not see, thou shalt not hear, thou shalt not walk, thou shalt not speak." One strength of traditional psychoanalysis was that it was able to decipher the language of the hysteric, but it still did not allow her story to be told directly. It is left to the new psychoanalysis to allow woman to express herself as subject of desire.

PHALLIC LANGUAGE AND *ECRITURE FEMININE*

Hysteria is a phallic representation for women. Ordinary language represents a phallic and therefore amputated language for men—and women. The language of the dominant discourse becomes a means of separating from the womb and the mother. Language is the tool that allows men to think they are giving up the preverbal. But in fact masculine domination through language represents the return of the repressed in a verbal masquerade, the return of the omnipotent infant in the adult. Male domination is not exclusively verbal, however; it includes the domination of the woman's body, which masks a return to the importance of the baby's body in the pre-Oedipal, when the baby perceives the mother's body as his. One might say that male domination is an attempt to return to the early space of childhood from which the male child is expelled. He then tries to recreate in the external world the feelings of grandiloquence that he had as a child by creating external institutions from which he excludes women. The woman can enter that public space only through the intermediary of the male. He becomes her umbilical cord to the outside world.

With the new child-rearing practices, however, in which fathers participate strongly, it may not be necessary to separate from the mother so forcibly. This will no doubt change male and female psychology and the configuration of the Oedipal, as well as language itself.

We are not there yet, however, and our very terminology militates against equality—for example, the use of the term *Oedipal* for the central drama of existence, when, as Donna Bassin indicates, there are many dramas.

At the moment of separation, by allowing an entrance into a shared world of representation and symbols, phallic, Oedipal language unifies, but mainly it aids separation by allowing discriminations to be made. Language, which individuates, separates, categorizes, defines, describes, and cuts the umbilical cord, is an intellectual and phallic production (as opposed to a maternal reproduction). One leaves the inchoate archaic, pre-Oedipal world, with its lack of boundaries between oneself and the world, and enters into a world of limits, definitions, and control.

But in fact this production is not simply phallic, although it appears to be. There is a whole aspect of language that is not sayable, that is more related to feeling, to the mystery of the body, to the pre-Oedipal, as Kristeva points out. It is as if official language has repressed this archaic element; the question is, What in the body does not pass into language, and how might it do so? In depriving women of their own voice, men are deprived of their own inner voice also. Their focus in language is on control and mastery.

Some women writers in France have been trying to break

through the verbal masquerade, to reach the language of the pre-Oedipal directly (at least as it applies to women). In doing so, they have advocated an *écriture féminine,* which has led to the unspoken and named it. It expresses what previously was inexpressible. It has given back her voice to Kore/Persephone. *Ecriture féminine* gives a large place to the body, to blood and milk, pleasure, cycles. Freud said that he learned everything that he knew from literature. Will the new psychoanalysis learn from literature again, this time from *écriture féminine?* And will the new psychoanalysis be more fundamental than the traditional Oedipal one in exploring what might be called the pre-Oedipal Jocasta complex, our relation to the early mother?

Or will *écriture féminine* close doors for women? French sociologist Christine Delphy, a representative of liberal feminism, feels that *écriture féminine* is simply another cage of femininity, a way of getting women back into the closet. The difference, however, between this "cage" and the narrow and locked cage of patriarchy is that the early one was structured by men, whereas this "cage" is without walls, varied, bottomless, multidimensional, ultimately unknown and unknowable.

It used to be assumed that certain experiences of the body could not pass into language. D. H. Lawrence tried to give expression to the sense of mastery and mystery in male *jouissance* (roughly but not exclusively orgasm). *Ecriture féminine* is trying to reproduce female *jouissance* in language, with *jouissance* meaning not merely the sexual.

It may be that American women's fear of essentialism, of biological determinism, has kept them from analyzing the female body in all of its cycles in new ways. But it is the experiences of menstruation, loss of virginity, sexuality, pregnancy, childbirth, lactation, and menopause that mark a woman's body in ways that will lead to her psychic growth or to physical pain, as Dinora Pines has indicated in some of her work. It is this journey that has been relatively ignored, even in the new psychoanalysis, perhaps because women, American women at least, have been so wary of sexual difference as the mark of subordination. But some, such as Bassin and Benjamin, are examining the relation of the body to psychology in new ways. Before we can get to a new symbolism, however, it seems to us necessary to examine why the old is so entrenched. Why does psychoanalysis remain so phallocentric?

THE SYMBOLISM OF THE PHALLUS

The phallus, as Joyce McDougall expresses it, is primarily an erect, triumphant symbol for the penis, what we might call a makeup for men, which makes them the creator, owner, and legislator of the world. This power is not a given. It has to be recognized like paternity. Like phallic language, the phallus (or glorified penis) allows the male to separate from the mother and thereby to enter the public world as colonizer of culture.

The phallus is also the representation of the suppression of the polymorphous expression of sexuality. Emphasis on the phallus ensures that reproduction will take place.

If we no longer needed erection for reproduction, would it disappear? Is man in danger of nonerection? Is it because erection has always been so fragile that the phallus is so valorized? This fragility, as St. Augustine pointed out, was one of the conse-quences of the Fall—one of Adam's punishments and Eve's too, we might add.

However, male and female pleasures are different. In contrast to Freud, who spoke of the need for women to shift from clitoral to vaginal orgasm, Lacan wrote of women's "supplementary" *jouissance,* which involves more of the body and which surpasses phallic *jouissance.* Man is fixated on the Oedipal, on the genital, this to the detriment of other parts of the body. (Traditional psychoanalysis never speaks of breasts with an *s.* It speaks only of "the breast," making of it a phallic representation.) The man in the danger of love must avoid being seduced in order to remain the master, must avoid the lure of the sirens. Men want to have mastery, to impose boundaries and extend control in sex, rather than to abandon themselves totally to pleasure. Why do men want power over women? One reason is that this is the way they can recreate the earliest relationship with the omnipotent mother, this time with the positions reversed. It may be that in the traditional relationship of the sexes, women find men's loss of mastery and abandonment to pleasure threatening also. In that role, the man is no longer the structuring, powerful phallic father but rather the vulnerable baby/penis.

In its grandeur, the penis is like the phallus, the transitional object that helps the penis become the landlord of the world. In its vulnerability, it is a pitiful instrument; little, weak, fragile, ineffectual, unpredictable, unreliable, passive, impotent. It has all the traits that men have stereotypically attributed to women. The impossible male dream and perhaps women's as well is the phallusization (fallacy-zation) of the penis.

Yet we all, female as well as male, want the phallus, for in the symbolic patriarchal order, it is the representation of desire. Why this monist configuration of the phallus in a humanity that is bisexual? Probably because of the way that our psychology is now constructed, there is Oedipal fixation on the phallus. Upon recognizing the difference between the sexes, the little boy fantasizes a huge, erect penis/phallus that could satisfy his mother. The phallus is also essential in order to close the mother's womb. Otherwise, he is in danger of reentering it. (Of course, he has an unconscious desire to do that also.) But why have women adopted the phallus and not created their own symbol? In the pre-Oedipal or in the retroactive construct of it, the little girl, like the little boy, sees the omnipotent mother as phallic. But once she recognizes sexual difference, the little girl realizes that the mother is deprived of the male organ. In her need to separate from the mother, she cannot glorify her own organ because that would lead her back to the mother. Besides, patriarchy sees her organ as debased. (Most of the psychoanalysts represented here, unlike traditional psychoanalysts, believe that the little girl is aware of her vagina.) What is more, in idealizing the father, women have tried to make themselves the phallus (an image of perfection) that he is looking for. The best representatives of the phallus in this sense are the movie star, the model, and finally the unattainble madonna. What about the wife and the whore? Are they the phallus? Probably not, since they are obtainable, and men are condemned forever to phallus envy. In order for the phallus to remain the phallus, it must belong to the realm of desire and signify lack.

THE MOTHER'S BODY, TECHNOLOGY, AND PSYCHOLOGICAL BIRTH

One of the questions that we asked some analysts is whether there could be an alternative to the symbol of the phallus. Juliet Mitchell answered that the metaphor of the phallus has a long history that could not be arbitrarily supplanted. However, Monique Wittig, the French writer, in her utopia *Les Guérillères,* and Judy Chicago, the American artist, in *The Dinner Party,* have given rich and convincing expression to the alternative symbolism of the circle, which encompasses the vulva, the vagina, and the womb. Woman, we would say, contains less a dark continent than a golden cunt/continent. The womb is the utopian place par excellence, or has been. What will happen if prenatal experience is destroyed as a result of the new reproductive technology is another question we asked some of our analysts.

It is something of an irony that although psychoanalysis has barely begun to discuss the experience of motherhood from the mother's point of view—Helene Deutsch is a major exception—the experience of pregnancy and birth is now in the process of being taken away from women, through the new technology. Although this technology of in vitro fertilization and implantation is ostensibly being employed for problems of infertility, there is no question that it represents the beginning of a movement toward mechanizing the body completely. Whereas formerly they were reified as sex objects, women are now utilized for their reproductive parts, which are the commodities, the products of largely male technicians. The Subject is now the Doctor/Technologist. The desire of the male scientist to control and replace the reproductive functions of women with devices of his own is perhaps partial proof that the answer to the question "What do men want?" is to be a woman. The desire is also to be God, to hold the power of creation in one's hands or at least in a test tube, if one does not have a womb.

From the point of view of the child, matters are also increasingly complicated. Formerly, it was assumed that one would have a mother of one's own, with all the attendant emotions and prohibitions of the pre-Oedipal and Oedipal periods. Now one cannot be sure of this. A child may now have three mothers—the genetic, who provides the ova, the gestational, who provides the uterine environment and who may be different from the genetic mother, and the nurturing mother, who provides the care. What we are beginning to have is a specialization of the functions of motherhood, a division of labor, a separation of the process from the product of creation. Will there be a similar split in the emotions of the child? Men, whose primary form of thinking, the binary, involves separation and division, are invading women's inner space and turning it into a marketplace. Motherhood now has a price attached to it. It is part of the consumer society.

What was formerly the domain of women and of one woman at a time is now becoming a battlefield for competing interests. Throughout history, woman's body has been compared to nature, to land. This is misogynistic only if she is allowed to be nothing else. (That is what is wrong with the dark continent image.) War involves an appropriation of land. Similarly, the new reproductive technology may be seen as a hostile act—an appropriation of space to which outsiders have no right.

If reproduction is taken out of the body entirely, which seems to be the direction of the new technology, what will be the consequences? If we change the mother/child bond, what else will change? What effect would eliminating gestation have on our emotional life? Certainly the fear and envy of women would diminish. But what would happen to sexual desire? Would it disappear or decrease? The answer to this question depends on whether desire is inherited, on how much desire relates to prenatal experience and how much to early childhood experience with the mother or caretaker. If sexual desire is simply nature's (or culture's) way of getting us to reproduce, one would expect that under these new conditions, it would eventually disappear. But if sexual desire also arose (in the evolutionary scheme) for purposes of bonding, for caring for the young, it may persist, for the need for early nurturance would remain even if Huxley's vision of test-tube babies becomes a reality. However, we must grant that not only couples may care for children. Many arrangements are possible, as we already see. As Julia Kristeva says, sexual desire depends not only on lack and difference, but also on similarity, and the experience of similarity or sameness relates back to the early experience of fusion with the mother, which will not disappear even if we are no longer of woman born, and even if the one doing the mothering is a man.

The question of how the relation to the mother's body affects artistic, intellectual, and scientific activity is one that we sometimes asked our analysts. We did not always get an answer. If creativity is in part an attempt to recover the sense of fusion and omnipotence of the infant, why have women so often been deprived of the creative process? Perhaps because, as Winnicott says, it is also the result of separation. And if, as Melanie Klein claims, there is a desire to make reparations to the mother's body through the creation of art and religion, then the male child would feel more of a need for these endeavors later than the little girl who has a closer identification with the mother. The main reason that has been given for men's hitherto greater artistic creativity is that it is a sublimation and substitution for the making of babies. Perhaps, but there has also been a cultural reason: the debasement of women. The question should be not why have women not contributed more to culture—this question is further complicated by the fact that women's contributions have often been hidden or ignored—but rather why, despite all the barbed wire that society has set up against them, they have contributed so much? Now that women are allowed greater access to creativity in the public world, might it be that they will be deprived of their biological creativity—in a kind of technological revenge by men in their attempt to retain dominance?

It may be that radical feminists laying claim to their right to be mothers—a right they only recently disclaimed—joining in an unholy alliance with the ultraconservatives and the Vatican, will keep us from reproduction ex utero. But surrogacy—a dreadful word, since the "surrogate" is not a substitute at all but a real mother—is probably here to stay, at least in this country if not in England, where the Warnock Committee commissioned by the Queen has recommended making it a criminal offense. The analysts we questioned on the consequences of surrogacy feel that much depends on the psychology of the surrogate. Some surrogates, they claim, enjoy pregnancy, in and of itself; some want to make reparations, perhaps for a child they gave up earlier in their lives. But while some women feel good about what they see as an altruistic act, others suffer depression after giving up the child. Françoise Petitot in 1985 saw surrogacy primarily as another means of control over women. In 1987, she expressed horror at the decision in the Baby M case, for it is now the courts seemingly that will decide on who or, even more chillingly, what makes a good mother.* The result is that the woman is totally at the mercy of the patriarchal system. Neither feminism nor the new psychoanalysis seems to have made any inroads here. We do not know yet what the larger psychological implications of "surrogacy" will be for the mothers or the child (although we have some inkling from adoption cases). And when we do know, no matter how negative they may turn out to be, it may be too late to do anything about them.**

There are many ways of being born, as men have been quick to tell us in their mythology. Birth from out the womb is only one of them. There are psychological as well as biological births. Among them is what Margaret Mahler calls separation-individuation: the process whereby the child tries to separate from the mother. Then, there is the Oedipal stage: upon recognizing sexual difference, the child further separates from the mother.

In the *Bildungsroman,* the male hero must break away from his parents, particularly the mother, in order to achieve autonomy. He must be born from himself. A different story is played out in the female version, where the heroine seeks a man to be the agent of her development. Literature has often described the feminine quest for the self through the male tutor/lover and the failure of

---

*Mary Beth Whitehead, the mother of Baby M, had contracted for surrogacy but then did not want to relinquish the child. She was forced to do so by the courts on the grounds that the biological father, William Stern, would be a better parent.
**It is of some interest that although Baruch and D'Adamo formerly saw surrogacy (despite its potential for exploitation of poor women) from a biological point of view as a way of enlarging women's options, from a psychoanalytic perspective, it seems more like a violation of their inner space. (See "Resetting the Biological Clock: Women and the New Reproductive Technologies," *Dissent* (Summer 1985): 273–76.

this quest to live vicariously, as in *Madame Bovary, Middlemarch,* and *Portrait of a Lady.*★

Literature is often a profound mirror of psychic reality. Formerly, the little girl, the adolescent girl, and the woman all had to turn to the father or his representatives in order to be women separate from the mother. Father, instructor, seducer, were one in their internal fantasy. It is now the analyst (often the woman analyst) who has become the mother/mentor, who allows the daughter to separate and individuate. Although it is true that the male analyst can and often does perform this function of mentoring also, the father has largely been replaced. Many of the analysts we interviewed say that most of their patients are women and that these women specifically wanted women analysts in their quest for the Mother. Why are so many women looking for emotional and psychological rebirth from a mother? Because women want to enter and define culture directly, not through the intermediary of a male surrogate. We believe that the new psychoanalysis presented in this book will further that quest.

★See E. Baruch. "The Feminine *Bildungsroman:* Education through Marriage." *The Massachusetts Review* (Summer 1981): pp. 335–57.

France

Dominique Guyomard holds a licence de lettres and a diplôme de psychologie. Her psychoanalytic training was under the supervision of Octave Mannoni and Françoise Dolto. In addition to working with adults, she is a child analyst, who has had extensive experience with psychotics.

SELECTED BIBLIOGRAPHY

"A propos de Oedipe-roi selon Freud." *Revue des Psychanalystes* (March 1982).
"Questions sur l'espace et le transfert dans une cure psychanalytique." *Revue de Psychiatrie Française* (April 1984).
"Filiation et engendrement." *Topique* (May 1985).

ONE

Dominique Guyomard

Paris, Summer 1985

Dominique Guyomard lives and works in an apartment in a nineteenth-century bourgeois quarter near the Eglise Russe de Paris. As with most Parisian apartment houses, a code is required to enter. After we pressed the buttons, we opened the door and found ourselves in a foyer with stained glass windows. We then proceeded to her office—a delightful space full of light and color. The white leather couch in the analytic office, tan leather chairs, blue lamp and a chair of the same hue, the large ceramic stove standing in one corner, the teak bookcases that went from floor to ceiling—all had a lightness to them. Charm and grace abounded. Nothing somber here in either the decor or the analyst, who with so much tact and kindness reminded us that Paris was for beauty and enjoyment, not just for work.

What led you to become an analyst?

What led me to become an analyst is a history of women: maternal grandmother, paternal grandmother, mother. In my paternal grandmother there was a problem of insanity, to which I as a child could not respond. There was no access to her through speech. What she said made no sense and yet it made a great deal of sense. I felt the need for reparations later.

I am primarily a child analyst. I also see adults who remain in large part children. What interests me most in dealing with children is the therapeutic cure, not only in relation to them but in relation to their parents—the unconscious desire for reparations, which may concern guilt, debt, redemption, narcissism. There are very different levels of reparation with regard to all these. During analysis we realize that our relations with our family change. We resign ourselves to the fact that the people don't change, but we are now able to say certain things because we change, because we separate from them.

Where do you place yourself in the psychoanalytic movement?

I was part of the Ecole Freudienne that Lacan founded and dissolved. After that I didn't feel like being part of an institute. (What an institute is is a difficult question.) With Maud Mannoni, her husband, and Patrick Guyomard as founders, we started the CRFP, the Center for Psychoanalytic Research and Training. Maud and Octave Mannoni are older, experienced analysts who don't have a total allegiance to Lacan, but rather follow a freer direction.

Above all, the Lacanians have an intense need for pure theory and are not concerned with the clinical aspects, with the cure. I consider psychoanalysis a reaching out and a return which is nourished by interaction with patients. There is in the Lacanian group an intransigence. The time and respect owed to the patient, the taking into account of his speech, is dismissed. I don't renounce Lacan. He gave us a remarkably exciting reading of Freud.

But there was a transference to Lacan which women dealt with better than men. Lacan had a very rigid relationship with his "sons," which could be destructive.

How do you see yourself in relation to the women's movement in France?

I accept the term feminism completely although I am not a militant. As a woman I cannot ignore the intelligent questions that the liberation movement has posed.

Are your patients women or men?

At the beginning, my patients were mainly women. Fifteen years ago, I was too young to represent the mother. Now it's not a problem any more. Of course, with children, it's different. They are brought to me by their parents, and I have more little boys than little girls.

Is your position as an analyst the same whether you are treating a male or a female patient?

One is never the same when facing different people. At the first meeting one doesn't know if one can be an analyst for someone. If I agree to analyze someone, this is a guarantee that the patient will be able to work through with the unconscious and overcome the difficulties. The analyst isn't there to act out on the social level. We aren't there to please but rather to do the work that has to be done. There are some people I cannot work with, but I would not say that there is a whole type that I cannot work with. We cannot just be an analyst for people we resemble. It wouldn't have been worth going through an analysis just for that.

Is the transference different with male and female patients?

My countertransference depends on the patient's transference. When one is a woman analyst, there is always the question of being a mother and a daughter. The identification as a sexed human being, Freud said, is transmitted through the father. I don't think that this is entirely true. It depends partly on what the little girl thinks of the inside of her body and what her mother might say about it. I have married patients with children who still don't know what their anatomy is like inside. It's not a question of what the physiology is but of what has been forbidden them to know. The imaginary, the symbolic, and the real all meet there. When a little girl discovers herself, does she, as in Freudian tradition, discover first what she is lacking, or does she discover something else? It's true that sexualization is expressed in relation to the phallus. But at the same time there is an identificaiton with the mother and the mother's body which the mother can speak about. There are also prohibitions here that are liable to be transmitted which are very destructive and that in the worst cases cause psychotic wounds.

Do you follow Freud in his account of the development of the little girl in the Oedipal stage?

Freud was more careful than is generally thought in his account. He tried to describe what *is* from what he heard. I diverge from him in the sense that he stopped at a certain point. For example, in "The Case of Dora," her mother is less present than any other character. But Dora's homosexuality can perhaps be understood as a return to the mother, an attempt to make her a desirable part of the parental couple from which Dora was born. Dora's homosexuality is not a definite position in her genital life. She identifies with the phallus mainly because of the power it confers, from which the mother is excluded. If the mother would be all-powerful, she could appropriate her children without them belonging to the power of law, society, exchange, language, in short, the father, who recognizes the child and allows it access to the symbolic order.

Is there a difference between what the father represents for the little boy and the little girl?

Freud says that the little girl never leaves the Oedipal stage. One of Freud's judgments is that the woman has a weaker superego than the man. But to say that this results in a weak woman who always needs a father or a husband is ridiculous. As far as I am concerned, both men and women—it doesn't matter who—have to deal with castration, loss, and the fact of mortality. It's true that sexuation is different for a man and a woman. Freud was right when he said anatomy is destiny; the way in which one imagines one's sex in one's body is extremely important. But there are little boys who have a greater femininity than little girls. The reverse might be said about some little girls. What is true is that there is nonetheless a reality of the body. The woman doesn't see a penis when she looks at herself. But to equate the phallus with the penis is not accurate. Neither men nor women have the phallus. One believes that it is always the other who has it. For the little boy, it's either the father or the mother. He may think that the mother has one, which she got from the father. The little girl thinks that she had one which was taken away from her. Therefore, she has already lost it. This is the basis of Freud's theory that the little girl has already mourned for her penis while the little boy is in danger of losing it. Therefore the Oedipal period gives a structure to the male child, who has to identify with the father in order to feel like a male, whereas a little girl is always waiting for a man to give her what she doesn't have. Thus the equation "phallus equals baby." Freud says that the little girl and the woman that she is going to become will always be in a seductive position with regard to men, but that's somewhat misleading also. Masculine fragility, of which we do not usually speak, is also terrifying. Men have all this panoply of macho; yet they can be totally empty. In fact, what we have is the fragility of the suffering human being — female and male.

What produces the female superego?

For me, the superego is the inheritance of the Oedipal stage, whether one is male or female. It involves something of an appropriation from the parental superego. The superego helps the subject to construct something for him or herself. It allows the child to affiliate with the parents and to belong to society. One is a child in a lineage, not just in any place. And places cannot be changed. This is very important. In the unconscious of some psychotic patients there is a question of incest. What is most destructive in incest is that the person no longer has a sense of filiation. In incest there is no difference between the generations. It represents omnipotence, that is, one no longer feels that one is mortal. I have seen this with patients. This is a way of defining incest which is different from the legal definition, which is also efficacious because it obliges one to be considered as the child of someone else.

Is there a biological basis to the superego?

There is a sexed identification of the superego. If one says that the superego is the interiorization of the parental superegos, one could say that the superego, that is, the positive superego, is sexed to the degree that one integrates it. I also see a negative superego, which condemns, destroys, and entraps one in an unpayable debt. It is in this sense that I speak of a pre-Oedipal superego which is not necessarily feminine or masculine. It can be transmitted by a woman or a man. But the superego of the little girl or boy after the resolution of the Oedipal stage is integrated into its male or female identity and therefore is part of the identification which feeds into positive narcissism.

The little girl is in danger of not forming a superego because she doesn't have to resolve the Oedipal stage. Therefore the feminine superego is less strong. But a little girl can achieve a masculine superego if she is very identified with her father. That is to say that her feminine narcissism is enlarged by the superego. There is more value on the phallic side, not just on the side of law but also on the side of power. In contrast, the feminine superego is more on the side of feminine narcissism since woman is more concerned with the image of her body, more in need of possession to achieve a sense of completeness.

I see the masculine side better than the feminine one. But as soon as one speaks of masculine and feminine, the one in relation to the other, one tries too much to see them as reverse images and ends by impoverishing them.

As for the feminine superego, I would say that it is a maternal superego. In order not to be destructive when the little girl becomes a woman, the superego has to be tied to what the Other represents, to the desire of the Other. It's a little bit of a caricature but the danger for a woman would be to remain riveted to the mother in the desire for omnipotence, an omnipotence which does not include a desire for alterity.

Do you see a split in the pre-Oedipal mother between the primitive mother, which is a sort of abyss, and the phallic mother, who is more structured?

The phallic mother is already bound to castration because there is a desire to have the phallus while knowing that one doesn't have it. In male and female sexuation, one lacks what the other has. The other *is* the other insofar as he or she is not us and belongs to the other sex.

I encounter this phallic mother in patients who have autistic children. These patients had all-powerful mothers who would not allow their daughters to become mothers themselves unless they imitated them totally. This produces astonishing effects. Sometimes these women find men who have an important feminine identification or who are only the genitors or don't exist at all. In such cases there are often dead children and an inability to work through the process of mourning. In one case, a patient was babysitting her brother when he died. It was not her fault, but she felt that she had killed her mother's child. She later had a son to whom she could only give a false narcissism, an empty envelope. The son was totally manic.

Mourning is impossible because these women cannot accept loss. After giving birth, some women have a short psychotic episode. I wonder what they have lost at that moment. Is it something that their mothers gave them that is here taken away? Do they see themselves as whole only when they are pregnant? The real and the imaginary are joined again, and when the infant is born, it is not seen as separation but as destruction. And the child outside the body cannot be accepted. What can such a mother give her daughter when it is her turn to be a mother some day, other than a sense of omnipotence and total possession? As for the father, one is also able to see terrifying things, as in the Schreber case. One can see omnipotence too but with variations. With men the desire to be omnipotent is different from the pre-Oedipal omnipotence, which is a power without any breach, which has no opening. It's a type of absolute.

What does the pre-Oedipal father represent for the little boy and the little girl?

The pre-Oedipal father must already be present in the mother's desire. When she carries her child, the mother knows that she is not all alone in creating it. I have heard women say that they want to have a child, but they don't want a man. This raises questions. Does one have the right to refuse a father to the human being that one brings into the world? Don't we then enclose the child in our desire to be everything for it, even if we don't go as far as the psychotic? There were women who were widowed during the war, whose children were not deprived of a father in the symbolic order. They missed the real presence of the father, but nonetheless, he existed in the mother's desire, memory, and story. They were semiorphans but they knew that they were born from the desire of two people. This is important.

Could there be an equivalent of the phallic mother in the father—a sort of womb father?

There are men who want to be everything also. I had a patient whose father had a very strong feminine identification. He was very jealous of his wife when she was pregnant, as if he didn't realize that he was not the one who would be pregnant. What's interesting is to see why. This father was an adopted child who met his biological mother in adolescence and began to develop a kind of narcissistic delirium at that moment. Nothing could be too good for his mother. The delirium disappeared only to reappear after the birth of his two children. For example, he rented a Rolls Royce to go and visit his mother, and, decked out with all the phallic attributes at that moment, he said to her, "Look at your son."

How would you describe such a father?

What such a father wants are all the feminine attributes. He will not accept being marked by another form of castration, the one of not being able to bear chidren. This raises another question. In the generations to come, will the fact of speaking to little girls about their physiological potential, about something that exists and is positive, give women a different way of situating themselves in their body? Girls used to reach menstruation without knowing anything, but if one tells them about their ovarian function, this becomes an enrichment and not a handicap. Understanding more about the unconscious identifications of little girls with the mother and the father, and also more about the mother's identification, will enable the little girls to grow up not to be all-powerful but to know what it is to be a woman.

What would be the effects of a more equally shared parenting on the development of the little boy and the little girl? Does a woman always have to play the role of the mother? Can the father also be mothering? How will parenting be different in the future?

Men are taking much more pleasure in their babies now. In the past, before a child could speak, they weren't interested. They weren't fathers in the same way. And I think that the pleasure that fathers now take in their babies has consequences for the infant's narcissism. The moment of individuation when the child turns to the father will be different since the father is already there, feeding the baby, changing the baby, and waking up at night for it. But I don't think that the roles should be totally mixed up.

At the level of pleasure that the father has in parenting, does he remember the pleasure that he gave his mother when he was a baby? Is there a possibility of transmitting that to the child? And what would this mean for the baby? Is this still part of mothering? Or is there something on the side of the father which is expressed? A father who doesn't take pleasure in nurturing the infant is not necessarily a bad father, but the question is whether there is something different in the narcissism that is then inscribed in the body.

I have in mind a young patient who didn't see her father when she was very little. The parents separated. She discovered him in adolescence and there was real father/daughter incest, without any guilt on the daughter's side. And the only guilt that she is starting to express now has to do exclusively with her rivalry with her mother. She says, "If my mother knew this, the world would collapse." Fundamentally there is the idea that she took her mother's place in relation to her father. She wanted her father to give her something that she never had. And I think that the father has to give something to the very small child. With the traditional father the pleasure passes solely through the mother. But with the present-day father, there is more sharing. Is he gratifying something which was repressed in the past of his unconscious feminine side? It's possible.

I have a forty-year-old male patient who had an extraordinary dream, in which he identified with a woman insofar as she was a mother. This was connected to an archaic identification in which, as a little child, he thought he could have a fetus inside his body. In the dream were the words *fétu de paille* (blade of straw), which were connected to the term *fœtus*. The interpretation of the dream was that he was mourning the loss of that maternal identification. In many men, there is this feeling of loss, which is different from the fear of castration, but which involves a renouncing, nonetheless. For a child, sexuation implies that one is masculine or feminine; one therefore renounces the possibility of being the other sex.

Do you think that the fear of castration is a screen for a greater fear, that of being engulfed in the mother's body?
The fear of castration is a construction at the Oedipal stage which allows separation from a more invasive anguish to take place. Castration expresses loss but at the same time it gives a place to filial identification. This allows the structuring of the subject with regard to the self.

I had a patient whose father had filmed the birth of his two children, and he later showed his children how they came into the world. One child, a boy who was ten or eleven when I saw him, was able to speak about it. He was not psychotic but had terrifying phobias. He realized that the most horrifying moment was when the film was reversed. That signified engulfment by the mother. In fact, boundaries had been eliminated. He was no longer outside the mother. I asked myself what this meant on the father's side. What was the father taking over with his eyes? There was a voyeuristic appropriation of his wife's giving birth, of her body, of a pregnancy for which he was only the genitor. There was doubtless an unconscious desire for omnipotence, on the part of the couple. The film was a way of saying, "We created you."

Phobias reveal an anguish of separation, in relation to two different spaces. The fear is that the phobic object will erupt in the same space and eventually destroy one. For me, the phobic object allows the separation from the engulfing maternal space to a space where the patient lives as separate from the mother and autonomous. The anxiety keeps the phobic patient from falling into psychosis. It's a kind of protective railing.

Gloria Bonder, an Argentinian analyst, says that men use women the way that Winnicott says that children use transitional objects. Do you agree?

It is true that there are more fetishists among men than among women. But which men? Some only sons, for example? Is it because these men had to deal with mothers who were more mothers than women? Who lacked eroticism with men and used their child like a hot water bottle, like a blanket, as Françoise Dolto has said? The child fulfills all the libidinal lack of the woman that she doesn't want to fulfill with a man.

I also think that there are women who demasculinize their lovers, making of them teddy bears, women who are not castrators but who put their partners in a child's role. They become the mother. What is eroticized is not sex but eating, caring.

As a woman analyst, I would say that men have a tendency to use women as objects and not as a total person. That is, there is a mutilation. One need only look at erotic literature. In the erotic magazines the woman is used in bits and pieces. There is a male eroticism which is not the same as a female eroticism. But female eroticism uses male eroticism for its fantasies. Women have fantasies that have been nurtured by all the panoply of masculine eroticism. I hear this from my patients. Now there are also magazines with nude men. But the women don't buy them. They aren't really interested. I don't think that women are excited by the sight of a young Ephebus.

What are women's erotic fantasies?

They say that women are masochists. But there are plenty of men who are masochists also in their fantasies. There are men who like to be whipped. And some women have sadistic fantasies.

This is not masculine or feminine. It depends on the libidinal organization of the person, the history, what was eroticized in one's life earlier, one's relation to the mother and father. Women's fantasies include everything. There are now women's journals which try to record women's fantasies since women are now speaking more freely about this. One might ask if fantasies always have to be a form of alienation. Not necessarily. One is at the same time the object of the other in a fantasy.

Do you think that Freud went beyond his models of anaclitic and narcissistic love?
Freud was extraordinarily free in naming parts of the body. But although he gives us models of the process of maturation, his theory of narcissism is his main theory of love.

Pleasure according to Freud is an attempt to master excitation. This attempt to master annihilates the object, the woman. Is all of this discourse founded on a matricide?
Freud speaks about pleasure as discharge, the lowering of the threshold of tension. It's true that the object is annihilated, but is this the equivalent of killing the mother?

Are women nearer to death than men because of their body and the experience of maternity? We are connected to something very mythical here. Insofar as women are guardians of the hearth and of life, are they not also before the doors of death? The fear of women is an enormous question. We can ask if men didn't try to tame women because there is this whole equation of women and power. We can't forget about the sorceresses, the fear that women cause men because they have something the men don't have. But this is not power that gets translated into law. It's something else. Melanie Klein has treated the pre-Oedipal period with great subtlety and the type of terrorizing superego that women exert especially as mothers.

In valorizing this all-powerful mother, this sort of engulfing abyss, are we not creating a neomisogyny?

We have to be careful about this. But male/female relationships allow the child to know that he is not the creation of the mother only. Women do not have the power of life by themselves, and neither do men.

Nonetheless men often think that women have this total power. And there is a complicity of women in this. There was also a whole generation of women who were terrible with their daughters and with other women, the so-called bitches and whores who allowed themselves sexual pleasure. These respectable women were the enemies of other women and their daughters by playing men's game. They didn't give a place to women's pleasure.

The omnipotence of the mother could also be shown in her prohibition of her own daughter to be a mother. That could also deprive *her* of pleasure. Women must give up destructive power for legitimate power.

What are the big questions that psychoanalysis faces today?

For me, the big questions now have to do with its ethics. At the moment of the dissolution of the Ecole Freudienne there was a splintering of the Lacanian groups over both theoretical and technical issues. This raised the question of what psychoanalytic training should be, and the problem of recognition since an analyst needs recognition. But what is it that one can acknowledge? What we know of her work and her training? These two questions of training and recognition are connected to the question of the different institutes. What is it that an institute can propose as training? What should it recognize in someone who wants to be recognized? There is the problem of theoretical training and supervision. There is also the question of the Freudian inheritance. With ethics comes another question that exists in the United States also, that of therapy, which is ambiguously based on more or less psychoanalytic principles. Ethics poses the question of the analytic act. What is it? This will be a vital question in the future. For me, it's an act of speaking. It begins when someone asks for help, in the preliminary interview(s), and the moment that one lies down on the couch. The analyst must dare to be rigorous and coherent, to have a conceptual apparatus, of course, but also to enter into the clinical, the practical side. Technique allows us to make connections between theory and practice. The analyst must be able to say why *she* works in one way and not another.

In Freud's psychoanalytic family, terrible things happened. Perhaps the analyst at certain times took a place that he shouldn't have taken. And perhaps we, the present generation, should question the psychoanalytic family lineage. These questions trouble me because we lived some crazy but very serious moments in the Ecole Freudienne. I can't run away from my history.

In the United States, we are asking whether psychoanalysis is a science. Do you have this same problem in France?

Lacan said that analysis is allied with science. I think that analysis works through a process of its own. What would be dangerous would be for analysts to engage in a process of proving, because psychoanalysis is not an exact science. Even if Freud's thinking was scientific in some ways, when we listen to a patient, we don't listen with an a priori theory. But we have some hypothesis. One should see someone two or three times in a preliminary interview. It's necessary to have some idea of what this person brings as an outline of a structure because if someone is psychotic, we are not going to put him or her on the couch. Freud says this in his papers on technique, which are still current. There is one called "The Beginning of Treatment," where he is very precise with reference to emergencies and the fact that the analyst carries an enormous responsibility.

The question of science is more a question for the theoreticians who want to prove that analytic discourse is a scientific one. As far as I am concerned, insofar as it is nourished by clinical experience, whether psychoanalysis is a science or not is not really a question for me. I don't have to prove that it is a science to my colleagues in the sciences.

This was a question for Lacan. But I don't consider myself a Lacanian even though I think that it is very important to know Lacan's work. To be a Lacanian would limit me. When he tried to systematize his own theories, he enclosed himself. One develops oneself through experience. And readings of Klein and Winnicott, even more so, and contemporary British analysts have been very fruitful. A particular system may be suggestive, but it is too confining. If the analyst limits herself to the Kleinian object, or the Lacanian signifier, where is the patient? Analysis should always be a creation. With each person, one has a different story. The patient brings fascinating questions, but if one is enclosed into a system, one is going to miss them.

Monique David-Ménard passed her agrégation de philosophie and studied psychoanalysis at the Ecole Freudienne de Paris. She holds a doctorate in clinical psychopathology and psychoanalysis. She is affiliated with the Centre National de la Recherche Scientifique and the Collège International de Philosophie. At the Centre de Formation et de Recherches Psychanalytiques, she conducts a seminar on clinical and theoretical psychoanalysis.

SELECTED BIBLIOGRAPHY

L'Hystérique entre Freud et Lacan: Corps et langage en psychanalyse. Paris: Editions Universitaires, 1983. (Forthcoming in English by Cornell University Press).
L'Objet comme obstacle au délire. Forthcoming.

TWO

Monique David-Ménard

Paris, Summer 1985

Monique David-Ménard practices near the Tuileries gardens, near a much-frequented marketplace, as lively at night as during the day with its profusion of restaurants. Her office is in a landmark building with a spacious, airy, and modern interior. The analytic couch looks deep and beckoning with its tapestried pillow. The analytic chair was placed not behind the beautiful wooden eighteenth-century desk but very close to the head of the couch as if it were an extension of it. The light streaming through the two large windows over the beige rug and purple flowers, the deep blue that dominated the large painting lent an air of grace and sensuousness to this warm room. During this first interview, David-Ménard smoked long, thin brown cigarettes. Dr. David-

Ménard, with her smiling, quiet but strong presence, gentleness, sparkling sensitivity and intelligence, could make smoking come back into style. When we left her, she was going off to celebrate her daughter's second birthday.

Our questions touch on the history of women and the road that they have traveled as women. That is why we are asking what led you to become an analyst.

I was a philosophy student and then a teacher of philosophy. I'm told that when I was eighteen years old, I always walked around with a copy of Lacan's *Ecrits*. It had just come out. I think that walking around with the *Ecrits* was an intellectualized way of saying that since a great man spoke of them, I had the right to express things that caused suffering in me also, even though I was a philosopher. What made me turn to psychoanalysis were things which weren't working in my life and were formulated at first in a very intellectual manner.

Where do you see yourself in the psychoanalytic movement?

I belong to the last generation, the Ecole Freudienne of Paris, but during all my psychoanalytic training, I didn't participate very closely in the internal history of the Lacanian school. I never went to see Lacan. I read what he wrote, but it was necessary for me to protect my analysis, to keep it separate from institutional questions. It was only when the Ecole Freudienne dissolved that I realized that there were problems in the history of the psychoanalytic movement. Besides, at the university, I wrote my thesis on psychopathology and psychoanalysis for a department which wasn't connected to the Ecole Freudienne. I therefore saw psychoanalysts who had a different allegiance also.

What was the subject of your thesis?

The biological metaphors in psychoanalysis.

Where do you see yourself in relation to the women's movement? Do you accept the term *feminism*?

I think that the question of feminism is very different in France and in the United States, in part, no doubt, because of the role that psychoanalysis has played in France. I will not say that I am a feminist but I think it. It is through the questions that do not concern feminism exclusively and directly that the work that we do or the positions that we take have feminist implications. I don't define myself as a feminist whether as a philosopher or as a psychoanalyst. But I am very aware that it isn't by chance that the questions that interest me are often those posed by women. Still, I have always been a little opposed to the exclusion of men from women's groups, even if I saw that this might be necessary at certain moments. I think that we may say more important things concerning people's relations when we don't address these questions directly. All in all, for historical reasons I refuse to define myself as a feminist.

Do you have more men than women patients?

I have more women patients than men. I don't know whether it is because more women are in analysis than men or because women often want to go to a woman analyst. But it hasn't always been like that. It's perhaps tied up with what I have written or said in public.

Do you agree with Freud on the development of the little girl in the Oedipal stage?

I feel completely Freudian but then again Freud didn't say everything. The development of the little girl during the Oedipal stage is one of the questions that Freud himself said he didn't advance in much. Nothing prevents us from saying things differently or from searching in another direction. Besides when you said, "the development of the little girl in the Oedipal stage," I asked myself, "What is that?" In analysis, I quickly forget the dogmas learned in books. I have the impression, and Freud said it—it's for that reason that I'm also Freudian—that the formulations which correspond to the history of someone are only efficacious if they are rediscovered each time and particularized according to that which is singular. We all end up with schematics, but it isn't with them that we can analyze.

What exactly do you have in mind when you ask about female development?

We are thinking about the little girl and the concept of castration, of what leads her to separate from the mother, and also of sexual monism, the absence of a female sexual organ in Freud's account of childhood fantasy. According to Freud, women don't have castration anxiety. Is the concept of castration used in a real or imaginary sense and is castration connected to the penis or the phallus?

To the phallus.

In this case, wouldn't the little girl suffer from castration anxiety also or should the question be not, "Do I or don't I have a penis?" but rather, "Does he love me? Does she love me?"

I don't believe that one excludes the other. I think that the two coexist and that they are located at different moments of structuration. It is at one and the same time, "Does he love me or does she love me?" that is to say, "Am I going to succeed in being all for the other, which would make me completely indispensable and therefore justify my life?" And it's also, "Will I be able to take from the man, this thing which seems to work so well, in no matter what domain?"

Are the women's liberation movement and psychoanalysis restoring the little girl's sexuality, or are we still in the scopic economy which sees her as deprived of a penis?

The accounts that I have read on the clitoris and the vagina always seemed to me very abstract. From the moment that a woman's identity starts expressing itself, there arise dreams that are important for the cure as if the patient knew of what she is made. When sexual representations enter into the dream material, they are in all ways more phantasmagoric, more imaginary, more surreal than the opposition between the clitoris and vagina, and refer to something archaic in sexuality.

Is it possible that our binary system, for example, the op-position clitoris/vagina, isn't real but rather a sort of cari-cature?

I think so. It is an imaginary system which is apparently scientific but which doesn't correspond to the order of the things that it treats.

You have spoken of women's dreams in which sex is repre-sented in a surrealist and complicated fashion, where there isn't simply a vagina or a clitoris, but perhaps a combina-tion of both. Do men have an equally surrealistic represen-tation, which doesn't depend so much on the penis?

That is a question that I never asked myself and I would have the tendency to give two somewhat contradictory answers. In one sense the sexual representations are as surrealistic among men as among women. But daily visual motifs also play a greater role in men's way of fantasizing sex and thus there may be—but I'm not sure—something of the scopic drive in the fantasies of sex that men have.

Is female identification with the mother during the Oedipal stage preceded by attraction to her?

Certainly. Identification is the residue, the scar of an impossible, forbidden, incestuous love—at least in most cases. But the mother does not qualify as an object because in the relation to her there is something more archaic than the formulation of a love object. Without doubt the infant loves or hates parts of the mother, somewhat the way that Melanie Klein has described it.

It's more a question of partial drives than of an object in the sense where object refers to something completely external. Then, too, in the obsessional neurosis, for example in the *The Wolf Man,* Freud acknowledges a level of identification with the father, a desire to be like him which is older than anything specifically sexual. It is perhaps to something of that sort that you alluded in your question. This nonsexual identification is something which is carried throughout life, which creates an image that is more resistant than strictly sexual identifications. Perhaps there is something of this type in the relation to the mother.

Are you speaking of the ego ideal?

I am speaking of something even more archaic, which has to do with incorporation. The ego ideal comes to pair itself with sexuality, without doubt with the resolution of the Oedipus complex.

An article by Catherine Millot in *Ornicar* (July 1984), treats the female superego differently from the masculine one, which brings the Oedipus complex to an end. The feminine superego, on the contrary, puts the little girl in a situation of dependence with regard to the father. But it is preceded in the pre-Oedipal period by the ego ideal, which has nothing to do with sexuality. It is an ego ideal which is more specular, which depends on the face as a mirror, whereas the suprerego is rather a creation belonging to language and made up of prohibitions.

That seems interesting to me for differentiating the sexes. What troubles me a little in what you have said about Millot's article is why call this image an ego ideal *(idéal du moi)*? Why not ideal ego *(moi idéal)*? The Lacanians have been struggling to differentiate the ideal ego from the ego ideal.

What is the difference?

It is perhaps what Catherine Millot is referring to, a Lacanian distinction that has become classic in Paris. The ideal ego refers more to an image. A patient of Lacan, Emmée, had as an ideal ego an actress whom she attacked one night. (She is an example of female paranoia.) The ideal ego is the perfection of a narcissistic image of which the subject appears as the negative. If a woman has the feeling of being stripped, her "ideal ego" will be all the women that she imagines as rich.

However, the ego ideal is completely different. Certainly it refers to the traits projected on another to the extent that it may refer to the father, but it corresponds much more to a task with which one identifies, to an image which captures you, or a quality of someone, like succeeding in a play for an actress or becoming rich in the riches fantasy. If I am a philosopher, it is because somewhere in my ego ideal, the rigor of philosophy has brought me back to things which in the history of my incestuous drives have been important erotically, which transformed themselves into a socially acceptable activity. That is a typical ego ideal which when more severe can be linked to the superego. It is an ego ideal to the extent that it permits the transformation of the residue of the Oedipus complex into something which profits the subject; and if the subject recognizes itself as faulty in relation to its task, that derives from the superego.

But the superego and the ego ideal are in this sense completely different from the ideal ego, that is to say, from the images which win by underhanded methods and which perhaps have more reference to the maternal. Women have problems of separation, without doubt, in connection to images that are different from those of men. I would say the question of separation is a problem of relation to the other, distinct from the relation to the superego. How can we separate ourselves from these ideal egos in order to act on our own? Separation is also important for men but it occurs in a more immediate fashion. The superego and the separation of the imagos are different in women and men.

Are you saying that separation from the imagos is more difficult for women because they are more deeply rooted in them?
Not more difficult but different.

In what sense?
What makes me unite the superego and the problem of separation of imagos is the question of guilt. It is the superego which engenders guilt, and separation, which gives oneself the right to be another, also engenders guilt.

What Millot is speaking of is perhaps a female superego which isn't internalized and which is in a situation of dependence with regard to another, the other being the man.

Pleasing a man, clinging to him, reveals a superego which constitutes itself by connection to an external structure.

Yes, that is able to happen in certain cases but not all. In hysteria, the connection to seduction, to the man, is so strong only because it masks terror of the maternal, the impossibility of picturing incest with the mother. The hysteric demands from the man that he guarantee that she will not have to confront that which binds her to the mother. Here we have to take into account fantasies concerning something like a paranoia of jealousy, a delirium of the homosexual type, which represents a sort of terror in connection to the maternal, which sometimes surfaces when the conversion of symptoms breaks down. And this has to be analyzed within a structure of its own and not be reduced to the relation to the father and the "symbolic castration," that is, to the phallic problematic. I think that it is in this sense that I am drawing implications that are without doubt feminist, even though I am not completely in agreement with using this term. What can change the dependence of women is the analysis of what is terrifying in the relation to the mother and finding forms for symbolizing that, forms of socialization which are autonomous, which don't proceed only in relation to the man. Otherwise, women will remain dependent in their daily life as well as in their fantasies. If they face their difficulty in separating from the mother while identifying with the mother in a certain way, they will be able to symbolize that which constitutes them without going through the intermediary of seduction of men. Doubtless this is one of the goals of the women's movement. I can also say that it is the purpose of certain analytic cures for women. That doesn't mean that they won't seduce men any more, but seduction will no longer serve to hide the difficulty in their relation to the mother.

What is the basic cause of hysteria? Why are there fewer hysterics now? What is the masculine counterpart for hysteria?

In Europe, the repression of sexuality at the end of the nineteenth century was the major cause. Through the spectacular side of hysteria, women expressed what was impossible to say concern-

ing sexuality. The men who examined the women, at the Salpétrière, were also part of the hysterical phenomenon, but they used
their medical power to distance themselves from the patients and
look at them as curious entities.

It's true that when I think about hysteria, I think about women
first. But it all depends on how one defines hysteria. In fact, I
don't know what masculine hysteria is. Sometimes I say to myself
when I hear a male patient who is very identified with a woman,
"Perhaps that comes from hysteria," but I always end up saying,
"It's not really that." Hysteria doesn't exist just because there is
an identification with a woman, a desire to be a woman, a mother,
or even a hesitation between being a man or a woman. But not
everybody agrees with me. There are persons who speak of masculine hysteria.

How do *you* define *hysteria?*

For me, it is a way of playing with neurotic erotism to the limit,
with a risk of psychosis, that is to say, to a delirium of homosexual jealousy. Hysterical women are women who enter into seduction in relation to men, in order not to become crazy in their
relation to their mother, but in a way that turns out badly with
men since they cannot satisfy the demand which is made of them.
I think that's where the hysteric lack of satisfaction comes from.
This means I do not agree with the definition of hysteria as a
desire to take the place of the man. It is true that that is able to
happen, for example, in Freud's Dora. In her second dream, she
takes the part of a young man who visits the city all alone and
doesn't allow a man to accompany her and show her the road
because she wants to be the man. But finally there is in her
identification with men many things which are more relevant to a
quasi paranoia than to hysteria, and the demand addressed to a
man—seduction, erotization, the fact of acting out a scene in the
hysteric crisis—is a failed attempt to transform the paranoia into
something else.

Is there more paranoia in men than in women?

Among men, paranoia tends to transform itself into competition,
which is acceptable socially by all the institutions that bind men

together. I believe that masculine paranoia is differently structured from female paranoia. Certainly in masculine paranoia, there
are symbolic and social guides for transformation that one learns
as a little boy. As for women, I would say that the social transformation of paranoia has yet to be invented.

**Does the little boy who is tending toward paranoia displace
it into an obsession by using symbols?**

Yes, a transformation into an obsessional neurosis is entirely possible when the paranoia isn't too serious. There is a very strong
investment in symbolic activities and sometimes an investment in
clear and distinct rigor of thought. That is, there is never any
incoherence.

Up to now, female paranoia hasn't been able to transform itself
by these means. It transforms itself rather into seduction in relation to men in order not to be overwhelming. Women have to
invent a means of sublimating the paranoia. There are some women
whose paranoia is founded on a hatred of the father, who are led
to a transformation that tends to the homosexual. This is a completely different fate from that of the hysteric, where the subject
leans as much as possible on the father, but at the wrong time and
in a manner such that something underneath remains unresolved.

**There is a whole psychoanalytic literature which treats the
primitive mother and opposes her to the phallic mother.
How do these two mothers coexist in the later development
of men and women? Do you agree with the concept of the
primitive mother as the figure who threatens engulfment?
Do you see this in your patients?**

Yes, that exists in my patients, men as much as women, a terror
of sinking into the mother mixed with a fascination of it. It is
undeniable.

**What differences do you see between the primitive mother
and the phallic mother?**

I would say that they belong to the same register. The mother
who may swallow her children is also the mother who has something fearful inside her, which is perhaps the phallus.

Isn't the phallic mother more structured than the primitive mother, who is without limits, a sort of abyss, as described in writings such as Jeanne Hyvrard's *Mère la Mort* (Mother Death), 1976? This archaic, primitive mother is without shape, a gulf which we risk falling into every moment of our lives, as opposed to the phallic mother, who is delineated, structured, and therefore less dangerous.

If one refers to Melanie Klein, the phallic mother has the phallus inside her. It is often the phallus swallowed by the mouth. It isn't a phallus like the one attributed to a man. It isn't a visible phallus if it is in the interior of the body. Therefore it is not conceived by the scopic consciousness. It is not encompassed by the term "phallic" if we mean by "phallic," fantasies which cling to the visual. In the phallic mother, who is also the primitive mother, there is a phallic material that is completely trapped in a primitive structure.

In mythology there are representations of this primitive mother, Medusa, for example. What does Athena represent? The phallic mother?

Athena isn't a mother; she is a virgin. She is only the daughter of the intelligence of her father and in this sense, she is phallic, but that doesn't stem from the phallic mother.

Is it possible to change mythology?

To change our reading of the myths or to change mythology?

Both.

We don't choose the myths. Not all societies have the same myths. This year I reread *The Symposium,* which treats the beginning of sexual difference and love, the establishment of sexuality and sexual desire. I realized that it is not at all the same as the biblical myth. There is a problematic of separation here also, but there isn't the problem of sin. Societies do not have the same fundamental representations of sexuality. And one isn't able to decide what myths one is going to have. I think that this is done unconsciously at the level of society.

In the United States, as without doubt elsewhere, we are asking what the biological facts are. What is the biology which supports the psychology of men and women? Is there a biological foundation which we are not able to change? If we should arrive at a reproduction ex utero, what will being a parent signify? What will happen to the relations between men and women?

In Freud, we find the language of energy, the idea that pleasure is the sensation of a discharge. I asked myself, "What is a masculine fantasy? Does it occur because the man sees the erection and detumescence of the penis?" In this context it is much more the man's idea of it than the physical apparatus which is weakened in pleasure and tends toward death, even though there is only a temporary loss of tension and complete emptying. Freud acted as if what he called the physical apparatus were either an electronic machine or an organism. And I asked myself, "Why this language?" This type of question is bound, I think, to the history of psychoanalysis because in the first period, psychoanalysts took the biological interpretations of Freud literally, at least in France. Afterward came Lacan who rejected all biologizing in Freud and redefined the structure of desire as originating in language. And every time that there was a formulation that was too biological, he transformed it into something topological.

For me, Freud's idea of speaking of desire in terms of energy wasn't only a male fantasy but was something which took account of symptoms. For example, in hysteria, in the spectacular crisis with so much excess, there is the will to actualize something crazy, to represent it in order for it to exist. The hysteric crises also bring into play a discharge but certainly not in a biological sense; rather they metaphorize or speak simply of the excess in sexual *jouissance*. Thus I reread Freud after Lacan, trying not to reject the biologizing language, but making it the metaphor of something else.

At the same time your question interests me because what you call biological represents two different things. One, it pertains to the recent discoveries in genetic engineering and the possible manipulations of reproduction and their potential connection to the problems of sexual identification. But it also refers to what we spoke about before. You asked me whether the clitoris or the vagina is the most important sexual organ in women. I told you that I am not sure if in the unconscious we are dealing with the vagina *or* the clitoris. The female sex is imagined in surrealist ways which at certain moments involve full forms and at others, empty ones. But I am not sure that this corresponds to what doctors call the clitoris or the vagina. That's another problem for biology. In this sense, I believe that biological sex is only raw material for the unconscious, without which homosexuality and transexuality would not be possible.

Biological sexuality, that is, the fact of being a boy or a girl, a man or a woman, has two meanings. There is a medical sense, but from the point of view of psychoanalysis, the problem is to know what a man or a woman does in the process of identification or in the history of desire. In truly human sexuality, there is a utilization of the biological material in the process of identification. Everything depends on what one does with the substratum.

What I have just said is very theoretical. Now I want to go to the other side. If I have a homosexual woman in analysis, what do I hope for her? Do I say to myself, "When she is better, will she be heterosexual?" Being basically heterosexual myself, I have my unconscious preferences. But from the analytic point of view, such an idea is inoperable. The only thing that I am able to say to myself is not, "Will she be homosexual or heterosexual?" but rather "Up to what point is she able to go in the discovery of what made her homosexual? Will she become heterosexual or will she be homosexual a little differently, with less difficulty in living?" I don't know. It is not for me to decide that and I even have the impression that if the analysis is to work, it is to the extent that I don't decide.

Joyce McDougall graduated from Otago University in New Zealand and underwent psychoanalytic training in London from 1950 to 1953, where she was a student at the Hampstead Child Training Centre. In 1954 she moved to Paris, where she became a candidate at the Paris Institute of Psychoanalysis. In 1961, she was nominated supervising and training analyst.

SELECTED BIBLIOGRAPHY

Dialogue with Sammy (co-authored with S. Lebovici). London: Hogarth Press, 1969.
Plea for a Measure of Abnormality. New York: International Universities Press, 1980.
Theaters of the Mind: Illusion and Truth on the Psychoanalytic Stage. New York: Basic Books, 1985.
Dialogue avec Sammy (rev. ed.). Paris: Payot, 1983.

THREE

Joyce McDougall

New York, Fall 1985

We saw Joyce McDougall not in her own country but in her
home away from home, The Algonquin, a small hotel packed
with history in midtown Manhattan, whose clientele has always
been largely literary. When we asked for her by her full name at
the desk—we were, we thought, being feminist and egalitarian
—the concierge hesitated for a moment. "Ah!" he exclaimed, a
look of recognition and admiration suffusing his face. "The doctor." He directed us to a small room, with a profusion of flowers
on the bedspread of the brass bed. Warm, vibrant, "the beautiful
grandmother," as she was described to us by a fond colleague,
was dressed in a flowing deep burgundy ensemble, a gold chain
around her neck. Like her clothes, McDougall's voice is alive and

dynamic. She sat on the bed, playing with her new tape recorder with the infectious enthusiasm of a child with a new toy. Generous and direct, she picked up our list of questions and with charming strength, which put us immediately at ease, she took gentle charge.

Why did you become an analyst?

I was about fourteen when I first came across *The Psychopathology of Everyday Life* by Sigmund Freud, and I thought it was the most exciting book I had ever known. It seemed to open up a whole world—the world of the mind actually. Then at Otago University in New Zealand (which is my home country) I decided to study abnormal psychology, and of course we had Freud as part of our required reading. In a sense I wanted to be a psychoanalyst from the time I was an adolescent. But I especially wanted to have a personal analysis. Like all analysts I had my share of neurotic symptoms. Psychoanalysts and psychiatrists are drawn to their field because of their own psychic conflicts. Through one's mental suffering one becomes interested in understanding that of others. Perhaps that's a partial answer to the question of why I became an analyst.

What were your important influences?

In 1950 my husband and I, in our twenties, with our two small children took the boat to England. His project was to further his experience in adult education work and mine was to study psychoanalysis. In London I wrote to everyone whose books I had read, and many of them said they would see me and allowed me to take part as a student observer of their work in psychiatric and psychoanalytic centers. I also met Anna Freud to see whether she would accept me for child training at the Hampstead Clinic. She was most surprised to learn that her father's work was studied in New Zealand universities and said that we were in advance of England in this respect! To my surprise and delight I was accepted as a candidate. My plan was to terminate this training and then apply for admission to the British Psychoanalytic Institute for training in adult work as well. I got a job at the Maudsley Hospital, and began my analysis. I believed my life was planned for

years to come. But my husband found practically no work anywhere in London and then suddenly was offered a job in Fundamental Education with UNESCO in Paris. I had done only eighteen months of the four-year training course and was heartbroken
to leave Hampstead, my analyst, my lovely job at the Maudsley.
Miss Freud said, "So? You are going to leave the course?" She
added that there was no child training in psychoanalysis in France.
But she did give me an introduction to Marie Bonaparte and there
I was, in 1953, in Paris. So I did the first years of my psychoanalytic training in a language that I scarcely spoke. I read everything
I could get my hands on: Freud, Abraham, Ferenczi, and then all
of Winnicott, Klein, Bion, and of course, Lacan.

Speaking of important influences, I would say that Winnicott
was for me the most moving. I had already been a number of
times to Paddington Green Hospital where he did his consulta-
tions. He was fantastic and we kept in touch. He had a profound
influence on my thinking. In France, Lacan was by far the most
stimulating theorist, but clinically I thought he was crazy. However, he did have the great virtue of making everybody *think,*
whether you agreed or not with his theoretical positions. Basically, I had a classically Freudian training in Paris, as I would have
had in England, but in France I felt free to read Melanie Klein and
the post-Kleinian writers who had been frowned upon in Hampstead in the 1950s.

Does the analyst's sex affect the transference?

I began my own analysis with a male analyst in London and
continued with another male analyst in France. Then many years
later when I went back for more analysis I looked for a woman
analyst but it wasn't possible to find one I didn't already know.
Those I liked were my friends and those I didn't like I didn't want
to choose for an analyst.

In the long run, the sex of the analyst probably does not make
a difference in the transference. You use the analyst to play male
and female roles, as a father, mother, giving him the idealized and
bad aspects of both at different times. That's what transference is
of course. It's always ambivalent and all the fantasy projections
one makes about the analyst have to be interpreted and under-

stood in their historical context. So the biological sex of the analyst is not a predominant factor. However, I don't think it's a negligible one either.

There comes a moment when the sex of the analyst does play a role. Also there's the fact that women and men have different ways of being analysts. There's something basically sexual, let's say, about one's way of listening and identifying with one's analysands. Perhaps something like the difference in the approach of each parent to his or her children. Fundamentally we are all working with the same metapsychological concepts, and all are aiming at the overall goal of making the unconscious conscious. But we do this by interpreting—through our own countertransference feelings—our way of understanding the other. Psychoanalysis is not one analyzing another but the analysis of the relationship between two people, and from there on, the establishing of its roots with the past. So I do think that male analysts at some point are probably listening and interpreting differently from female analysts. Still the analyst should be gifted enough to be both male and female in his identifications with patients of both sexes. A male analyst should not be frightened of his female wishes and should be capable of being both the bad and forbidding mother as well as the idealized, nurturing mother. In the same way a woman analyst should not be afraid of her own masculine wishes or of interpreting the phallic roles that may be attributed to her. She should be able to make interpretations about her "penis" if that is the direction in which the patient's fantasy is moving, such as at times when the paternal transference is the most important. We must all learn to recognize projections onto us of both mother and father parts and in this way help our analysands to recognize the many different mothers and fathers they carry around inside them.

Some of my male colleagues write most sensitively about the use made of them as seductive or castrating mothers by their female as well as their male patients. Perhaps it depends also on how far the analyst has been able to go in his own, or her own, personal analysis, particularly in continuing self-analysis. With childlike megalomania we all once wanted to be *both* sexes, and to *have* both sexes.

Are your patients male or female?

Over the years I've had as many patients of one sex as the other. The fact of being a woman analyst doesn't seem to make much difference in the request for psychoanalytic help. As far as countertransference, I'm most interested in those of my analysands, whether male or female, who are keenly interested in their analytical adventure. Those who constantly resist, come late, miss sessions, or remain stubbornly silent for long periods of time, are more difficult to work with. And these problems arise with analysands of both sexes. Over and beyond this I probably have a deeper identification with my female patients and with the difficulties of growing into womanhood for the little girl. I feel the sexual difficulties of women are in some ways more complicated than those of men. Also their "castration anxiety," as the jargon puts it, is more widespread. I'm not at all in agreement with Freud's ideas on the basic elements of female sexuality. Freud attached the little girl's anxieties about her body solely to the fact that she doesn't have a penis. Of course this worries her, as it does her little brother. But her sexual sensations are all felt on the inside of her body. And it is difficult for her to form a mental representation of them. So when she fantasizes, just as the little boy does, that she may be punished for her guilty Oedipal longings—to take her mother's place with her father and to make a baby with him—she's more likely to imagine that the angry mother will attack her whole inside. Whereas the little boy in the same circumstances imagines he may have his penis taken away. But he's able to verify it constantly and tends to have less frantic fears for his sex organs than the girl when faced with inevitable sexual interdictions, such as masturbation. The girl-child often equates masturbation with death.

Does this give us a biological reason why little girls tend to be more obedient than little boys? Their whole body might seem to be in danger?

Yes it's quite possible. Especially since the girl doesn't have a clear representation of her genital organs and sexual sensations. They are readily confused with oral and anal representations, and this is often a contributing factor to feminine frigidity. We discover in analysis that, unconsciously, many women give to their vaginas the quality of a mouth or an anus, with all the good and bad qualities associated with each. In a sense Freud was right to say that "anatomy is destiny." But he stopped short at the girl's wish for a penis. Of course she would like a penis like her father. Why not? Little boys are also envious of the mother's role and her power to attract the father and make babies with him. They would like to be able to do that too.

Freud did a lot for women of the Victorian era—at least he *listened* to them which was rather rare in this phallocratic age. But he took the Victorian woman as the model for all womanhood. Still he was always doubtful of his theories in this area. You know he didn't publish his first article on the subject until seventy-five years of age! And at the end of his life he said that he had lived to know that he understood nothing about female sexuality. He was both fascinated and scared of the subject, I guess.

Are your patients your readers?

A certain number of people come to me because they've read things I've written: often psychiatrists or analysts wanting further analysis. But on the whole my analysands refuse to read what I've written until their analysis is finished—which I always regard as a good sign. That way they are more spontaneous in imagining what I am thinking or feeling.

How do you see yourself in regard to feminism?

A certain faction of the feminist movement in France has been rather violent. But on the whole I'm in favor of the feminist movement. We probably need violent extremists to bring about any revolutionary movement—like the suffragettes. Some of the leaders in the women's liberation movement probably have profound neurotic problems, but then these are the people who so often lead revolutions. Passionate feeling born out of deep pain and suffering inside oneself will often lead not only to neurotic symptoms but also to doing something creative with the pain, even if it leads to violence. Violence is not necessarily destructive.

The women's liberation movement was socially inevitable. I don't imagine that many analysts, male or female, would be opposed to it.

I don't think the liberation movement has influenced my theory and treatment, since I had always been in agreement with the basic tenets of the movement, before it became a socially recognized one. But the problems in psychoanalysis go far beyond this. However liberated today's women may feel, little girls still have specific *female* problems in growing into adulthood. Just as the boys have theirs.

We have a reverse question. How has psychoanalysis affected feminism?

I would think quite a bit, from reading the books that have been published. Mitchell, Millett, and many others have a considerable psychoanalytic cultural background and this is obvious in their approach. But then the whole Western world has been profoundly affected by psychoanalysis. Of course the feminists themselves would be the people to ask. Some of them have been strongly motivated against Freud's concept of making "penis envy" the basis of femininity. Many analysts, such as myself, also question Freud's concepts in this respect. Melanie Klein was probably the first analyst to challenge the specific importance of penis envy. Little boys are also envious of the father's penis because it is so big and so important in the relationship with the mother. And Klein pointed out that boys are equally envious of the mother's ability to attract the father and to make babies.

These male and female fantasies play an important role in any patient's analysis, but the analytic process deals with many more primitive anxieties as well, more archaic than the sophisticated level of the feminist movement, which is after all centered on adult socioeconomic problems and on woman's place in the adult world. In analysis we are equally concerned with the child inside every adult and the slow reconstruction of that child's history.

What about the emphasis on the pre-Oedipal mother that is so important right now? Don't the feminists have something to do with that interest?

The interest in the pre-Oedipal mother far antedates the modern feminist movement. Ruth Mack Brunswick first published an article with that title in 1940. She was working on the subject while Freud was still alive. I imagine Freud was interested in the questions that were being raised. And of course Karen Horney was another pioneer in the theory of female sexual development, who well preceded the feminist movement of today.

It seems to us there is a closer relationship between mother and daughter in the United States than in France, where it seems that the mother's relationship to her little boy is closer. We don't know whether you agree with that.
I don't agree in so far as my own experience goes. What I have noticed more particularly are the *religious* influences that affect child-rearing practices. In Jewish families one is very aware of the extreme importance of a son to the mother. (I would imagine this to be just as true in the United States.) Whereas in Catholic families I see a closer mother-daughter tie. Perhaps it has something to do with the central importance of the Virgin Mary? But this is a purely personal observation. Having had a Protestant background, I have tried to understand as much as I can about Judaic and Catholic upbringings to sense to what extent this may affect parent-child relationships.

However, leaving aside possible religious attitudes, I think also that the United States is a pioneering country in which women obviously had a particularly important role to play. As a New Zealander, I too am a "New World" citizen. In these countries, so much depended on the pioneer woman, politically and financially. So the narcissistic investment in the daughters as the guardians of the future generations and their importance for survival of these new countries perhaps plays an important role, whereas in European countries, men had the more dominant position as the upholders of the social structure.

I've often thought that national differences also have a subtle effect on the development of psychoanalytic thought in each country. To my mind it is no accident that in the United States so much emphasis was placed on adaptation—especially by those who had emigrated to your country. In a pioneering country if you don't adapt, you don't get by. And certain philosophical and sectarian aspects of European psychoanalytic thought seem to me to be connected with the ethos and cultural histories of the different countries involved.

What do you see as the differences between American and French psychoanalysis and the English schools?

Although I can only talk adequately about the country where I did my training—France, I did spend eighteen months in England as I told you. At that time the analytic scene was dominated by the struggle between those two passionate middle-European women—Anna Freud and Melanie Klein. They were the leaders in the movement that gave rise to what is known as the "British School." The real Britisher was, of course, Ernest Jones. It was largely due to his influence that the movement didn't split up—as well as the English talent for compromise. The French don't really know what that means. They tend to split infinitely into separate groups. Of course there is an overall impregnation of Lacan's thought in French psychoanalysis, even among those who would claim to be anti-Lacanian. Just as in Britain there is the profound influence of Kleinism, even in those who would never wish to be thought of as Kleinians. In the United States there is another form of theoretical terrorism, that is, the Hartmanian influence of what is known as the "ego psychology" school. There seems to be a curious resistance among many American analysts even to read anything coming from modern European research in psychoanalysis, particularly Kleinian and post-Kleinian thought, which after all has been of considerable importance, whether one is in agreement on all points or not. It's as though many prefer to be out of the stream of psychoanalytic history. This of course is not true in California, where the influence of Bion has been considerable.

But these comparisons that I am making are rather superficial no doubt. It would require a whole book to do justice to your question. Many gifted thinkers in different countries have contributed to furthering psychoanalytic research in both practice and theory. The important thing is not to close one's mind to any aspects of this research. The purists in any "school," whether they be pure Hartmanians, Kleinians, Bionians, Sullivanians or Lacanians, often do not wish to know anything outside their own "church." They frequently have a quasi-religious attitude that I find dangerous. I personally do not wish to belong to anybody's sect. When psychoanalytic theory becomes an article of faith (rather than a set of postulates that have never been proved—for that is the definition of "theory"), then this puts an end to questioning and to further discovery. And you no longer have patients or students but disciples!

How do you explain this narrow-mindedness in psychoanalysis?

Perhaps it has something to do with the nature of psychoanalytic training. This is transmitted with powerful transference feelings. There is not only the positive-negative attachment to one's personal analyst which may well leave lasting traces in the form of idealization or denigration, but also the transference effects of personal supervision and the experience of psychoanalytic seminars. Thus all one's initial psychoanalytic discoveries come about in a highly transferential way. Also analytic writers sometimes become very identified with their theories, so that when you criticize a certain concept they may feel you are attacking a person rather than questioning a theory. The followers, in particular, are often the most virulent and feel personally attacked when their spiritual leaders are put into question.

Who was it who said that theory is autobiography?

Theory is metaphor anyway. And metaphors are very personal and sometimes revealing.

Would it be possible to eliminate the Oedipal stage?

Would it be possible not to have parents?

If children were communally raised, for example? Or if you had a situation, such as Plato describes in the fifth book of *The Republic*, where children don't know who their parents are, could you eliminate the Oedipal stage?

Children have to learn from somebody how to grow up, and these child rearers would become the parental substitutes. Someone must teach a child how to talk, what the rules and regulations of the society are, of which he or she is one day to become a member. Reality in all its dimensions has to be created for children. It doesn't exist per se. And therefore somebody inevitably plays what we call the "Oedipal" role.

You say "somebody"; what if several people shared this function?

Then they will be invested as parental figures are and the struggle will be both for and against them. Even children brought up initially by their own parents transfer onto several people—teachers, and, later, social and intellectual leaders—the same attitudes that they had toward, and against, their parents. The Oedipal organization really refers to the *structure of law and order* in any given society. In occidental societies this tends to begin in the family unit, and the prohibition of incest also. But as Lévi-Strauss demonstrated, the prohibited figures are not necessarily the mothers and fathers. There must be some kind of sexual laws to construct the rudiments of a society rather than a primitive horde. So the prohibiting figures of childhood are unavoidable since children are not allowed in any society to make their own laws. Somebody playing the role of parents and educators, even in a Platonic society, will be required to transmit these social structures.

It was Winnicott who said there is no such thing as a baby all on its own. The first care-taking people are destined to be invested libidinally and narcissistically by the growing infant. They are the people who first give it the will to live by meeting its needs for nourishment and love. What we might call the Oedipal crisis is concerned with these people. The child has to learn that it will never possess these people and must wait for adulthood to satisfy the instinctual and narcissistic demands that all children make. If children could have and do anything they wanted, no society would survive.

What if incest were allowed?

If it's allowed it isn't regarded as incest. The prohibitions vary with different societies. In some ethnic groups what *we* call incest is permitted. But if there were no sexual laws of any kind, and no recognized affiliations with a family or a group, then people would have an organization closer to that of packs of animals, where there are rigorous pecking orders, rather than rigorous sexual do's and don't's.

There seems to be some form of sexual structure imposed on any kind of society, and of course this then includes property and space structures when societies move from being nomadic to becoming agricultural. The same underlying concern for law and order exists—who has rights over what.

If we try to apply the notion of Oedipal structure as concerned with social law and order, there will always be conflicts—and these in turn can be understood in dialectical terms.

So there has to be hierarchy, inequality between the generations, no matter how egalitarian the society?

In my opinion, yes. Otherwise a society would run the risk of dying out. Children cannot bring themselves up, or do whatever they want. There is no generational equality, and anger and jealousy about dependency is inevitable. And this spreads over into social and political situations.

Returning to Western society specifically, are women more capable than men of reconciling tender and erotic feelings?

They certainly deal with them differently. If I may oversimplify the question, I would say that women tend constantly to stabilize their love-relations and, within those, their sexual relations. They are always afraid of being abandoned, of losing their lovers. Men on the other hand are frantic about getting trapped into a situation from which they cannot escape, as terrified of this, as women are of losing their security.

How do you explain this psychoanalytically?

I suppose there could be evolutionary reasons. In a deeply phylogenetic sense, I imagine that if women had not been interested in creating a stable situation and hanging on to their mates, there would have been no nest for their young. Had a woman tended to leave her mate and go elsewhere, her babies might not have survived. And if the male had not been somewhere outside all the time, hunting with the rest of the males and bringing home the mastodon or whatever, maybe the whole tribe would have died. I don't know whether such ideas might explain something of the personality differences between men and women, and their relation to each other.

Not all anthropologists agree with this view of hunting/ gathering societies. Some feel that the food supply was provided largely by the women.

There are other important factors also. Often men are afraid to admit to their immense desire for tenderness and mothering, as well as possession of their women. The male also seeks something of the erotic and sensual things he had to give up with regard to his own mother. But then women also want their mates to be caring mothers at certain times. Perhaps the whole world is looking for a mother! Feeling more fragile, women tend to think that men more easily separate sexuality from love. But women of today are perhaps changing in this respect too. For example, since the widespread use of contraceptive pills, a young woman no longer associates sexuality and maternity. And on the other hand the men are now permitted to be maternal and to look after their young infants if they so wish. I think we are in a period of transition which could change our opinion of sexual roles. Perhaps the men of tomorrow may reconcile tender and erotic feelings better than the older generation.

Why does Lacan appeal to many women theorists at the same time that Derrida and others accuse him of being phallocentric?

Well phallocentric, even in the popular sense, I guess he was, but this wasn't the reason that women analysts were interested in his theoretical conceptions. By his provocative statements he pushed everybody to *think*, women as well as men. And we're always grateful to anyone who makes us think, even if in the long run we come up with quite different ideas. This is the reason I consider Lacan, Bion, and Winnicott important influences in forming my own psychoanalytic thought. But to get back to Lacan's phallocentrism—taking this term in a narrower sense, it must be said that Lacan did not believe that the phallus as a *symbol* belonged to either sex; rather it belonged to both. For Lacan, the phallus was the fundamental signifier of desire for the two sexes and from this standpoint his theory might be said to be *phallocentric,* but not sexist.

But there is still the association of the phallus more with the male than with the female.

That's because people take *penis* to be the strict equivalence of *phallus.* The phallus cults of ancient Egypt and the old Greco-Roman ceremonies were centered on *the penis in erection* and therefore this emblem became the symbol of fertility and desire—of that which links the two sexes together. The erect phallus presupposes, in its fundamental significance, a response to the female genitals.

We want to ask you if you could suggest another system of symbolization.

Why not, yes. The great darkness inside the female body might symbolize mystery. The womb, the breasts are symbols of maternity. One difficulty is that into a mystical darkness you can project more archaic significance. Thus you might get anything from Kali, or other death-dealing goddesses, to the Virgin Mary. Other civilizations have had symbols based on female signifiers.

But would that be an improvement for us?

It would be just a different mode of thought, a different ethos, a different religious structure perhaps. Many ancient religions were based on female godheads.

Why do we retain the term *penis envy* with all its load of patriarchal associations?

The trouble is that metaphors become entrenched and form a jargon, so that it becomes difficult to get people to change them.

Metaphors of course do have an insidious effect on our thinking and can be noxious in the sense of hindering us from thinking more clearly about what such terms mean fundamentally, and what the concept is behind them.

We are having a problem with the terms *phallus* and *penis envy*. As we said before, it seems that the man is much more privileged even if the phallus is something that neither sex can have, or that joins the two sexes.

This is probably because the male genitals are visible and the female genitals are hidden from sight.

But particularly since you have written that the first phallic object is the breast, why retain the term *phallic*, since the association is predominantly male?

It's hard to change these theoretical terms. It's a question of definition.

It's like grammatical terminology?

Exactly. We might ask "But why retain it?" But can we change it?

You write that you use the term *breast*, not to indicate a corporeal part object, but as the concept in the sense elaborated by Melanie Klein, of the mother in her totality. So why use the word *breast* then? Or even the term *breast-mother*, which we think is analogous to phallic reductionism, that is, it's taking a part and again investing it.

All figures of speech do this. The only alternative is to give the full definition or summary of the concept each time. I use the term *breast-mother* to refer to the way a baby sees the world. For the baby the breast is the whole mother, its whole world. I often use the term *environmental mother* or *the mother as universe*.

We prefer that. Another question. Many people blame the mother for being seductive, but in contrast you write that it is the mother's task to seduce her child to want to live.

Well this time we could say that the term is not well chosen. Perhaps we should say that the mother's task is to "induce" (rather than "seduce") her baby to want to live?* A mother's narcissistic and libidinal investment in her infant in normal circumstances is profound. This makes her baby excited about being alive and about all contact with her. A very depressed mother who might be prevented from investing her baby this way because of inner distress, or because she feels it is forbidden for her to love this baby, runs the risk of having a sickly and unhappy infant. Babies that are brought up with food and warmth but no love sometimes become marasmic and die. Something has to make a baby want to live. The spark of life doesn't keep going all by itself. Someone has to constantly fan the flame. That's what I meant by "seduction to life."

But the mother is in a Catch-22 situation. She has to seduce and she is later blamed for this.

Let's say she is normally "seductive" to her infant by her very love for her baby. To the baby she's magical and omnipotent and erotically arousing. She is not aware of seducing or erotically arousing her baby any more than she is of the fact that she is responsible for keeping life burgeoning in that baby. That she becomes the first figure of sexual desire is inevitable—and creates a great human problem for children of both sexes.

Certain French analysts that we spoke to made a distinction between the archaic, dangerous mother who threatens to overwhelm us and the more structured, balanced mother. Are these concepts parallel to your concept of the pregenital, oral, or anal-sadistic mother?

They could be. Presumably we are all talking about the same clinical phenomena, and these can be conceptualized using different metaphors. I've noticed that analysts, even of widely divergent theoretical schools, can all get together and understand each other well when they're discussing clinical material. It's only

---

*We prefer the term *seduce*, for we feel that this primary seduction by the mother points ahead to one of men's fears of women later.

when they begin propounding their theories that each one wants to sing his own aria. Maybe we're a lot of prima donnas? To come back to the significance of your question, I think we can talk about the "archaic" mother as representative of the way the baby experiences her—*as a life or death factor.* Babies have such violent reactions of love and hate (if we can already call them that). Wild instinctual expressions in any case. So the mother is experienced on one hand as the most frightening and hateful one. She is both the fairy queen and the witch. Of course, objects of need become hated objects as well, because one is so utterly dependent on them. You worship them when they respond, and you want to destroy them when they don't. Infants believe they *are* the omnipotent mother when she responds adequately, but they want to throw her out, and feel different from her, when she refuses their needs.

These are archaic elements in the early structurizing of the psyche. But the "bad" and "good" mothers inside every baby's mind are not all pure projections. Most mothers are doing their best because they do love their babies and want to give them what they need in order to grow. But some mothers have problems. In this I am more in agreement with Winnicott's concepts than those of Klein, who tends—like Freud—to say that all mothers are essentially good. Some mothers are not "good enough" in the Winnicottian sense. They have inner problems that prevent their helping their babies to come together, to become individuals, and as individuals to feel that life is a creative and worthwhile adventure.

The primitive, destructive feelings about the mother (which are universal) may find some *support* when the mother is not able to respond adequately to her baby's needs because of her own psychological problems. The latter may get in the way of her intuitive being-at-one with her baby: listening to its needs, trying to understand why it is restless or crying, wanting to help it develop, feeling good and alive with it.

With regard to the concepts of "oral" and "anal" libidinal and sadistic impulses that you referred to—these again should not be too concretized. They are terms that are intended to sum up a whole complex of instinctual and relational interreactions. They include the concept of different erogenous zones, all of which draw different kinds of fantasies to their representation. Through these experiences and their mental storage, the baby slowly comes to have a unified picture of its body—and eventually of itself as an individual mind in an individual body.

What happens if a baby is bottlefed?

I don't know that it makes all that much difference. The cardinal factor is the mother's attitude to her baby. Whether she breast-feeds or bottlefeeds, the baby regards her as the source of nourishment and life, and drinks in her image with his or her eyes at the same time . . . just devouring *her,* her smell, her touch, her voice. This is the image that I call the breast-mother. And she can be all of this even if she bottlefeeds. A mother who is hesitant about breastfeeding and would only do it because she is made to feel guilty or obliged, would probably be better off not to breastfeed, both from her own and the baby's point of view.

In the United States breastfeeding was played down for so long. Now it's in favor. Dorothy Dinnerstein speaks of the ravishing smiles of the nurturing mother. Again it's seducing. If there were a more equal parenting between mother and father, male and female, what consequences could this have, do you think, on the development of the little girl and the little boy?

That way the infants would be "seduced" by two parents! And why not? Today many young parents do share in the caretaking and upbringing of their babies. It is also more generally accepted, I think, that the father has a right to enjoy his babies as much as the mother, and she has the right to get away from them at times. It's surely good for both parents as well as for the baby's future development. As the growing child comes to learn that he or she is loved by both parents equally, and that the parents love and respect each other, but also that they sexually desire each other— a relationship from which the child is excluded—then that child is pretty much guaranteed a safe passage into adolescence and adulthood. As long as the parents love and desire each other, and as long as they don't give the child the impression that *it* is the central object of desire and narcissistic enhancement, then not only will the child add something profound to the parents' relationship, but it will also feel it has the right to its own identity.

I might add that I don't think the male and female roles should become confused. Children need to feel that father and mother are two distinct beings. And they need to be aware of each parent as having a special and different relationship with them.

So you would not want to eliminate gender (to use the term that is so popular in the United States)?

No, I certainly wouldn't. It would be a denial of reality for one thing. But it's also a way of dehumanizing people to deny their specific differences from one another and their different sexual identities. In any case the baby would not be fooled by that!

Ah, good point. The adults can try to fool themselves, but the babies are not fooled. Are the essential differences sexual differences?

Yes. But what are sexual differences? We need to define this term in an enlarged sense. Sexual differences are far more than simple gender differences. Although anatomical differentiation includes hormonal and emotional differences as well as different specific gender and sexual role experiences in growing into adulthood, this does not exclude the fact that each parent plays a vital and different role. These are in accordance with the concepts of masculinity and femininity for any given society, and play an important part in the bringing up of children right from the beginning.

With the new reproductive technologies, we may eventually get to the point where babies are reproduced or produced ex utero. Would all religion and art disappear if we were no longer carried in the mother's body, or would nurturing itself lead to sublimation? That is, would just the closeness of another body lead us to want to recover that feeling later so that art and literature and all civilization would still be very important as forms of sublimation?

You mean the fact that the baby grows outside its mother's womb? If we were to have test-tube babies, I imagine that in this

Brave New World they would have very different psyches from the children of today. That reminds me of a time when we used to raise chickens in our country house just outside of Paris. We had a couple of mother hens who raised their own chicks and then every so often we would buy one hundred day-old chicks that had a special lamp in their quarters to which they cuddled up for warmth. One day there was a tremendous thunderstorm, something quite rare in that region. Immediately the chicks raised by hens rushed under their mothers' wings and all the others rushed to the lamp! It's difficult to tell with chickens, but they certainly behaved differently.

We have the impression that you were more positive about homosexual relationships in your article "Eve's Reflection: On the Homosexual Components of Female Sexuality" than in the chapter in your book *Plea for a Measure of Abnormality*. Is that correct?

The chapter in the book was written some twenty years earlier. (In fact, it was the first article dealing with adult psychoanalytic work that I ever published.) My views have changed considerably since then. But also the article to which you refer deals only with the heterosexual woman and not at all with the manifest homosexual.

Do you still consider homosexuality a perversion?

I don't think I ever did. The last two chapters of my recent book *Theaters of the Mind* deal with what I call "neosexualities," that is, deviant sexuality which is usually heterosexual, and excludes homosexuality, although some homosexualities might deserve the name of perversion. I've written a follow-up to those chapters in *Theaters*, based on a talk I gave at the International Psychoanalytic Congress last year, where I discuss the differences between homosexualities and other deviancies. (It was published in *The International Journal of Psycho-Analysis* under the title "Identifications, Neoneeds and Neosexualities.")

You said in *Plea for a Measure of Abnormality* that it takes two problem parents to produce homosexual offspring. Do you still believe that?

On the whole, yes. This doesn't exclude the possibility that some baby boys are born with a predisposition to more effeminate ways of reacting and some girl babies with more masculine propensities. But I'm inclined to think that these inborn dispositions are not the decisive factors, that children who later discover themselves as homosexual had little choice in the matter because of the kind of family discourse and parental attitudes with which they were faced since infancy. Nobody freely chooses to be homosexual in a predominantly heterosexual society. I believe that homosexual adults feel strongly in most cases that this is the only possible sexuality for them.

Perversions, which I prefer to call neosexualities, are very different. Most fetishistic and sadomasochistic rituals, for example, are usually attempts to maintain a heterosexual relationship. Few of these individuals are interested in homosexual relations. And the majority of homosexuals say they are not interested in whipping or being whipped, etc. We probably have to talk in the plural—of "heterosexualities" and "homosexualities."

How do you treat the homosexual couple that seems to be mimicking traditional male-female relationships, in which you have the strong "masculine" figure and then the weak "feminine" figure? What about the very "feminine" figure?
Are you talking of males or females?

Female homosexuals. How do they arrive at their sexuality and what is their relationship to their father?
We have to beware of a fallacy in projecting onto homosexual couples, male or female, the image of a heterosexual couple. This is a heterosexual fantasy. There are many different kinds of lesbian couples. They aren't all alike. On the whole, they tend to have more stable relations than male homosexual couples do. And there is often an attempt to exclude the male world—the world of the father—and to recreate something of a mother-child relationship that did not work out harmoniously with the girl's own mother when she was small. For some reason, there is still a desperate need for contact with another woman for the exclusively homosexual girl, in order for her to feel complete as a

woman and know that she possesses her own sexuality in her own body. She discovers her body through the body of another woman.

Sometimes both partners in a lesbian relationship are seeking a fusional relationship of this kind with each other. When this is the case, it is one of the causes of passionate, angry fights. Lesbian couples sometimes come to consult because of the violence that breaks out between them that risks destroying their relationship. It seems to me that they are afraid of their wish to fuse and lose themselves within the partner so that they become only one body, only one mind. And of course such a wish is frightening, because it would be the equivalent of psychic death. The quarrels serve to reestablish separate identity.

Catherine Millot holds a doctorate in philosophy from the Sorbonne and teaches psychoanalysis at the Université de Paris VIII. She is a member of the Ecole de la Cause Freudienne.

SELECTED BIBLIOGRAPHY

Freud antipédagogue. Paris: Editions Navarin, 1979.
Horsexe: Essai sur le transsexualisme. Paris: Editions Point Hors Ligne, 1983. (Forthcoming in English by Autonomedia).

FOUR

Catherine Millot

Paris, Summer 1986

Catherine Millot lives near St. Germain des Prés, a neighborhood very popular with intellectuals and the avant garde. Over early morning coffee served on a silver tray, with the wind blowing through transparent white curtains that billowed out over the open windows, Millot smoked American cigarettes and answered questions with grace and élan. At ease in her body, her clothes, her brilliance, Millot spoke of her impending travels to South America and the United States. One felt that she would be at home anywhere. We can attest to this after seeing her at Columbia University and the MLA, where she presented papers.

What led you to become an analyst? What was important in your formation? Who are your patients?

I was led to psychoanalysis because I felt myself at an impasse. Before that, I had studied and taught philosophy. In 1971, I began an analysis with Lacan, which lasted eight years. After his death I continued with another analyst. Besides that I attended Lacan's seminars from 1971 to the end. I had also attended his presentation of cases at St. Anne's from 1973 on. My training was also connected to my own teaching in the department of psychoanalysis at Paris VIII, which began in 1975 and which was directed at this time by Lacan. I am still teaching there. At the same time I worked on Lacan's theories and on the history of psychoanalysis, beginning with Freud.

I wrote a thesis on Freud and pedagogy, which was published by Navarin, with the title *Freud antipédagogue*. And since 1975 I have also written many articles in *Ornicar*, a review edited by J. A. Miller, and in *Scilicet*, which was Lacan's review, published by Seuil. I would say that, in addition to Lacan's teaching, it was the work that I did for my own teaching that formed me. Besides that, I was in control [supervision] analysis. In the Lacanian training structure, controls aren't necessary, and I practiced for a certain time without feeling the need for it. I think that psychoanalytic training is essentially one's own analysis, then one's work on texts, and finally one's practice.

I have more women than men patients. This corresponds to the current figures in France. Most often, my patients are referred by my students or my readers.

Do you consider yourself a feminist?

I don't think that the women's liberation movement has the same meaning in the United States as in France, where to my knowledge there have been two directions in feminism. The direction of the struggle for certain rights is called the M.L.F. (Mouvement de la libération des femmes). These initials were also taken over by the group of Antoinette Foulke, who along with Hélène Cixous, founded Psych et Po, or Psychoanalysis and Politics. This first current I would call legalistic. It struggled for abortion rights and equality. It is the classical feminist position, inspired by Simone de Beauvoir. This position, which led to social reforms, is important but I didn't participate in it. Sometimes I attended meetings of the group called Psychanalyse et Politique, which was active for more than a dozen years. But I wasn't particularly interested in following this movement either. Nonetheless, it was stimulating. This group centered on examining the specificity of the feminine condition.

I was going through my own analysis at the time. Perhaps that is what drew me away from the group. In addition, group reflections didn't interest me. Besides I remember the big debates at that time on the question of whether there was a specific women's writing, which didn't seem completely convincing to me. There is certainly a different relation between women and men to the symbolic, but from that to say that there is a feminine writing is only possible if one considers it an invention, that is, an invention of language. To posit that there is a feminine writing is to want to make it exist, to produce it in some way and why not? But I would say that it has a dimension of artifice. It is a creation. But after all, woman is a creation also.

The movement Psychanalyse et Politique was inspired by Lacan's teaching. And Lacan in a way answered the feminists in his seminars, such as *Encore*.

In France psychoanalysts are more theoretical than in the United States. The Americans are very careful to remain close to practice and they distrust theoretical abstraction. I am not sure that they are right. In the American movement from the beginning of its history, there was an emphasis on ego functions, which was criticized by Lacan.

Do you agree with Freud on the development of the little girl in the Oedipal stage?

In the first stage of his formulation, Freud emphasizes the predilection of the little boy for the mother, a predilection which is interfered with by the prohibition of the father. He also sees the little girl as having the father as an object of choice. That's the first stage. But it seems to me that in the second stage of formulation, he underlines the fact that the mother is also the first object choice of the girl and that in changing the object, the girl also has to change her sex in some way.

What I present can be deduced from Lacan. In Freud there is

also an orientation of the son toward the father. The son chooses the father as object. It is part of the Oedipal stage. We can say that the Oedipal stage consists of what Lacan in the last phase of his teaching called the *père* (father) *version,* that is, a turning toward the father. And the pivot of this turning toward the father for the two sexes comes from the discovery of the mother's castration. It is because the mother appears phantasmatically castrated by the father that the two sexes turn toward the father as toward someone who is able to master life, to respond to demands.

The little boy withdraws quickly from the father because of his castration anxiety. To turn toward the father in a passive manner would be to put the son's virility in danger. Thus he is obliged to renounce the father as an object and to make an identification with him instead. As for the little girl, according to Freud, this obstacle of castration anxiety doesn't exist except in a few cases, and she isn't led to make this identification with the father.

In contrast, Lacan believes that the little girl is led very often to make an identification with the father. That is part of her Oedipus complex, according to him.

In Freud, the boy's identification with the father brings a set of imperatives which involves submission to the ideal of acting like the father; at the same time it brings a set of prohibitions. In particular the mother is forbidden as an object by the father.

The forbidding aspect in the Oedipus complex, which corresponds to the superego, is structured by the fear of castration in the boy. It is thus renunciation of the mother which gives the superego all its force. As for the girl, she renounces the mother because the mother appears castrated and not able to respond to the daughter's own desire for the phallus. The girl's orientation toward the father, in which she awaits the satisfaction of her demand for the phallus, isn't barred by prohibition. In Freudian terms, one can say that she remains in a position of expectation and that this expectation is resolved to the extent that she is satisfied by the baby that she receives from a man other than her father. In some sense, for Freud, this means that the girl remains bound to the father or to a substitute for the father as the one from whom she expects the phallus. She remains in a position of demand, of dependence in relation to the other. The castration complex makes the boy, who also has a demand for the phallus, renounce it. This constitutes the Oedipus complex for him. It is this renunciation that constitutes the core of his superego, which consists of all the imperatives that weigh on him but is also the source of his independence.

The situation is much more complicated in the girl. Childhood is long; so is adolescence. It will be a long time before she receives the response to her demand for the phallus. In the meantime she has been confronted with a deception which is liable to inscribe itself in her story, and which will end with her not receiving anything from the father. She is sometimes led to renounce this demand, and to proceed like the boy to an identification with the father. That is, she renounces the father as sexual object, but at the same time she keeps her father as object in the form of identification. And at that moment, there is a development that Lacan discussed in the seminar on *The Formation of the Unconscious* (1957–1958). The mother recovers her position as object in relation to her daughter: to the extent that the girl recovers a position of earlier dependence, in relation to her mother, this isn't a resolution of the Oedipus complex.

The identification with the father, which leads the boy to a positive disengagement, in the girl has rather the tendency to enclose her in a fixation at one and the same time to the father insofar as she identifies with him and to the mother inasmuch as she is reinstated as object. This is liable to produce a regression, in which she appeals to a mother for whom she would be the phallus. This is one of the aspects of the feminine Oedipus. But if this develops in all its amplitude, it becomes a handicap with regard to the possibility of orientation. Finally, what one can say is that the little girl, in this case, exchanges her demand for a substitute for the phallus for a phantasm that she has already had.

How do you define *narcissism*?

Freud has spoken of feminine narcissism as one of the seductive elements that women exert over men. He says that certain women love themselves above all, that they take themselves as objects and that that is the cause of their capacity for fascinating, for seducing men.

Taking up the question again in Lacan's terms, the situation that Freud outlines corresponds to the acceptance by the woman of her position as the object of masculine desire; she has an identification with the cause of the man's desire. It is what Lacan calls the object little "a" *(objet petit "a")*. One might also say that in this position, the woman is identified with the phallus inasmuch as masculine desire is oriented toward that. I think that, in effect, it concerns a sort of phallicization of being, which corresponds to the equation "girl equals phallus." It is in relation to the man's desire that she identifies herself as his object in some way. It is that which we call narcissism.

I would say that this is very different from the narcissism that Lacan describes in the mirror stage. And if one views narcissism in its dimension of relation to the similar, to rivalry, to competition, men aren't deprived of it at all. Quite the contrary. We see very well that this isn't narcissism of the same order, however.

Women also relate to the other woman, which is a more complicated relation than a simple connection to a similar object, since the other woman is something which links up with the fantasy of what a woman would be who is truly a woman, that is, it involves a questioning of the essence of femininity. It is not so much similarity that fascinates the woman in the other woman. It is what she can't succeed in rejoining, that is, Woman.

What are your thoughts on the nature of desire?

Men's desire is often the direct cause of woman's desire. This is also true in reverse for the man, but the fetishist side of masculine sexuality masks this dimension. Freud spoke about feminine passivity, but what he refers to isn't really passivity. The woman's desire is aroused by the fact of being desired by the Other. Some men may wonder: "This desire which appears suddenly in a woman, where was it before? Was she really hypocritical in hiding it until just now?" How should we situate this desire which emerges from his? There seems to be something scandalous here because it is enough to desire a woman for her to desire the man. Therefore where are we? Is she the prey of all desires? Evidently not. It may happen and it is a symptom (of illness) that a woman could be the offered prey to no matter what masculine desire. But it doesn't ordinarily work that way because there are always specific traits involved. She too has her connection with the particular. However, the man's desire is absolutely essential in creating feminine desire.

I wouldn't say that it is solely created by the man, however. It goes through the man's desire insofar as the man is the Other. It is to the extent that the desire of the man comes from the place that one might call the Other (with a capital *A: Autre*), to the extent that her desire joins with his desire, that he is the cause of her desire. For a man, the fetishist dimension makes him desire a woman because she has a physical trait which plays a role equivalent to the fetish, which allows him to ignore feminine desire. There are even men for whom it is a condition of their desire that the woman not have desire, and if the woman appears desirous in front of them, they panic and run away.

The desire of a middle-aged man to leave his wife for a much younger woman represents the resurgence of desire for the woman as the equivalent of the phallus.

Lacan spoke of a bigamy (although that is not the term he used), an essential bigamy in the masculine position. There is on one side, for the man, his desire which pulls him toward women who represent the phallus. The virgin and the whore are the most traditional representatives of this pole. On the other side, there is the pole of love which is concerned with the woman insofar as she is lacking. She is loved for what she lacks and responds to the love demands which are addressed to her by giving what she does not have, which is the definition of love for Lacan. I have the impression that men often maintain the two types of objects in their lives. This double vision of masculine desire exists in the woman also, but she can make them converge. One man alone is able to play both parts: (1) as bearer of the phallus, the carrier of the organ corresponding to her own desire for the phallus; (2) and beyond as the castrated or dead lover. The same man is able to support the two functions but they can also be separated.

What difference do you see between masculine and feminine *jouissance?*

The question of masculine and feminine pleasure is not one that Freud posed himself. In his seminar *Encore,* Lacan introduced the idea that there was in women what he called a supplementary *jouissance* in addition to what he called the phallic *jouissance,* which belongs to both sexes to the extent that the two sexes refer themselves to the phallus. Phallic *jouissance* comprises the *jouissance* of the organ but it isn't only that. There is a symbolic dimension also. Then what is supplementary *jouissance?* Supplementary isn't complementary. That is, *jouissance,* as Lacan sees it, is defective. There is something missing. He expressed feminine *jouissance* as the *jouissance qu'il ne faudrait pas* (which isn't necessary). There is a dimension of mistake that is at stake.

Supplementary *jouissance* does not complete phallic *jouissance.* That would be complementary. Rather it is a supplement. In the idea of supplement there is also the dimension of substitution, which relates to Lacan's term for the *jouissance* of the Other. This *jouissance* of the Other is the absolute *jouissance* but it is forbidden in the Oedipus and anyway it is impossible.

Traditionally one distinguishes—and Freud did so—between clitoral orgasm in women and the vaginal orgasm, the other orgasm that is proper to them. What Lacan challenged is precisely this organic dimension which is posited at the level of the vagina, which has no feeling. There aren't any nerve endings there. The vagina is one of the least sensitive zones of the body. Lacan deals with a *jouissance* which is not linked to this anatomical organ. He was able to connect this supplementary *jouissance* with the *jouissance* of the mystic insofar as it isn't bound to the organ. With regard to this, he referred to St. Theresa of Avila and St. John of the Cross. For St. Theresa, the body participated but not the organ.

What Lacan indicated on this subject is that men could have access to this supplementary *jouissance* as long as they placed themselves in a feminine position. This position Lacan defined as having a certain connection to the phallus, but not all, not completely, not entirely, not exclusively phallic. This articulation of the "not all" rejoins Freud, in dealing with what creates limit. What Lacan calls the phallic function, the phallic *jouissance,* is bound to what imposes limits, that is to say, the prohibitions emanating from the father, the menace of castration, the interdiction of the mother as object, the prohibition of absolute *jouissance* that the mother incarnates. It is on this limit that all of phallicism is founded.

On the woman's side, what creates limits is missing. The fear of castration cannot overcome her, even though she is liable to castration anxiety also, insofar as she makes a masculine identification. One can't eliminate anatomy entirely. There is an anatomical substratum in the male which gives consistency to the fear of castration. The woman's lack of limit ensures that she isn't just constituted by phallicism. The lack of limit allows her access to the other *jouissance,* to this supplementary *jouissance* of which Lacan speaks. One could say that the prohibition of incest is not valid for women and that in a way supplementary *jouissance* is linked to the incestuous one, that is, to an absolute *jouissance* which is not forbidden but which is impossible. Nonetheless, the supplementary *jouissance* is real although it is connected with that impossible *jouissance* also insofar as the woman incarnates the Other, a radical alterity. It is an important element in relation to which men find the subterfuge to defend themselves. This subterfuge takes the form of indifference to this *jouissance,* with the postulate that women don't enjoy themselves sexually. It's less current now because there is a whole ideology which emphasizes the feminine *jouissance.* But I think that in certain cultures, this assumption is still important and manifests itself in men's choice of frigid women as objects.

The virgin and the whore are representatives of the equation: girl equals phallus. The two of them are not supposed to enjoy themselves. It is well known that the prostitute doesn't enjoy herself. Even if that isn't true, the principle is there nonetheless. And that explains in part the attraction of some men toward prostitutes: the men are at least guaranteed that the women will not enjoy themselves. There is in women's *jouissance* something without limits, a sense of abyss.

Some women are fascinated by the prostitute also because as a figure of completeness, she is capable of having all the men. This includes the father. Therefore the interest in the prostitute is connected to the Oedipus.

How important is the pre–Oedipal for you?

For Lacan, there is no pre–Oedipal. What is called the pre–Oedipal is a retroactive construct which is effected after the Oedipal stage. It is because of this that one is able to speak of a phallic woman, that is, to the extent that that implies that there is the term *phallus*, which is introduced by the paternal function. If this dimension exists, it is because the father is part of the setting. So what is called the primitive mother is a phantasm which Lacan calls the big A (the Other), which would not be castrated, not marked by lack, but is in the register of omnipotence. And it is in this regard that there is an equivalence between the figure of the *femme/mère* as nonlacking, complete, and the figure of the father as the imaginary father, who is also in the place of omnipotence and totality. It is because of this strict equivalence that we speak at certain moments of the combined parent, this figure which joins together the masculine and the feminine. This figure of totality posits the subject as the phallus: he/she is the one who completes the other. It's complex because identifying oneself with the phallus of this Other who is complete makes oneself equal nothing. This connection to the other's totality is destructive, essentially deadly.

What is the place of myth in psychoanalysis?

Mythology is a production, a formation of the unconscious, the discovery of which allows us to analyze the structure of myths. Lacan has a formula which states, "Truth is structured like fiction." That is to say, myth is a construction which makes the state of truth conscious. Analysts are often engaged in analyzing myths and using them, that of Oedipus, for example. Freud also invented an analytic myth of his own, that of the primitive father.

We wonder if new myths aren't now being created by women analysts.

Our first interview with Françoise Petitot took place in the Palais Royal, a place where the French writer Colette used to live. Petitot's spacious and airy office overlooks the beautiful gardens and gravel walks. We met Françoise Petitot another time for brunch in a restaurant full of flowers in Greenwich Village. Once again, we were charmed by her warmth, intelligence, dynamism, and her giving of herself.

Françoise Petitot has published many articles in the French feminist review *Sorcières*.

FIVE

Françoise Petitot

Paris, Summer 1985 and New York, Summer 1986

Where do you place yourself as an analyst?

I am very much influenced by the reading that Lacan made of Freud. I also have an alliance with the women's movement and I founded the Editions Tierce★ with Françoise Pasquier. At present I am working on a research project at the CNRS (National Center for Scientific Research) called "Women's Discourse in the Age of Psychoanalysis and Freud."

Do women participate in the same way as men in the creation of language and myth? Is there a difference between the male and female unconscious?

★A feminist publishing house in Paris.

Language and myth are structures in which women as well as men are encoded. In this register, women participate like men and are produced by it, for I believe that women like men are created as subjects by language. I think that the unconscious, insofar as it is a product drenched in language, is the same for all speaking beings. The question is how in this sea of language, this discourse and structure, one subjectivizes a sexed position as a man or a woman. In fact, this subjectification doesn't have to correspond to one's anatomical sex. Therefore, I would never say that there is a male unconscious or a female unconscious.

The difference between the sexes seems to be essential to psychoanalysis. Do you agree? What are the consequences of this?

Freud says that there isn't any difference between the little boy and the little girl until the moment of the Oedipus complex, which according to him is the moment when they subjectivize themselves as male or as female in their identifications and in their positions with regard to *jouissance. Jouissance* is not sexual pleasure alone. It is what enables us to live and function, and it belongs to different registers, such as complaint, sorrow, even hate. It is during the Oedipal stage that the little boy and the little girl have to choose an active or passive identity which puts them in a masculine or feminine position. They face their subjective position in relation to the structure of discourse which will encode them. Therefore, there isn't a male or a female unconscious but rather subjective positions which are different from one individual to the other.

Psychoanalysis asks how a speaking being functions and how the differences in the sexes are managed by a speaking being. It holds that the difference in the sexes is the paradigm for all differences and that to the extent that humans are creatures of language, the production of the difference of the sexes is also a production of language and not just an anatomical production. How does a creature of language go from its anatomical sex to a psychic sex, a position which is bound to anatomical sex but not exclusively?

There remains the question of the phallus, that is, the question of what is the sign of difference, which is anatomically the penis but symbolically the phallus, representing what Lacan called the master signifier, that which permits language to exist. There is a displacement of the anatomical organ to this symbolic production, the phallus, which no matter how far one goes in the displacement toward symbolization remains attached to the organ. It is a question on which many of us at the CNRS are working. Freud would say that if it is the penis which becomes the support for this differentiation, even in the phallic symbolization, that is because it is seen. Freud says that the little girl sees that the little boy has a penis and that she doesn't have one. Therefore, everything here is bound to vision. This is what all analysts in one way or another take up again, even when they are Lacanians. When they are asked, "Why is the phallus the signifier of lack, of the name of the father, etc.?" they answer, "This is what attracts us the most easily." This is equivalent to saying, "That is what is seen," what is bound to the question of tumescence and detumescence. It is something which is able to be the mark of what could be lost, and there is an "ease" in this representation. But this is unsatisfying as a response at the same time that it is satisfying. For we recognize that something visual which constitutes the mark of difference, this part of the body which is able to be lost, is in fact a privileged support. That which links the mark to an organ has certain consequences.

Freud made some effort to detach the organ; Lacan made much more, but the phallus remains attached and here is where the problem lies. One always wonders if psychoanalysis has worked out a new way of seeing things or if it tries to put what has always been said under a new form. Monique Schneider, for example, claims that Freud only put things into a different form, that he dragged out all the imaginary discourse about women, the connection of women to nature, the essence of the feminine, while making feminine equivalences with the passive, the unknown, the nonverbal, "the dark continent."

Are the feminine and the masculine condemned to be separated?

In the very structured formulations of sexuality with Lacan, not everything is in the phallic register—the register of representation, of language, and of (phallic) *jouissance*. There is a remainder which is on the side of the female position, it being understood that not all women are exclusively on that side; there are men who are able to be there also. For example, many male analysts say that being an analyst allows them to recover their feminine side, that is, not the phallic *jouissance,* but the other *jouissance,* which Lacan called feminine. But there always remains the mystery of the body, where reproduction resides. What is real in the body doesn't pass into language, into representation, but nonetheless experiences *jouissance.*

If we posit the hypothesis that the phallic register is everything which is able to represent itself verbally, to enter into the organization of language, there always remains the question of that which is inexpressible because it doesn't have a means of representation. We can speak ultimately of a feminine essence, feminitude, a connection to the body, the ineffability of sensation, and the reproduction of babies.

One part of us escapes the strictly Oedipal organization to which all speaking beings belong, whether we are men or women; it is what is sometimes called the pre-Oedipal, to which Freud alluded when he spoke of a "dark continent," which he compares to the discovery of the Minoan-Mycenean civilization under the Greek civilization, that is to say, an unknown territory, very little penetrated where the mother/daughter relation in particular resides. We can call this period the archaic.

The archaic is as mythical as the unconscious through which we try to take account of that which is beyond representation, that which has been repressed.

The question isn't really to say what hasn't been said but rather to explore the realm of the inexpressible. One always ends up with this well-known statement: "The name of God cannot be said." And this is why one finds equivalences even in Lacan between the question of the feminine *jouissance,* the mystical *jouissance,* and the name of God which is unsayable. Is there a reality which is actually unpronounceable not because society doesn't accept its existence but because it hasn't reached representation? Is there a way of writing which can render the inexpressible? These are some of the questions which are embedded in Marguerite Duras's work. In the analytic structure, it is true that the feminine is able to be the carrier of this inexpressible because women are, in large part, in the other register.

Freud's question, Lacan also posed. "What do women want?" Freud said, "Women don't tell us anything." He also said to the women analysts who worked with him, "You are like men." A question remains. Why is the feminine the carrier? Is it in large part because women are the ones who have the babies? The mystery of mysteries is this possibility that women carry in them of procreation. It is a question of the body, and it isn't by chance that there are more women hysterics than men, who become obsessional instead.

What is the so-called primitive mother? How different is she from the phallic mother?

The first mother is the placenta, which threatens us with the risk of not being separated, of not acquiring our own subjective position, that is, of being only a piece of flesh appendixed to another. After birth, the "primitive mother" is like an abyss; we feel the vertigo of returning to nothingness, which is sometimes fantasized as a place of ineffable pleasure. The parasitic, vegetative life that we have lost is felt as something which would be marvelous. But its recovery is entirely imaginary.

Myths deal with beginnings. Through them, we represent the creation of the world and its organization. Whether it be God who has created the world by his word, or the primitive mother, it is always a question of origin and of nothingness. The abyss represents a return to nothingness, which is completely imaginary. It is not enough to leave the mother's womb to be born. Most psychotic children are never born. To be born one must be a speaking being, for language has the function of separation.

Like the primitive mother, the phallic mother is also imaginary. In an early stage, the child thinks that the mother possesses the phallus. That would be a position of omnipotence, for the representation of a mother who doesn't lack anything is, at one and the same time, man and woman, mother and father, castrated and phallic. She is therefore an imaginary representation of the idea that the mother is everything, and the child wants to give itself to her so that she would have even more. People who are not autonomous might be in this position of giving themselves endlessly to the mother or her representation. Therefore one offers to her one's body with all its symptoms, its maladies, its being, for her missing anything would be intolerable. It is lack which would make her desire, for in order to desire, it is necessary to lack something. The object of desire has to be elsewhere; it is in the other. The phallic mother is precisely that which hasn't been amputated; in my view she is just another version of what is called the primitive mother. These different formulations aren't entirely recoverable. The primitive mother and the phallic mother are different representations of a mother who wouldn't have need of another to procreate. Sex here doesn't make any sense, for the difference between the sexes doesn't have a representation that is bound to language, that is cultural.

It is probable that insofar as the imaginary is tied to images of the body that that will have its effects. But difference in the sexed position isn't given at the outset, it is something which is constructed. "One isn't born a woman, one becomes one." This phrase is Simone de Beauvoir's but Freud said it also. There isn't any difference between little boys and little girls until the Oedipal stage. Or as he put it, until the Oedipal, there are only little boys. As I said before, it is primarily language that creates the difference.

How is this difference worked through?

With language, there is of necessity an enunciator, who may be God, the great Other. There is someone somewhere who has created language and who would be the imaginary representative of this Other. For the child, it is the fused body of the parents that has produced her or him; it is a type of bisexual monster. But at the same time we aren't able to say that it is bisexual because the difference between the sexes makes no sense to the infant. I think that it is a representation of the imaginary combined parental couple which supports beginnings.

Language presupposes a speaker who is in reality also spoken by language. The individual has to deal with parents who are themselves encoded by language that goes beyond their social roles, their psychological position, their personal fantasy, their personal structure. It is very complicated, because to the extent that one speaks of the relation to the mother or the father, I feel like saying that they aren't real persons, they are only roles. One might say that what the infant has to deal with in the earliest moments of its life is motherhood, whether the baby is held by the real mother or by another person. This nurturing person is able to be multiple and can be male or female.

I don't think that these things change much. What will change is men, the fathers who are putting themselves into a particular position with regard to paternity. The two great questions in psychoanalysis are: "What does a woman want?" and "What is a father?" The positions that a man may take with regard to what it is to be a father will certainly have repercussions. It isn't what he does alone, but what he does as signs of a position in relation to paternity. This includes not being able to play the role of a father or playing the maternal role or only being a progenitor. There are probably subjective questions on paternity which are changing; furthermore, all the new technologies of reproduction put into question what constitutes paternity.

Could you elaborate on what is also in the process of changing, the new instrumentalization of maternity?

Are you referring to surrogate mothers, the production of children, the "right" to have a child? Just this morning I heard a colleague speak, for whom there is no reason not to have baby buyers the way that there are meat buyers. The position that children will have as objects of production makes me shudder. But we haven't thought enough about this. We have gone from the desire for a child to the right to have a child. There will certainly be effects from that. Children will not be born into the same type of discourse, of representation. Women don't totally realize what they are initiating when they demand the *right* to have a child. Whether I am homosexual or celibate, I will be able to have a child if I want to, when I want to, without sexual relations. Prenatality is now impregnated with scientific, medical and economic discourse. In this perspective, the child would become something like merchandise.

Now when I hear my patients tell me that when they were little, they were told that babies were bought at the supermarket, I say to myself, "After all, we aren't very far from that in what we are now talking about." We are outside the sexual and sexual pleasure, outside the relation of a man and a woman, and also outside of the usual relation between women and children in the case of surrogacy. I don't know if this will be better or worse. It is frightening with regard to the criterion of values.

With reproductive technology there is a manipulation of the woman's body which is very important. Is maternity something that anyone should be able to possess and something that one can demand? The manipulators are the doctors who are usually men. Basically, what is involved here is the question of origin. It isn't surprising that the seekers have a desire to know more and that they want to tear the secret out of the bodies of women, the mothers. There are women who participate in this also.

Is feminism influencing psychoanalysis?

There is no question that the women's movement is posing questions to psychoanalysis. Freud wrote a number of texts which touch on the differences between the sexes at the moment that he was questioned by the German feminists in the 1920s and 1930s. And Lacan's texts such as *Encore* date from the 1970s and are contemporary with feminist questions. I think that the questions of the feminists have led analysts to try to answer them. In some ways, psychoanalysis and feminism are antithetical. Feminism is an active social and political movement but its discourse has brought questions to psychoanalysis. Texts like those of Michèle Montrelay on feminine sexuality or those of Lacan are the effects of a feminist discourse.

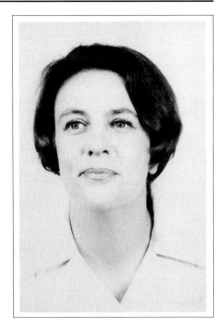

Janine Chasseguet-Smirgel holds a diploma in political science and a Ph.D. in psychology. She is also a Docteur d'Etat ès Lettres et Sciences Humaines. From 1982–1983, she occupied the "Freud Memorial Chair" at University College, London and in 1984, she was André Ballard Lecturer at Columbia University. At present, she is a training analyst at the Paris Psychoanalytical Society and Vice President of the International Psychoanalytical Association.

SELECTED BIBLIOGRAPHY

Female Sexuality (ed.). Ann Arbor: University of Michigan Press, 1970.
Freud or Reich? (coauthored with Béla Grunberger). New Haven: Yale University Press, 1986.
Creativity and Perversion. New York: Norton, 1984.
The Ego Ideal. New York: Norton, 1985.
Sexuality and Mind. New York: New York University Press, 1986.
Ethique et Esthétique de la Perversion. Seyssel: Champ Vallon, 1984; in press in Germany: Deutsch Verlag.

SIX

Janine Chasseguet-Smirgel

Paris, Summer 1985

Janine Chasseguet-Smirgel lives and practices in a beautiful seventeenth-century *hôtel particulier,* formerly inhabited by the nobility who wanted to live near the Louvre. Inside is a paved courtyard through which horses and carriages once passed. Walking up the white marble staircase, we came upon frescoes. Chasseguet-Smirgel had just returned from a conference in Hamburg. She asked if it were all right if her dog, so happy to see his mistress return, could stay in the room. We were delighted with the big, black, curly haired, friendly creature, who barked for emphasis at seemingly just the right moments. Despite her fatigue, Chasseguet-Smirgel was warm, generous, and always psychologically acute and impressive.

What was your psychoanalytic training like? In what school do you see yourself now? Have you moved from one school to another?

I have not moved between different schools. I am a member of the Psychoanalytic Society of Paris, and I began my analysis in 1953, that is to say, at the moment when there was a split between different schools, but I totally ignored the existence of problems within French psychoanalysis. I underwent analysis for myself and I didn't care about anything else. I was lucky to begin very young, and I thank my neurosis for having pushed me into analysis.

I became an analyst for two reasons. First of all there was my neurosis. I was able to test the therapeutic effects of analysis on myself. I wasn't led by an intellectual interest. In fact, nobody is led there by purely intellectual interest. That is an illusion. Besides I had a training that was a little peculiar because I received a degree in political science. From this I got the impression that behind political phenomena there were always psychological ones that one had to investigate. That was a second, more intellectual reason which impelled me to psychoanalysis.

In the book *Feminine Sexuality,* which is so popular in the United States, you speak a great deal about Freud and other analysts, such as Jones, Horney, Deutsch, but you don't mention Lacan? Why not?

First of all, that book is a collection which dates from 1964. Lacan was already known but he wasn't the celebrity that he became later. Besides I must say that I continue to be very reserved with regard to Lacan. His theory seems to me negative for women. His system pushes phallocentrism, which already exists in Freud, to the most extreme conclusions. I have never been able to understand why there are feminists (more in foreign countries than in France, by the way) who relate to Lacan.

Perhaps you know that I held the Freud chair during the year 1982–83 at the University College, London. When I was in England, I met women who asked me all sorts of questions about Freud and feminism and about the fact that there are French feminist writers who were influenced by Lacan. For example, J. Hyvert, whose books I read when I was in London, refers to Lacan's theory of language while trying to recover or to recreate a language which would be a primitive maternal language in place of the paternal one. I believe that this is completely contrary to what Lacan wanted; furthermore, in Lacanian theory this would signify a return to psychosis, to a language which would be a nonlanguage.

In *Feminine Sexuality*, you interpret the myth of genesis in a way which seems to perpetuate matricide. Even if this myth is only the expression of a desire, shouldn't it be the role of psychoanalysis to go beyond the decoding that you provide to denounce the myth as a fantasy which structures the unconscious?

As I recall, I speak of the myth as an inversion of reality: it isn't the woman who is the mother of the man, but rather the man who is the mother of the woman. It isn't that I accept or don't accept the myth. What seems important is to listen to the desires that are expressed by the myth. Even though it negates reality, it legitimizes certain needs. In a paper in 1975, I develop the idea of the importance for the baby boy or girl to leave the maternal universe at a certain moment of development and to transfer power to the father. In this transfer of power, "patriarchal society" is marked by problems connected to a particularly negative relation to the mother and also to what I would call masculine uncertainty concerning male identity and worth. These narcissistic problems for men which demand that they transfer power from the mother to the father also exist in many women. In my practice—but also in daily life—one sees women who are deeply hostile to women and not only during the Oedipus complex, which is normal. Not long ago I heard some women on a bus protest that there are so many women bus drivers, saying that they take men's places. I think it would be completely unjust to say that this position simply reflects the male one. I believe that there are deep feminine attitudes which are tied to the need to separate oneself from the mother's bondage. It is inaccurate to think that patriarchal society results simply from men's oppression of women. Women also desire to confer power on men or on fathers to liberate themselves from maternal dominance.

One of the essential problems that psychoanalysis should consider is to define what belongs to reaction formations or the defenses concerning the primitive archaic conflicts with the mother and to determine what is necessary structurally for the development of the two sexes. This displacement of power from the mother to the father is important in the formation of the human being. At a certain moment, it is necessary to leave the maternal bond and to draw nearer the father and confer certain powers on him. One then achieves an equilibrium between that which is structuring and that which is pure defense, a way of attaching oneself to the father to avoid falling again into the maternal universe, which would be psychotic.

This is perhaps something that Lacan saw well. But the Oedipus complex as he sees it refers simply to the fact that the father arrives at a certain moment and cuts the bond between the infant and the mother, that is, when the infant is no longer the phallus of the mother, and separates from the mother. But that is merely a pure defense against the archaic mother, not the Oedipus complex. In fact, what exists in the Oedipus is a positive bond with the mother; the father interferes with the love that the child has for the mother. In the Lacanian system as I understand it, the mother is driven by her desire to have a penis—which is a controversial point even in Freudian theory. Now Lacan takes this point of Freudian theory to structure the Oedipus. But at the moment of the Oedipus, one has already left the archaic maternal world and has changed one's attitude toward the mother. There is not only rebellion against her omnipotence, there is also love. And here is one of the tragic aspects of the Oedipus complex: the father and the mother are both invested positively and negatively at the same time. It is not that one has the part of the savior and the other the role of the sorceress as in Poe's tale "The Pit and the Pendulum." In that story, the hero is enclosed in a pit which constantly changes its form and threatens to crush him completely. At the end, the Napoleonic army arrives with General Lassalle, who rescues the hero from this strange place where he is buried. He draws him out and saves him from what seems to be the mother's body, but this is not the Oedipus. It is a vision of an archaic, dangerous relation to the primitive mother.

What consequences would a more equal sharing of child rearing by the mother and father have on the development of the little girl and the little boy?

This question leaves me perplexed because what does a more equal share mean? The absence of the father from the child's early infancy doesn't exist any more. The father is close to his baby. A total confusion of roles—the father who gives the child something to eat, who stays at home, the mother who goes to work—one can see in certain Scandinavian countries, and also in the United States, but much more rarely in France and not at all in Eastern Europe. I wonder if this is really positive. I believe that an excess in this sense leads to a confusion of roles in the child who at a certain moment ought to be able to face the need of turning from the mother to the father. This requires a differentiation between the two parents. A confusion in the roles may lead to a confusion of images of the father and the mother in the unconscious, which would be destructive.

The more one goes from neurosis to psychosis, the more one sees this confusion between the imagos of the father and the mother dominating the psychic tableau. Neurosis is a structured mental response to problems that the neurotic has the capacity to solve. Thanks to analysis, the patient is able to give up the crippling aspects of the neurotic solution. What dominates the psychic picture in psychosis is the confusion between the father and the mother's imagos which tend toward a nondifferentiation. I am aware that what I am saying is not very fashionable, but I think that the confusion of roles has reinforced the sliding from the neurotic solution toward the psychotic one.

Having said that, I would also like to make a qualification. I don't think that roles alone are the determinants in nurturing. There is something more important, which goes beyond the simple fact of whether the father changes the diapers or not. The respective attitudes of the father and the mother structure the psyche of the infant and permit it to differentiate the paternal and maternal imagos, if the father and the mother occupy a settled place in each other's unconscious. This is essential in the psychic structuration of the child of either sex. A confusion of roles reflects another confusion that exists inside each of the parents with regard to their own parents.

What would be the consequences of a reproduction *ex utero?*

I don't know if that will ever take place, and I don't know why biologists would want to have it.

Don't you think that it could be part of a quest for power, a masculine usurpation which would take away from women that which is unique about them?

I think so. Certain feminists seem to me to go in a direction that is unconsciously antifeminist, those who don't see how maternity and the fact of being pregnant is tied to a great enhancement. It is an enormous pleasure. One often sees postpartum depressions which are connected to no longer having a mother/child unity in which the mother identifies herself with the infant in utero. In pregnancy lies the possibility of the woman's complete fusion with her mother, something which a man can never recover exactly. Thus, in spite of all the prophets who want it, I hope—for the mothers' and infants' sake—that children will be born naturally, except in cases where mothers aren't able to have children otherwise—and even then what is going to take the place of the mother's womb, of this state of union between the mother and child?

My husband, Béla Grunberger, has placed a particular emphasis on this existence in utero for psychic development. He sees the desire to recover this existence as the source of enormous accomplishments, religion being one of them. He thinks that Freud in speaking of monotheistic religions was wrong to find only the representation of the father in God. It is also the representation of the omnipotence that the infant loses after birth and after he distinguishes between the self and the object. He tries to overcome these limits by searching for the lost narcissistic unity through all sorts of achievements and through incest. Ferenczi insists that incest is a way of recovering the situation in utero at another level.

In your book *The Ego Ideal,* **you say that eating the forbidden fruit represents incest with the mother. How do you interpret the fact that Eve is the first to eat it?**

If I remember correctly—my book was published in 1973—I based this on the idea that eating the forbidden fruit is eating from the tree of knowledge and knowledge in the Bible is carnal knowledge. The prohibition of knowledge is also the supreme prohibition of knowing God. It is knowledge which is forbidden in the Bible, but which in contrast is possible to get in the gnostic heresies. Eve makes Adam taste the fruit. The desire for knowledge is a sign of hubris among the Greeks and a sign of pride in the Bible, which is here projected on the woman. It is she who represents evil, temptation, sex. Because she is the origin of life, woman becomes the point of departure for projections that we know can take all sorts of forms and all sorts of objects.

Do women project less than men? It seems that men project all the time.

Projection is a mechanism that is universal and normal. In *The Ego Ideal,* I speak of the projection of the lost omnipotence onto the first object, which is the mother. One loses this omnipotence at the moment one perceives that one is no longer without limits as one felt in the womb. At the moment that we differentiate between the self and the object, projection begins. As Freud says, when one has known satisfaction, one is obliged to recover it, one way or another. Therefore one projects omnipotence on the first object, the mother. It is only later that one projects divinity onto the father.

I don't think that women project less than men. But perhaps this projection on the second object, the father, gives preponderance to the sociocultural universe in which men dominate women. The great ideas which dominate our world are the masculine projections. Racism, one of the most massive projections of our epoch, has been developed essentially by men. But that doesn't mean that there aren't women who have adhered to it and still adhere to it.

Yet when we study the psyche of the sexes closely, we perceive —and I am not the first to say it—that there is probably a greater importance for the inverse mechanism for women—that is, for introjection. This mechanism consists of taking something into oneself, of swallowing, incorporating, and not of going out from the self. This mechanism exists in both sexes, and is necessary for the enrichment of the ego, but there is a preponderance in the woman, which is without doubt bound to her capacity for maternity, and for incorporating the penis to create an infant. This concrete incorporation extends to more abstract mechanisms. That women use this mechanism more frequently than men explains the quantitative difference between women and men's psychic problems. For example, the great number of depressions in women are bound up with introjection.

Both incorporation and introjection, however, are essential for the phenomenon of identification. It is thanks to them that we become relatively autonomous. In fact, the child will become autonomous and be able to take on the capacities of the person who takes care of him to the extent that the child identifies with that person. Furthermore, all that we learn is bound to the mechanisms of incorporation, introjection, and identification. But there is always one sex which has a greater propensity toward one or the other of these mechanisms.

Do you accept the two representations of the pre-Oedipal mother that certain feminists speak of: the primitive, archaic, and dangerous mother and the more structured phallic mother? How do these two mothers exist together in the individual's psyche?

I spoke a great deal about the archaic, primitive mother at the London Congress (see *The International Journal of Psycho-Analysis,* 1976). The phallic mother was first seen by Freud as the male's projection of his own sex on both female and male beings. One day he perceives—with horror according to Freud—that his mother has no penis. At the moment of the Oedipus complex, the child perceives castration and not sexual difference. Castration becomes an event that is liable to happen to him. In a defensive way, he projects a penis on all women, in particular, on his mother, and denies his perception of the lack of a penis. According to Freud, the phallic mother is a purely defensive construct. The fetishist continues all of his life to have a type of double register, in which one part of him knows very well that a woman doesn't have a penis, but another part continues to think that she does.

After Freud, Ruth Mack Brunswick wrote an article called "The Pre-Oedipal Organization of the Libido," in which she says that the infant of both sexes imagines that the primitive mother is all-powerful and is therefore provided with all the most enviable organs, including the penis. Therefore the little girl wants a penis like the primitive mother. Alas, it's not this way in Freudian theory. This article by Brunswick was probably written in 1938. It was annotated by Freud and published after his death in 1940. According to the author, she has incorporated Freud's annotations; therefore, this article would represent Freud's final ideas on the phallic mother. For my part, I attribute the structure of the imago of the phallic mother to a complex process. To be engulfed in the maternal abyss is dangerous. Rather than that, the young child attributes a phallus to the mother which eliminates the possibility of being swallowed up in the vagina. The child then associates the danger coming from the mother with the penis. And there would then be in the child of either sex a desire to castrate the mother.

When we reread Freud's essay *The Wolf Man* (I give a reading of it in my book *Creation and Perversion*), we see that all the activity of the wolf man is aimed at castrating women and making them inferior in order to suppress the dangerous phallus and also to prevent it from penetrating the infant.

I would also like to add that in *The Ego Ideal* as well as in my subsequent studies of perversion, I give a central importance to Freud's idea that the absence of the knowledge of the vagina is common in both sexes, that before puberty (this is something that Lacan had always continued to affirm), this ignorance protects the two sexes. Above all, this enables the male child to avoid being cognizant that the father has a more satisfying organ than his for gratifying the mother, and saves him from an intolerable narcissistic injury.

Is this negation of the vagina Freud's defense or the defense of the little boy?

Freudian theory expresses the defense of the little boy facing the Oedipal drama. The success of the Freudian theory of the ignorance of the vagina is bound to the fact that it avoids a great narcissistic injury. One of the things that I find completely inadmissible in Lacan's theory is that it takes this part of Freud's theory that is most controversial and makes it the center of the theory. I think that is completely defensive.

Do you know the work of Judith Kestenberg in the United States on the subject of the knowledge of the vagina?

A little. It seems to me that she says that the little girl is aware of her vagina but is afraid to localize her vaginal impressions. She caresses her doll because it is at the same time a means of discharging a diffuse sexual excitement and a way of projecting limits of an object. I believe that her theory recognizes an early and inner awareness of the vagina in both sexes.

What does the Oedipal father represent for the two sexes?

First I would be sufficiently in accord with the Kleinians and the Lacanians of another register, who refuse the distinction between the Oedipal and pre-Oedipal. The Kleinian groups would speak of genital and pregenital. According to Melanie Klein, the Oedipus arrives very quickly in the second half of the first year. In a paper presented in New York in December 1984, when I was the André Ballard lecturer at Columbia University, and entitled "The Archaic Mother in the Oedipus Complex," I tried to show that there is an extremely archaic Oedipus complex in which the reality principle enters into a struggle with the pleasure principle, which is represented by the mother's womb to which the child desires to return. The reality principle is represented by all the obstacles that the child finds to his desire to return to the mother's body: the father, his penis, the siblings. All the obstacles to the return to the mother's body are perhaps to be considered as part of the paternal essence and as bound to reality since it is reality that prevents the return to the mother's womb. There is therefore a confusion between the paternal universe and reality. What I also tried to say in this paper is that thought itself is a way of introducing reality into the universe of the pleasure principle. In his article

"The Two Principles of Mental Functioning" (1911), Freud re veals the opposition between the pleasure and the reality principles. There wouldn't be a need to think if one didn't find obstacles. I try to show how thought itself is tied precisely to the impossibility of returning to the mother's body, which would be the smooth universe of the pleasure principle.

Therefore, for me, there is no pre-Oedipal or Oedipal father. The father is by definition tied to something that I have called the archaic mother of the Oedipus complex. He is all which comes to oppose this soft universe of pleasure which is mingled in the maternal body without obstacle and where thought does not yet exist.

Is there is a difference between men and women's pleasure? We often speak of the need for mastery in male pleasure.

I think that there is a difference but that mastery isn't the particular property of one sex. Mastery, like a total lack of mastery, can be a defense in either sex. A man has to affirm that he is provided with different organs from those of the mother. This may be a reaction against the fear of being engulfed by the mother while trying to master her and impose himself in a phallic way; it is aggressive and defensive at the same time. But there is also the prize of possession of the other in the sexual act, which is normal in both sexes. It is evident that for the woman, the sexual act, which consists of being penetrated and also of retaining the incorporated penis, psychologically is tied up with the mechanisms of incorporation and introjection. When this sexual act isn't prohibited, when it isn't stopped by a need of mastery or by a fear of mastery (for the two exist), it leads to a desire to incorporate the penis into a body which has lost its boundaries. There is a kind of need to be invaded by a man's penis.

Symmetrically but not identically, the man has a desire to be swallowed up entirely in the body of the woman and to return inside the mother in this way. The man and the woman are essentially bisexual at the psychological level, for each of them identifies with the two parents and not only with the parent of the same sex, and each sex ought to be able to integrate the opposite sex also, not just the parent of the same sex. There is a possibility for the two sexes to identify with the pleasure of the partner and during the sexual act to experience by identification, indeed by fusion, the pleasure of the other sex. At the same time, I believe that the pleasure is different and that there is also a possibility of being able to live vicariously something which is more appropriate for the other sex. There isn't a complete separation of the sexes. On the contrary, a successful sexual act indicates a possibility of fusing with the other sex in a temporary way and forming a unity with one's partner.

In the feminine imagination, the seducer and the instructor are able to coexist. Is there an equivalent representation in the male imagination?

Here one falls into all sorts of questions. For example, it is accepted that a woman might have a lover much older than she. However, it is less acceptable for a man to have an older mistress. I think that the woman naturally finds help confronting the maternal power in the man to whom she easily transfers the image of the father. The desire to find or to be at the same time the lover, the instructor, and the seducer is similar for the two sexes. But it is very difficult and in a sense perhaps partially pathological for men to consider the woman as their instructor to the extent that that implies that their identification with the father and their own feeling of identity haven't been achieved. Yet having said all that, we know that there is nothing absolute here. Young men who are initiated by older women are a widespread phenomenon, but this is a "rite of passage," which ought to be passed through like all passages. If the woman has a need to be protected, it is in relation to the mother, and if the man has a need to be stronger, that is also in relation to the mother. Finally, the couple in which the woman depends on the man isn't something purely ridiculous as long as that doesn't enclose each sex into a rigid role. It is hard to be a virile man—I don't speak of machismo—it is something which is natural and positive and which probably aids the child of a couple to growth and health.

These considerations allow us to say that what we call patriarchal society is finally all that which is macho, a society which is bound to attitudes in which virility isn't represented in what should have been integrated, but rather in a parody of virility. There is a well-known article by Joan Rivière called "Femininity as a Masquerade." I think that what's happening in the macho attitude is that it isn't true virility but rather a masquerade also. True virility does not have such fear of the mother but rests on a good identification with the genital father.

At the Congress in Germany that I recently attended, there was a discussion on Nazi fathers and children. I asked whether the Nazi fathers were truly fathers in the sense of a paternal image differentiated from the maternal imago. Surely Hitler wasn't such a father even if he presented himself as such to the German people. Rather he was the dangerous, archaic mother, provided with all the apparatus of a regressive phallicism: boots, whips, arms. . . . That isn't virility.

Does the split into virgin/whore stem from the macho virility complex? Do women make a similar split of men?

Concerning women, I think that there is sometimes a cleavage. The paternal transference as I have described it in *Feminine Sexuality* represents an idealization of the man, the father, who protects the girl from the all-powerful mother. At that moment, he is totally forbidden, for all the components that we just spoke about, the mastery and aggressivity which are inherent in the sexuality of both sexes are repressed and counterinvested. Some women have a lack of success in sexual relations, indeed a frigidity with a certain type of man but a satisfying sexual relation with men who are passers-by, gross, a little sadistic. The woman doesn't fear using these men sadistically since she herself is being used that way. This is something which corresponds to splitting. The sexual man might be something of a bum; on the other side is a man who is idealized. This is a little like the virgin and the whore. Nowadays the virgin/whore split exists less at the level of the collective imagination. Novels would be completely ridiculed if they adopted this type of split. Men have less need to find a virgin today, except perhaps those who are completely paranoid. They fear finding a penis in the nonvirgin. Furthermore, paranoia is linked to the fear of homosexual desire. But something still exists which is similar to the virgin/whore split. There are men who are impotent with women who aren't prostitutes. Because their aggressivity toward the mother is neither accepted nor integrated, these men fear hurting women. Having relations with a prostitute is more acceptable to their superego than having a relation with a "respectable" woman. It is the reason for the desire to dirty, to sully, which is often unconscious.

Do you think that there are differences between the masculine superego and the feminine one?

This is an extremely difficult question. You know that for Freud the woman has a less severe superego than the man. For Melanie Klein, it is the opposite. I also think that there is a difference. If one judges by women's descriptions as well as clinically, at first sight, one would think that the woman has a more severe superego.

That is a generalization and obviously there are lots of exceptions. Women undoubtedly have more prohibitions than men, and I would be inclined to think that that is the result of a more severe superego. But Freud has insisted on the fact—and this is completely true—that a fully developed superego, which results from the resolution of the Oedipus complex, is an impersonal superego, one which hardly reveals any traces of the people with whom the person had identified. It becomes independent; there is no longer a question of obeying orders or opinions, but rather the subject is capable of differentiating good and bad without caring about the opinion of his neighbors, the public, or the boss. According to Freud, men arrive at that point but not women. Therefore when I say that a woman has a superego which is at least as severe as that of the man, there is perhaps a contradiction there because often the woman is obliged to rely on a man's opinion. Yet there is something here that is much more superficial than one might think.

When a totalitarian regime is installed in a country, one has the impression that the wives accept the opinions of their husbands or those of the groups to which they belong, which are principally masculine opinions. But when women are concerned with saving human lives, they know as well as men how to be independent and impersonal, not better but as well. During the Resistance, for example, there were numerous women who were able to have an independent and objective opinion.

Is there a difference between the ego ideal of men and women?

The ego ideal touches the collective more than the superego does. When Freud introduced it in an article on narcissism, it was a concept which joined the individual and the collective. Perhaps because a woman has the possibility of reunion with the mother through her capacity to have children, she projects her ego ideal on extremist ideologies less often than men do. I just returned from Germany and I know how many women terrorists are in that country. Therefore what I am saying has many exceptions. But in general women have less need to project their ego ideal on extremist formations which promise them the realization of paradise. In my book on the ego ideal, I connect the extremist ideologies to the possibility of returning to a lost paradise which is the mother's body. Now if one fixes upon this return to a lost paradise as an objective, reality is always opposed to it. Whether it be the ideologies of the extreme left or of the extreme right, they are always tied to something violent and aggressive. Because he doesn't have the capacity for motherhood, the man perhaps fixes his ego ideal on the extremist ideologies more often and that leads him to revolutionary groups which want to sweep away the superego, to make all culpability disappear totally. However, among the Russian nihilists, there were many women, and among the Nazis, there were female guards in the concentration camps. What in their structure made them choose this more masculine mode of resolving the ego ideal? Not all ego ideals lead simply to destruction. But in my book I stressed those which are connected with the disorders of ideality.

In *The Ego Ideal* you make a distinction between the amorous state and love. What psychoanalytic interpretation do you give to the fact that the amorous state is so often found in literature, for example, in courtly love and romantic love?

I think that the nonconsummation of sexual desire in the amorous state always remains the carrier of the ego ideal, and that at the same time this includes an incestuous aspiration which itself contains the primitive desire to return to the mother's body, to the lost paradise. The amorous state remains magically invested with this desire and therefore gives the reader the illusion of being satisfiable one day. But once satiated, desire becomes something completely limited. It becomes human and is no longer the carrier of this total accomplishment of being that persists in the amorous state if one defines that as the carrier of a desire that doesn't end. The tragedy of human love is that unhappily when this love is realized, it loses much of its attraction. It is necessary to add many other things to the fascination of the first moments of love, in particular, the possibility of consoling each other for its loss, and of loving each other not only because one reaches paradise together but also because one remains outside the door. Successful love is love which accepts the limits that are inherent in the human condition.

What about the relation between sex and gender? In the United States, one defines gender as what society does with the differences in the sexes, as the roles which it imposes. Gender might be called cultural sex. What is your position on gender in relation to sex?

Gender is cultural in a large sense. I had the occasion a number of years ago to go to a hospital in Paris where there was a department that treated sexual ambiguities, that is to say, children who were declared boys or girls at birth and then were found to be genetically opposite. The parents raised their girl as a boy or their boy as a girl for several years. Now one knows that after a period of time, even if it were possible physiologically to restore them to their true sex, it would be a tragedy in the children's lives if one said to them, one day, "You aren't a little girl, but rather a boy" or vice versa. I didn't work in that hospital, I simply observed, but there were psychoanalysts there who decided that it was necessary to perform surgical and hormonal interventions to allow the child to remain in the assigned sex and not the biological one. This depended on a number of factors, connected, of course,

to the imprint that was already made on the child, to the investment that the child had made as a boy or as a girl. And there was
therefore no absolute response. Even so, one knew by a certain
time that the game was over. If one then transformed a boy into
a girl, a psychosis would occur as if the ancient sex of assignation
returned under a delirious form.

Margaret Mead wrote a great deal about social roles. It seems
that they are very different depending on the culture. There is no
social role which is universally accepted.

Do you think that roles are necessary?

I can only answer by taking up again what I said before: it seems
to me indispensable for the mental health of a child that there be a
difference between the father and the mother, not just a physiological difference but also a psychological one. This difference
passes in part into roles without our having to fall into an excess,
consisting, for example, of saying that a woman must absolutely
have children, nourish them, stay at home. Without going to
extremes, this differentiation ought to be found somewhere in the
man and the woman, in whatever might be the acceptable social
roles without its leading to a total imprisonment of the man and
the woman in these roles. One knows that there are functions and
professions which have been considered masculine for a long time
that belong to something completely feminine, for example, being
a doctor. For reasons which tend to shut women up in secondary
roles, it is considered completely natural that she should be a
nurse and not a doctor. That's not what I want, but I think that a
total confusion of roles is probably harmful to a child; there ought
to be a differentiation which doesn't entail superior and inferior,
subordinate or dominant.

At the end of *The Wolf Man,* Freud speaks of the fact that the
child feels a need to classify its impressions in categories, and
Freud connects this need to phylogenesis. The classification into
categories is something which permits the child to depart from a
primitive chaos and to enter into a universe of significations, of
differentiations. Reality is made up of differences. If all is equal,
there is no reality, there is chaos. To leave this chaos, which is the
same as psychosis, it is necessary to have differences. But the

differences don't signify that there is more on one side, less on the other. Differences are necessary. It is perhaps very difficult to arrive at roles in which one isn't more and the other less. But it is necessary to help the child classify, to make categories, and the first category is the category mother/father.

PHOTO: JACQUES SASSIER

Julia Kristeva was born in Bulgaria and now lives in France, where she is a psychoanalyst and teaches at the University of Paris. She has a regular teaching appointment at Columbia University in New York as well. She has written extensively on linguistics, psychoanalysis, philosophy, literature, and the condition of women. In her theories of textual analysis, she is part of the international avant garde.

SELECTED BIBLIOGRAPHY

Essais de Sémiotique. Paris: Mouton, 1971.
About Chinese Women. London: M. Boyars Publications, 1986.
Revolution in Poetic Language. New York: Columbia University Press, 1984.
Polylogue. Paris: Editions du Seuil, 1977.
Desire in Language: A Semiotic Approach in Literature and Art. New York: Columbia University Press, 1980.
Powers of Horror: An Essay on Abjection. New York: Columbia University Press, 1984.
Le langage, cet inconnu: une initiation à la linguistique. Paris: Editions du Seuil, 1981.
Tales of Love. New York: Columbia University Press, 1987.
Au Commencement était l'amour: psychanalyse et foi. Paris: Hachette, 1985.
The Black Sun: On Melancholia and Depression. New York: Columbia University Press. Forthcoming.

SEVEN

Julia Kristeva

Paris, Summer 1980

The following interview with Julia Kristeva took place in the summer of 1980 at the Closerie des Lilas, a popular café in the Montparnasse district and a favorite of Kristeva's. In direct contrast to the Café des Deux Magots, where everyone goes to watch the street entertainment, La Closerie is more exclusive. Even so there were disturbances and we had to go inside. But Kristeva's warmth, charm, and friendliness made one forget the abrasive effects of the street noises. Although her English is excellent, Kristeva chose to answer questions in French, for she felt that this would allow her greater accuracy and subtlety. Kristeva was first a literary critic and then an analyst. She has had a great influence on the linguistic, literary, and feminist psychoanalytic scene in

France and the United States, in part because of the ease, the freedom, and the brilliance with which she deals with the most difficult ideas.

Would you agree, in the words of Sherry Turkle, that there was a psychoanalytic revolution in France, and that now the culture is very much oriented toward a psychoanalytic point of view, which it had not been before?

Yes. There was an enormous delay in France on the question of psychoanalysis. For its mass diffusion, it had to await the arrival of Lacan; and on account of this delay, I think that the diffusion of psychoanalysis was more intense. Moreover, it touched important spheres of cultural life: the universities, the domain of art, even the question of mass communication. The whole of French society—at least in the cultural dimension—has been profoundly shaken up and influenced by, let us say, Freudo-Lacanism.

Do you feel that France is as narcissistic a society as critics such as Christopher Lasch have said that the United States is? Are the French also concerned solely with gratification of the self?

What I can say is that French culture is extremely chauvinistic; it is preoccupied with national values, it is interested in its own past, it treats its tradition as a model, and it suffers from a closedness toward the outer world. Yes, it's a form of narcissism.

Very interesting, but this is a group, a social form of narcissism.

On the other hand the idea of the "self" is not a French idea. It belonged originally to Anglo-Saxon psychoanalysis, and it doesn't fare very well in French psychoanalytic literature. It's not a key idea, if one is talking about psychoanalysis; and moreover, if you're talking about subjectivity, are individuals in France narcissistic, I wouldn't say that. One would have to make use of other categories—it's more hysterical, more paranoid, not so much narcissistic—if one can generalize in this area. Personally, I would avoid national diagnoses. I don't think there is a national psychology. I think there are individual differences.

But you do have what is called the borderline personality in France also? What direction will psychoanalysis have to take in order to treat the borderline?

Yes, well, that is a very interesting question. I think that the idea of the "borderline" comes from Anglo-Saxon psychoanalysis. The French authors who are interested in this problem are people who have been influenced by Winnicott and Fairbairn. So what is the direction one would have to take to come to terms with this problematic? First of all, I think, a very great attention to the writings of Freud, for despite appearances I am convinced that there are, in Freud, "flashes," very rapid perceptions, perhaps rather summary ones, which he quickly turns away from, but there are nevertheless approaches to those problematics. These occur when he is discussing obsessional neurosis, phobias, and hysteria. He quickly turns away from these questions. Nevertheless, one would have first of all to reread Freud, and to see, every time he speaks of his neurotic cases, how he treats the problem of narcissism, for it is at these moments that the question of the borderline might be understood. For this has to do with serious deficiencies at the level of narcissism.

Another direction that we should perhaps take to understand these patients is a very great attention to two things which seem paradoxical: on the one hand, to speech (discourse)—and it's here that the contribution of Lacan is important. Because he taught us to listen to what he calls, following linguistics, the signifier. So, one would have to try to follow these patients at the level of their speech, with all the implications that their speaking may have, of which they are not conscious, but which are inscribed in their speech at the level of the signifier. And that is a rather difficult sort of attention because the discourse of the borderline is fragmentary, it's difficult to follow, it's full of gaps, it doesn't have much logical order. And on the other hand, one would not be able to stay at this level of the signifier. It would be necessary for the analyst to be implicated much more profoundly than in the cure of neurotics in order to be able to associate on behalf of the patient. That is to say, to do all the work of free association, of which the borderline patient is not yet capable, and that presupposes two sorts of intervention. There is work to be done at the level of free association, at the level of mental functioning of the patient, to try to make the logical relations which he or she cannot make at first. But on the other hand the analyst has to put oneself in the place of the patient in order to try to relive the pre-Oedipal traumas. Therefore, it requires a great regression on the part of the analyst, to be able to follow the regressions of the patient, and this possibility of regression on the part of the analyst must be accompanied, of course, by a strong presence of the ego so that the analyst can perform the pre-Oedipal submersions and at the same time permit the patient to construct a relation to the object and to the other. Such a position can be, logically and linguistically, formulated by very strongly condensed interpretation. But, in brief, the cure of borderlines would require a use of the whole range of psychoanalytical ways of listening, which one can use in bits, in a fragmentary way, with different patients.

When did you decide to become an analyst?

I was working on language, and in particular on language in limit situations where it does not yet exist—that is to say, the language of children; and where it no longer exists, that is to say, psychotic language. And as I worked in these linguistic situations, I realized that I found myself or put myself in a relation of transference to the people I was observing, and I wanted to experience these transferences more personally. Because in fact I came to realize that there is no such thing as a neutral meaning, and that a signification is a signification that is made between two who are at least four. It was therefore necessary to contest the whole of positivist linguistics; I wanted to put positivist linguistics on trial by starting from a precise experience of the transference.

In an interview that you had done once for Psych et Po, which was translated in an anthology edited by Elaine Marks and Isabelle de Courtivron called *New French Feminisms,* **you said, and here is the translation: "There can be no sociopolitical transformation without a transformation of subjects, in other words, in our relation to social constraints, to pleasure and, more deeply, to language." Else-**

where you have spoken about the importance of language for structuring experience, and so have other French theorists. American feminists speak about the importance of language also, but they are talking about something quite different from what you are talking about. How could we go about changing our relation, particularly women's relation, to social constraints, to pleasure, and, especially, to language?

When I spoke the sentence you have quoted, it had to do with the following: very often, in France, a certain sort of feminism had posed itself solely as a movement of sociological protest, which consisted in making of women a sort of social force or motor which would ultimately take on the role played in Marxist theory by the proletariat. Here is a class or social group which is oppressed, which is not paid well enough, which does not have its proper place in production and in political representation, and this oppressed class, this oppressed social stratum, should fight, essentially, to obtain this recognition—economic, political, and ideological. I, on the other hand—and I am not alone in this; a large part of the French feminist movement, I think, is aware of this problematic—think that women's protest is situated at an altogether different level. It is not first of all a social protest, although it is also that. It is a protest which consists in demanding that attention be paid to the subjective particularity which an individual represents, in the social order, of course, but also and above all in relation to what essentially differentiates that individual, which is the individual's sexual difference. Well then: how can one define this sexual difference? It is not solely biological; it is, above all, given in the representations which we make ourselves of this difference, and we have no other means of constructing this representation than through language, through tools for symbolizing. Now these tools for symbolizing are common to the two sexes. Everyone speaks English if you're English; everyone speaks French if you're French, whether we are men or women. So how do we situate ourselves in relation to these universal tools in order to try to mark our difference?

Here the position of some feminists has seemed to me rather

strange and regressive. Certain feminists, in France, particularly, say that whatever is in language is of the order of strict designation, of understanding, of logic, and is male. Ultimately, theory, science, is phallic, is male. On the other hand, that which in language, according to the same feminists, is feminine, is whatever has to do with the imprecise, with the whisper, with impulses, perhaps with primary processes, with rhetoric—in other words, speaking roughly, the domain of literary expression, the region of the tacit, the vague, and where one would escape from the too-tight tailoring of the linguistic sign and of logic. I think that this is, so to speak, a Manichean position which consists in designating as feminine a phase or a modality in the functioning of language. And if one assigns to women that phase alone, this in fact amounts to maintaining women in a position of inferiority, and in any case of marginality, to reserving them the place of the childish, of the unsayable, or of the hysteric.

That the valorization of this modality of expression can have a critical, if not a subversive function, is obvious; but I think that it is not sufficient either. On the other hand, other women say that we must equip ourselves with or appropriate the logical, mastering, scientific, theoretical apparatus. They consider it as an extremely gratifying promotion that there are women physicists, theorists, and philosophers. In saying this, they preserve for women an extremely important place in the domain of culture. But these attitudes can be accompanied by a denial of two things; on the one hand, of the question of power, and on the other of the particularity of women. One can be a theoretician and a woman, or only a theoretician and not a woman. In other words one can fit oneself to the dominant discourse—theoretical discourse, scientific discourse—and on the basis of that find an extremely gratifying slot in society, but this to the detriment of the expression of the particularity belonging to the individual as a woman.

On the basis of this fact, it seems to me that what one must try to do is not to deny these two aspects of linguistic communication, the mastering aspect and the aspect which is more of the body and of the impulses, but to try, in every situation and for every woman, to find a proper articulation of these two elements. What does "proper" mean? That which best fits the specific history of each woman, which expresses her better. So you see that I would be just as much against the slogan, "All women should master the dominant discourse." I am also against the position which asserts that all that is part of the game of power and that women must express themselves in literature. I think that the time has come when we must no longer speak of "all women." We have to talk in terms of individual women and that each should try to find her place inside these two poles. I gave a talk on this some time ago which appeared in *Les Cahiers du Grif,* which is the Belgian women's paper, and it was called "Unes Femmes," spelled "unes" with an "s" on the end and "femmes" with an "s." What I meant by that is that there is a community of women, but what seemed to me important is that this community should be made up of particularities and that it not be a uniform mass. And one of the gravest dangers that now presents itself in feminism is the impulse to practice feminism in a herd. I think that at first this was perhaps something important because people cried out, "We demand abortion," "We demand the social advantages we have been denied," but now this "we" is becoming troublesome. There have to be "I's" and women have to become authors, actors, not to hypostasize or overvalue those particular kinds of work, but I say this so that this perspective will push each one of us to find her own individual language.

Would you say something about your concept of "abjection" in your book *Powers of Horror?*

The term in French has a much more violent sense than in English. It means something disgusting.

Abasement **perhaps?** *Degradation?* **It doesn't quite cover it but are these terms closer?**

Yes, there is all that; there is also the aspect of nausea, of wanting to vomit. *L'abjection* is something that disgusts you. For example, you see something rotting and you want to vomit. It's "abject" on the level of matter. It can also be a notion that concerns moral matters—an *abjection* in the face of crime, for example. But it is an extremely strong feeling which is at once somatic and symbolic, and which is above all a revolt of the person against an external menace from which one wants to keep oneself at a distance, but of which one has the impression that it is not only an external menace but that it may menace us from the inside. So it is a desire for separation, for becoming autonomous and also the feeling of an impossibility of doing so—whence the element of crisis which the notion of abjection carries within it. Taken to its logical consequences, it is an impossible assemblage of elements, with a connotation of a "fragile limit."

Would you say that women's experience of abjection, to use the English word for a moment, is the same as men's, or is it different? Is there a sexual differentiation?

To tell the truth, I did that work without asking myself that question. I wanted first of all to scan the notion in a more general way. But obviously I did it also on the basis of my own experience, because it is mainly a psychoanalytical book, but which like all psychoanalytical books is somewhat self-analytical, like—I am going to make a pretentious comparison—Freud's *Interpretation of Dreams,* which was based essentially on his dreams—and so this book is in great measure based on my own experience. I would say that abjection is a category which cuts across the two sexes, as one can be phobic whether one is a man or a woman or as one can be schizophrenic whether one is a man or a woman. On the other hand I have asked myself whether men and women behave in the same way when abjection becomes a source of pleasure. When, in other words, there are eroticizations of abjection, as for example one finds in the case of perversions: sexual pleasure in the face of disgusting things or in the face of disgusting actions. And in fact I think that here I can say that there is a difference in the relations of man and woman in this regard. I think that a woman does not eroticize abjection or the abject by herself. She does it if she is in a relationship with a man. In other words, if she does it, it is to carry out the desire of a man.

I do not think that there is a propensity to perversion in women. Cases of feminine perversion are very rare, and are above all perversions which are meant to satisfy the perversion of a man. Why? Because this relation to abjection is finally rooted in the combat which every human being carries on with one's mother.

In order that we become autonomous it is necessary that one cut the instinctual dyad of the mother and the child and that one become something other.

Now a woman gets rid of her mother in a much more complex way than a man. Either we don't succeed in doing so, and we carry with us this living corpse—but in that case we women (and, once again, it's very difficult to generalize) close our eyes: that is to say, we don't want to know, we don't eroticize this relationship. There is, as it were, a veil, like the hysterical veil which one sees in the gaze, very often, of the hysterical woman, which is extremely brilliant but sees nothing—a veiled gaze at a region of forgetfulness, which is the archaic relationship with the mother. Or one recognizes this relationship with the archaic mother, but in this case there are different forms of defense, of which feminism can be one, or again, if one enters the combat, this gives rise to fairly serious forms of psychosis. And this retreat, the eroticization of the mother, which produces abjection as a source of pleasure, does not seem to me something built in.

Is what you have said about the eroticization of abjection connected with Freud's theory of the splitting of the sexual object into the degraded and the exalted?

Yes. Exactly.

And would you agree that women do not split the sexual object in the same way that men do?

Exactly. They don't have to divide the object—the feminine sexual object has only to be abandoned: one abandons the mother for the father. And therefore the cleavage happens differently.

That's the cleavage.

Right. The question of the eroticization of abjection—it's interesting, what you asked—can present itself in another form as well, not only that of the desire which a woman can have for a man but also in the case of female homosexuality. That is, when one has not made the move to a male object but chooses as an erotic object an object of the same sex. Thus, inside a certain sort of female homosexuality one can find an eroticization of "abjection." This is not the case for all female homosexuality, for here we have a rather interesting range of variations.

There are two rather well-known books in the United States: one by Dorothy Dinnerstein, called *The Mermaid and the Minotaur*, and the other by Nancy Chodorow called *The Reproduction of Mothering*, whose thesis is that the exaltation and the degradation of the woman stem from the fact that it is mothers who rear children, and that if fathers or men were to have equal responsibility for the rearing of infants, this would eliminate all of our sexual malaise and end all of the problems having to do with women's inaccessibility to culture.

I don't think so. Because if there is a sort of rage against mothers it is not only because they take care of the child, it's because they carry it in their bodies. And that is something which men, even if they handle the diapers, can't do. I think that there is rooted a negative desire, a certain rejection of the maternal function—a fascinated rejection. Moreover the fact that men do the same work as women with regard to the education of children or their early upbringing will certainly change things in the psychic functioning of children. But I don't know if it will do so in the way foreseen by these feminists. In fact it will first displace and then decimate the paternal function. It will render ambiguous the paternal role. Up to the present, in the division of sexual roles, the mother takes care of the child, the father is farther away. The father represents the symbolic moment of separation.

And you feel that that should be retained?

If we do what they call for, that is, if the fathers are always present, if fathers become mothers, one may well ask, who will play the role of separators?

Couldn't they both be? Couldn't both sexes be nurturers and differentiators somehow?

I would like to think so. But it would be very difficult. What seems more likely is just that there will be many borderline children produced, and it will become necessary to find a third party, for example, the child psychotherapist, the school, all those medical sectors of the different "psy's": psychoanalysts, psychiatrists, psychotherapists, et cetera, who will play the paternal role. The number of helping institutions for early childhood, for school children, that are forming now in our society, is extraordinary, and one may well ask oneself what their function is. Well, every time I have looked closely at what these people do, it is, of course, to replace a failed mother, as is remarked only too often. But it is above all to replace a nonexistent father: to play the role of the separator, to play the role of someone who comforts the mother in order to permit her to take her role in hand, but at the same time the role is one of a third party. The question I think one ought to ask is not so much what must be done in order that women be happy, it is: what is to be done in order that children have a development—not a normal development—but let us say a development which permits them to accede to the various elements of human culture? And I think that what interferes with that access is the underestimation of the paternal function.

Nancy Chodorow would say that the function of the father has nothing to do with his sex, and that someone female could play the same role of separator.

Yes, certainly; that's why I say "a third party"—who could be the woman psychotherapist of the hospital where one can go with the child. In the family, the mother can be this third party, in relation to the father, or further, to a symbolic institution (religion, morality, social and professional goal). But how can a mother gain access to this third or symbolic function? That is the problem.

To return to that problem of not being able to overcome the biological fact of the mother carrying the child, never mind rearing it. How would you feel if the biological revolution were to go so far that the reproduction of the infant would take place outside the womb? Would you welcome that possibility, which is no longer quite so much of a fantasy as we had considered it even five years ago?

It's a very grave question and in fact I think about it often. We are all caught up in moral scruples, and we tell ourselves that in the near future such a prospect is to be avoided for ontological and ethical reasons, for the various experiments which could be done in this area should have guarantees. People have the impression that they are exposing themselves to kinds of arbitrariness which are not very far from the experiments of the Nazis, which hover on the horizon. This is a defensive attitude, which I cannot keep myself from having. But I think that nothing will stop "progress" and that, as you say, this will be the case some day. Assuming that, the question to ask ourselves is, how will sexual roles be distributed? What will fathers do and what will mothers do, when the child is no longer carried in the uterus?

Here we are in the face of a humanity whose character is completely unforeseeable. In the present state of things, there are two attitudes one might have. One, a defensive one, would consist in saying: there must be preserved, along a straight Freudian line, the distribution of the paternal function on the one side and the maternal function on the other, so that the speaking subjects who are constructed, psychically and not just biologically, can have the "normality" which we think of as theirs; and what is this normality? It is that which succeeds in getting along, surviving, in the Oedipal triangle. That is the defensive position. It seems to be more and more untenable. Hence the interest that I have in the cases of "borderlines." For I think that we will not be able to hold on for very long to this position—the fathers on one side, the mothers on the other. There will be mixtures of these two functions, which will give rise to a very different psychic map of humanity. One will no longer see, or very rarely—we are daydreaming, but perhaps it is not altogether a mere daydream, that hypothesis of which you spoke—if the production of children outside the uterus were to be realized, the good neurotic caught between Daddy and Mommy. One will have a psychic structure much closer to what is now seen as borderline, I suppose. Which does not necessarily mean that it will be outside the social order.

For a modern individual, who has had to manage the array of information of our times, which is scientific information, which is the mixture of the media along with television, there are ten thousand sorts of information which bombard us constantly—if an individual wants to be, not someone who lives in the middle of the seventeenth, the eighteenth, the nineteenth centuries, but contemporary with that information, one should be an individual who is not individual, but an explosion of either polyvalence or polymorphism. Well, that is someone of whom one cannot yet have the map, the precise representation. But I think that what some are trying to address today starting from these cases of borderlines, or indeed what a certain sort of modern art today displays as subjectivity, will approach that sort of individual. So what I can say is that the interest which the psychoanalyst can bring at the present moment to subjectivities which are not neurotic, but which have something to do with what is called psychosis, well, that interest will permit us to address with more assurance the psychic problems which will pose themselves in the face of this new, artificially manufactured humanity. For the moment, this is, again, a dream.

Or a nightmare.

Or a nightmare. It is fairly terrifying. But perhaps one must not close one's eyes to it. There is going to be a great battle around this; the opposite attitude will be taken by the moral authorities: the Church, a certain part of the psychoanalytic profession, which will fight for the classic Oedipus, and initially this will be a safety belt—perhaps a saving one—which will permit us to push away this experiment or at least to protect humanity from a certain number of moral risks which this experiment implies. But I think that if one calculates over the long term, if science were capable of what you say, the moral authorities would not be able to resist very long. And at that moment it would be necessary to have a knowledge of the human psychic structure in order to have a response or a way of acting toward those individuals. And for the moment I don't know what means we can have for knowing what problems these people can pose, except for these cases of borderlines and even psychosis.

Do you feel that desire between the sexes depends on difference, on differentiation? Could it possibly be founded on something else?

I don't think that it's founded only on difference, it's also founded on sameness. Anyway, one must know what one means by "desire." If you mean a desire as Freud defined it or as it functions in Western literature, for example, or when one takes the texts of Hegel, desire is founded on the notion of negativity, of lack, and therefore always on difference. But if you mean by desire, the attraction of the sexes to each other or of individuals to each other which makes it possible for the sexual act to take place, I think that, in great part, that functions on the basis of identification. For example, all homosexuality (but not only homosexuality, also the attraction of many men to women) has arisen on the basis of the similarity or identification which one may feel with another. This is not necessarily desire in the Hegelian sense of the term, but it is an attraction in the sense of the Freudian eros.

What do you see as the place of love in the new conservatism of the family?

It's the only thing which can save us. My seminar, this year, at Paris VII University, is on the "Love object."* One would have to try, in this situation, to save some territories of freedom. What is a territory of freedom? It is, in what concerns affective work, let us say, a place where people could explore the limits of their discourse, of their thought, of their manipulation of colors and sounds, of words, whatever you like. But the space of freedom for the individual is love—it is the only place, the only moment in life, where the various precautions, defenses, conservatism break down and one tries to go to the limit of one's being, so it's fundamental. The love relation is a situation where the limits between the *Ego* and the *Other* are constantly abolished and established.

Well, that is an assumption that many women today would not accept at all.

*Kristeva subsequently published *Histoires d'Amour,* translated as *Tales of Love.*

Yes. An assumption, yes.

People like Kate Millett in *Sexual Politics,* or Shulamith Firestone in the *Dialectic of Sex* say that love is a myth propagated by men for the control of women, that, in effect, what it has done is to perpetuate the hierarchy of the sexes and make women accept their oppressive place within the family. Firestone has said that men don't really know how to love at all—it's only women who know how to love. So this would seem totally opposed to your point of view, which is that love can be a species of freedom, the only means of defense against an oppressive state.

There are many things to be said about that. First of all, love is not something fixed; there is a history of love. When one takes the evolution of this concept in the West, one realizes that love for the Greeks was not the same thing as medieval love—courtly love—Romantic love, and existentialist love. So there is an evolution which is not necessarily progress. I would call it a recreation, but in any case a movement in what is called love, and it is obvious that in certain situations and some of the time, it has been possible that it is a means of blackmail by one sex of the other—and essentially by the male in the history of humanity as we have experienced it in relation to the female. But that is a vision, perhaps, through the wrong end of the telescope, which doesn't interest me very much because if you look at things that way, the whole of culture oppresses women—a madrigal or Shakespeare is antiwoman. Fine, if one wants to put it that way, but, on that basis, long live genetic manipulation or whatever. What is one supposed to do about it? What does one suggest as an alternative? It doesn't seem to me a very exalted view of things. On the contrary, I am not in favor of decimating men or of believing that patriarchy is a horror. I think that culture—in particular Occidental culture, which is founded on patriarchy and expressed in the great religions which were—which still are— Judaism and Christianity—has produced profoundly true visions of the human being as the symbolical being, as the being who lives in language and who is not reduced just to the womb and to reproduction. Now love is a moment in the life of a speaking being who, all the while caught in the body, opens oneself to the symbolic dimension. I love the other, who is not necessarily me, and who gives me the possibility of opening myself to something other than myself. This can take place through an imaginary fusion with this outer body, but if it is experienced not in a merely narcissistic way but as the governing principle of my whole subsequent existence, what I call love is openness to the other, and it is what gives me my human dimension, my symbolic dimension, my cultural and historical dimension. So if one says that it's patriarchy which produces that, long live patriarchy.

I for my part say that the love relation is the only chance to go through narcissism toward the recognition of the symbolic moment. And I would look with horror on a humanity which would decapitate or wipe out this symbolic moment. If that's what some feminists propose, I don't want any of it.

Well, I guess that some of them, at least, would say that what they propose is a different form of love than has existed in the past. As you point out there is a history of love, there are changes, and no doubt there will be transformations.

As you say, they will probably say that there are forms of love, but I don't know if they would recognize that love is a relation not merely to another self (*moi*) as we come together in order to get ourselves narcissistic gratifications, but it is also, by means of that, an *opening of my self* toward a symbolic dimension. Love is not simply when you give pleasure to each other, it can even be very different; it's above all when I am able to listen to Gesualdo, or to see a Rothko painting. Those can be moments of love. I am not capable of seeing them or of hearing those objects if I am caught in an essentially biological dimension or the dimension of protest. And I think that the feminists now, after a phase which was essentially critical or protesting, are trying to find a way of talking to people — to women — about that opening, the symbolic dimension where women ought to place themselves, and not to shut themselves up in wombs, or in machines which make children outside wombs. Can you imagine a humanity having as an objective or as sole horizon the reproduction of the species? The symbolic is a matter for speaking beings, and we women are first of all speaking beings. That must not be left to the patriarchy alone.

Luce Irigaray is a dissident psychoanalyst and writer; she has also been extremely active in the French women's movement. Her revolutionary quality lies in her exploration and deconstruction of existing mythological, philosophical, and psychoanalytic systems.

SELECTED BIBLIOGRAPHY

Speculum of the Other Woman. Ithaca: Cornell University Press, 1985.
The Sex Which Is Not One. Ithaca: Cornell University Press, 1985.
"And the One Doesn't Stir Without the Other." Trans. by Hélène Vivienne Wenzel. *Signs* 7, no. 1 (1981).
Amante Marine, de Friedrich Nietzche. Paris: Minuit, 1980.
Passions Elémentaires. Paris: Minuit, 1982.
Le Corps à Corps avec la Mère. Paris: Pleine Lune, 1982.
L'Oubli de L'Air. Paris: Minuit, 1983.
Ethique de la Différence Sexuelle. Paris: Minuit, 1984.
Parler n'est pas neutre. Paris: Minuit, 1985.

EIGHT

Luce Irigaray

Paris, Summer 1980

Luce Irigaray lives on the top floor of a very modern building located in the fifteenth Paris arrondissement in an apartment full of light, with huge bay windows, white cabinets, beige shag rugs, abstract paintings, and a superb African sculpture.

This interview took place while we were drinking strong black coffee on the floor of the room where Irigaray practices analysis. The floor-to-ceiling window, through which light flooded, the couch, chairs and rug, all white, with a few rocks scattered here and there, created the atmosphere of a surrealistic beach under Paris skies.

Luce Irigaray was tired and was not sure that she would be able to sustain a long interview, but slowly, after the first questions, she became immersed in deep analytic thinking. Recognizing Serrano's practice of yoga, Irigaray attributed to it her feelings of strength and serenity when the interview was over.

Feminism has been considered simply another *ism* in the phallocratic system. Considering feminism in France, do you share this opinion?

I don't particularly care for the term *feminism*. It is the word by which the social system designates the struggle of women. I am completely willing to abandon this word, namely because it is formed on the same model as the other great words of the culture that oppress us. I prefer to say "the struggles of women," which reveals a plural and polymorphous character. But I think that when certain groups of women criticize and fight against feminism, they don't take into account the gesture they are making with regard to the dominant culture. After all, it is necessary to consider the way they attack us, and it is most generally under the label of feminism. In this case, it is necessary to claim the term back and then to refine it and say something else.

At present, in France, do you discern several feminisms, several currents in the women's movement?

Yes, and I may perhaps forget to mention some of them. But I want to say first that the ideas that were defended by the militants in 1970 have now reached many strata of the population. That which interests me the most—and it is very important—is that women's liberation has gotten away from its old fights. It makes me very happy to know that women today are able to strike, not for the purposes of salary but in order to say, "You can no longer treat me like that," that is to say, on the basis of a sexist ideology. Certain women will no longer tolerate being treated no matter how. I remember a TV show called "Women's Work" ("Le Travail au féminin"), which showed a bank clerk, a worker, a high school teacher, a bus driver, apprentices in a factory who used the discourse of women's liberation. Before then I was a little discouraged by the conflicts among the militants, but while hearing these women I said to myself, "In all ways, we are winning." There may be conflicts, but the important thing is that it is spreading all over and that it be irreversible.

How then can one categorize the French current? It is, in my opinion, very split, from which comes the necessity to regroup people according to practical objectives. For example, I worked a great deal for the October 6, 1979, demonstration for abortion because it brought together all the different strains. We were not from one special group. The demonstration tried to mobilize all the women who were interested in legalizing abortion, whatever their persuasion.

To describe how the French movement is structured isn't easy. I would say that there is one faction which holds that feminism (and here I *am* using the word *feminism*) is secondary, and can arrive only after Marxism. The women in this group say that the struggle of the sexes can only occur after the resolution of the class struggle. But there are other feminists who are antisexists before all, and who emphasize the phenomenon of sexist exploitation before all class phenomena. Personally, I think that if one takes into account what Marx says, that the exploitation of man by man starts with the exploitation of the woman by the man, then the realization of Marxism would be the liberation of women, that is to say, the abolition of private property, the family, the state. This may look utopian, but this doesn't bother me. The most resistant, and at the same time the most explosive point in capitalist society would in fact be the liberation of women because women reproduce and nurture the labor force. In my opinion, the only thing which would be capable of upsetting capitalist society would be a general strike of women, not only the women in the field of production but a general strike of women; we would no longer submit to the social function in which they enclose us, that is to say, we would no longer do the housework, we would no longer have children, we would no longer make love, nor would we go to the factory any more. But it's not in the factory that we are most trapped—it is in the reproductive function.

In the description of the French movement, I haven't spoken until now of Psych et Po [Psychanalyse et Politique, a movement against all *isms,* in charge of and, according to some, exerting a

tyranny over the important publishing house Librairie des femmes].
To tell the truth, I don't see very well how it is connected today
with the other two big alternatives. This group sometimes attacks
the term *feminism* in what seems to be a nontactical way. I don't
see what the practical politics of this group is, what its aims are. I
would prefer that they themselves speak of these.

**What is *your* connection with the women's liberation move-
ment?**

I have already answered that in part. I am in the French movement and also in the international one because I work with the
women of other countries besides France and that is very important to me. Since 1970, I have refused to belong to any one
faction. If a group excludes me, it is the group that excludes me,
it is not me who excludes it, because I think that women's liberation is spreading everywhere, and there are things to say and to
do everywhere. Without doubt I will never belong to any party
in the cause of the women's struggle because I believe that my
objective world and my political practice are above that. I don't
want my commitment to be subjected to a contest of parties,
which ultimately takes over and encodes it for electoral purposes.
If the parties, under the pressures of the women's struggle, take
into consideration the exploitation of women and make things
happen, I would be delighted. But I think that, for what concerns
me, I have to retain my total freedom. I make myself available
beyond my analytic practice (and I do not standardize anyone in
analysis; I don't think that anyone could say that I have directed
her/him in one way or another) because women come to speak to
me when they are lost and need me to listen to them, to guide
them. My marginal position and my position in the struggle of
women make me the one that they choose to call on. There are
also my books, my writing. And politically, there is the fact of
aiming, let us say, at practical objectives. I spoke to you about the
October 6, 1979, demonstration. I also just went to Montreal
where I was invited to speak in a colloquium on women and
madness. When I participate in such a conference, I think that I
am putting on an act, given what I say about militant feminism.
But things happen which make me very happy—at least in for-

eign countries. Often, given my nonbelonging to any group, women from different groups come to me to regroup. I like that very much and it is very important to me.

What should women do in order to liberate themselves without falling into the quest for power like men?

I have the impression that power is a substitution or a palliative for impotence or the anxiety of impotence. To put this another way, power is like death; it is the work of the death drive, and if one wants to protect the values of the body, if one cares about a certain impulse toward pleasure and sensuality, power has no great interest. What's painful for me is the impression that with what I say, or write, or am, people are able to project distortions on me and can enfold me in those rags with which I have nothing to do. However, there is a question of political strategy. Is it good that at certain moments certain women occupy certain positions? Surely, if they can use them in order to make things move. The problem is whether they can remain women and not become total men. I think that this is not easy. But I am totally ready if they so desire to discuss things with women who are in this kind of position, and not to exclude them systematically. It depends on the women. I won't reject the women of the left who have chosen to be in political contests, for it is important to speak with them because of the place where they are. They can express certain things, on the making of laws for example.

For many women, equality is the most important concept. Do you think it would be possible to have difference and equality at the same time? Wouldn't hierarchy impose itself automatically with difference?

In a way that continues the question asked previously. I would say that equality signifies becoming totally like men. Do you agree?

Would it be possible to see equality as a halfway road between man and woman, the result of concessions made by one side and the other to reach a state of being instead of a state of possession?

I agree, but do you see that happening anywhere? As far as I am concerned, the overturn of power, the return to a matriarchy doesn't interest me at all. That which interests me is precisely sexual difference without hierarchy. As you have said, two parts of the world coming together is my wish. I don't think that could happen today. It could perhaps happen tomorrow. Let us say that my condition is feminine and that I try to speak from where I am and of the exploitation that is imposed on me without the least wish that women take power. On the contrary, I wish that women could succeed in checking certain power, that they would arrive at deconstructing and reconstructing another mode of living in society.

As for difference, just because it has always functioned in a hierarchical fashion doesn't mean that we have to reject it. I believe that it is necessary to make a double gesture, that is to say, both to interpret and deny that sexual difference should return to exploitation, to subordination, but at the same time to affirm the positive character of difference. To give a very simple example: just because there are anti-Semites doesn't mean that one should have to renounce the fact that one is Jewish. I believe that by putting it this way, people understand very easily what I mean— because I have searched for a long time how to say this in a very simple formula. There are many women today who are trapped by their refusals of difference, because difference has always served to exploit and I think that that is equivalent to saying: "I don't want to be Jewish any more because I have been exploited as a Jew." That is in effect to submit and to sacrifice oneself to hierarchy. The question is to discover the positive values in difference and to affirm them.

For you, to be a woman is to be different, but isn't vindicating this difference, in a sense, going along with the social structure which has constructed difference on the basis of so-called biological fact? In what way is your insistence on difference different from that of society?

The men and the women today who deny difference are, in my opinion, indulging themselves in a type of unbridled idealism, for difference exists and society has been constructed on it. It's fine that the so-called intellectual militant women say: "Let's develop our masculine side and let the men develop their feminine side, and abolish difference since it has always served to exploit us." I would like that but it is to forget that women are enclosed as and in private property; that women are the underpaid workers, the foreigners subjected to all kinds of sexual mutilations. It is to deny the material, materialistic, social, and cultural reality of difference. That reality exists. In fact it returns us to the question of how to distribute this difference. Women cannot be liberated from a reality other than a sexual one because this is the starting point from which they are exploited. Therefore one isn't able to renounce difference. That would be a false utopia.

How can we discover the positive characteristics of this difference? What I am trying to do is not to return to no matter what biology or anatomy, but rather to discover the specific morphological characteristics of the feminine. When others confront us with the concept of a feminine nature, we shouldn't let ourselves be taken in; it's important to answer that all of our culture in which we live depends on a masculine nature and a masculine morphology. All that which is valorized is connected to a masculine sexual morphology. So then, let us discover our own morphology and realize that our own vision of the world and our own fashion of creating, of building, is not, and is not able to be the same as that of men. Biology, anatomy have always made us the reproducers. The question to ask oneself is: "What can women in their difference produce?—Produce not in the sense of capitalist production?" There is something else on the imaginary level, on the symbolic, and beyond all consideration of reproduction.

With regard to the symbolic, how do you define the term *eternal feminine?* **Is there a connection between the eternal feminine and woman as merchandise, as object of exchange?**

The *eternal feminine* is not ours. It is a concept of patriarchal culture which, I think, idealizes us in a deathlike fashion. Within

Christian culture, the eternal feminine refers to certain conceptions of the Virgin Mary. It is how men order their own ambiva-
lence toward their mother and their wife to dissociate virgin and
whore. I think that woman as merchandise belongs on the side of
woman as whore, that is to say, that one exchanges her among
men for use. It is complicated because merchandise is on the side
of the fetish that measures itself according to a certain standard.
There, I would say, there would be something of the phallus.
And without doubt there is something of the phallic mother in
the Virgin Mary. But it is not exactly a feminine phallic; it is a
phallicism which is imputed to us. Therefore the eternal feminine
is merchandise insofar as it is fetish, but there is also its value as
use and usury, and there, it is on the side of the whore.

**What do you think of the position taken by certain analysts
that the major source of oppression stems from the mother?**
That is true at a certain descriptive level. But it is to forget that
even if this mother exerts a certain phantasmagoric power, in fact
she has no social, economic, or cultural power. Given the exploitation that she submits to on the part of her father/husband, given
her exclusion from social and creative activity, she reproduces the
oppression to which she is subject. I understand what one wishes
to say in denouncing the mother, and it's true at a certain level of
the family. But the important thing is not to still and always
crush the mother. The important thing is to try to understand
why and how the mother could change in the actual system. But
it is impossible; she cannot change. One might as well believe in
Santa Claus. What can we do? Condemn her a little more? Freud
says that our culture is built on a parricide. More fundamentally,
our culture is built on a matricide: the matricide of the mother/
lover—not of the woman as reproducer but of the woman as a
lover, as a creator who has a specific desire and who fights for her
desire. One sees this matricide at the beginning of our culture;
our culture has been founded on it. When the fathers took power,
they had already annihilated the mother. This can be seen in
mythology, in Greek tragedy.

Therefore, according to you, the mother/daughter struggle is inscribed in the alienation to which a little girl is condemned from her birth by a mother who confirms this alienation and who is her sole respondent?

I have in a way answered that. If the mother is the alienator, it is because she has no identity as a woman. And this effectively plunges the mother and the little girl in the same nothingness. But the problem is neither to accuse the mother nor to say that it is the father who comes to liberate the little girl. The mother has to find her identity as a woman and from that point, she would be able to give an identity to her daughter. But this is the key point to which our system is most blind.

There is a theme that I take up again in *Amante marine,* which can be found in mythology and which seems to be at the foundation of patriarchal culture—in the great mythological figures one sees the structuring of the imaginary system. It is the relationship of Demeter and Kore. Demeter, goddess of the earth, has a little girl, Kore, who is grievously manipulated. She is given by Zeus to his brother Hades, king of the underworld, both as a bond between them and as an impossibility of a bond because one is in the sky and the other is in the underworld. One day, a crevice opens up under Kore's feet; she is abducted by Hades. The little girl is thus separated from her mother. At that moment she loses her voice and her name is changed; she becomes Persephone. But since the patriarchal regime is not completely in effect, Demeter refuses to reproduce without her daughter. Then Hades is obliged to give back Kore for two seasons of the year: spring and summer. One sees there the separation of the daughter and the mother. One might say that at the beginning there was Demeter and Kore and that then there was a good mother/daughter relationship outside the patriarchal regime. One sees how this rapport was destroyed and how there was still a resistance, that is to say, Demeter didn't allow it to happen completely.

That said, I think it is interesting that today this mother/daughter relationship is questioned because it is the most obscure and most explosive relationship in patriarchal culture. If one were to succeed in creating again a good relationship between mother and daughter, women would no longer subordinate themselves. There would be a feminine identity and women would not submit themselves to what is called the exchange of women among men.

What are the basic representations in the symbolic masculine world by which the oppression of women is articulated?

Virgin, mother, whore. One might also add the mask of femininity that one sees in mythology beginning with Athena. Athena is always veiled and that is, I think, the basic ornamentation of the female body. And Athena is also called Pallas which means wound. The ornamentation becomes the veil over the wound.

I was thinking just now of Oedipus.

In reflecting recently on matricide, I thought that, for me, Oedipus is a repetition of Orestes; it is in fact a repetition of matricide. What do you mean when you refer to Oedipus?

It seems to me that the Oedipus theory represents submission to a unique system that annihilates the woman.

A unique system which would articulate itself on the murder of the mother and the identification with the father? If one touches the mother, one becomes blind. I would rather reverse that and say that one becomes blind because one forgets and one denies the beginning, that is to say, the connection with the mother. The fundamental blindness of our culture is there. And if this denial of the connection to the mother posits in some fashion the murder of the woman who gives us life, it is necessary to understand that one doesn't dare to touch that again without fear because it would be to participate again in the same crime. Therefore I believe that the sexual anxieties of men are explicable in great part by the fact that they are constrained in the functioning of the sole patriarchal order to kill the mother but they don't cease having the desire to return to this mother, to their birth, to their bodies, to their house of flesh. And it is at the same time a lunatic anguish because they have to kill their mother in order to become men.

How might the language of women deconstruct the representations of which you have spoken before?

I want to say that that is what I have tried to do more and more in certain texts. I think it is necessary to act in two ways. First, to criticize the existing system and that is perhaps what is pardoned the least, because people are not going to accept that you might put in question a theoretical system. So it is necessary to act in two ways: to question the systems and to show how we can deconstruct them because we are at the same time inside and outside them. We have to reject all the great systems of opposition on which our culture is constructed. Reject, for example, the oppositions: fiction/truth, sensible/intelligible, empirical/transcendental, materialist/idealist. All these opposing pairs function as an exploitation and a negation of a relation at the beginning and of a certain mode of connection between the body and the word for which we have paid everything.

So when someone tells me that the beginning of *Amante marine* is fiction, I say no. It is not fiction. Or otherwise everything is fiction and the "truth" which is imposed on us is a formidable fiction. This has posed a very interesting and complicated problem in the publication of books by women insofar as they were unclassifiable. They didn't fit into the existing categories because in fact they were not exactly literature, nor were they exactly essays or theory. What were they? One didn't know where to put them. I think that one of the important functions of the publication of women would be to create a "genre," a language which doesn't adhere to the existing categories, which refuses to submit itself to the established order.

To change reality, one has to change the symbolic order. Do you agree?

Completely. The symbolic order is an imaginary order which becomes law. Therefore it is very important to question again the foundations of our symbolic order in mythology and in tragedy, because they deal with a landscape which installs itself in the imagination and then, all of a sudden, becomes law. But that only means that it is an imaginary system that wins out over another one. This victorious imaginary system is what we call the symbolic order.

It seems—and you have already spoken about this—that the binary values are now being questioned. Does this questioning affect the masculine/feminine opposition?

This is at the same time a simple and difficult question. The binary values are now put into question; it is necessary that they be so, for we are the victims of this opposition. But the opposition feminine/masculine is a false opposition which doesn't truly belong to binarism, or, if it does belong there, it is to a binarism which is completely hierarchized. As with a certain number of opposing values that I mentioned before—materialist/idealist, etc.—there isn't truly an opposition. Rather, there is one pole of the opposition (the masculine) which constitutes the limit of the system and which plays with the other pole (the feminine) according to its needs. One is not able to say that this is a true binarism.

What we have to do is affirm the two poles, recognizing that the feminine will not be in the same mode as the masculine. In our present culture, to want to say that there is no difference is, I think, the politics of the neuter, a nihilistic politics in the worst sense of the term. I feel like asking how it happens that at the moment when something valuable occurs on the women's side, immediately a discourse of androgyny, of nonsexual difference arises. It is necessary to pay a great deal of attention to this because we risk being swallowed again by a new "humanism." Recently at the University of Vincennes, someone said, "We are all human beings," and I answered, "I totally refuse to be a human being. What is this abstract reality, this ideal that doesn't exist?" I refuse to be a human being because I cannot be one; I was not given the possibility of being a complete human being; therefore, I have no desire to be that. To affirm that the two poles exist is, in my opinion, liberating; it is to affirm a social, economic, cultural, religious, ideological reality which underlies everything. Once this affirmation is made, how does one find—if the earth does not blow up in the years to come, not an impossibility—a meeting place which would recast this opposition? I think it is first necessary to affirm the difference in order to find again the place of alliance between the two poles.

Can you conceive of a discourse liberated from oppression, a place where masculine and feminine would be able to coexist peacefully?

That continues what I was just saying. I hope so. I work for it. But that does not depend exclusively on me; that depends also on the other pole of difference. Unhappily, I fear that it's not going to happen tomorrow. To return to Nietzsche, when he says that God is dead, it seems that the collapse of this keystone of a transcendental system leads to the carriers of the phallus becoming gods themselves. Why is phallic culture so important after the fall of the gods? Because the carriers of the phallus want to be gods themselves. It is terrifying. Therefore, in my opinion, the meeting of the poles would be a type of sharing. If to be the carrier of the phallus is to wish to be an absolute power, there is no sharing. It is a very difficult question; one has to answer by means of a philosophical detour. In order that there not be a hierarchy and in order that there be a possible place of reconciliation, one has to have a double mirror, that is to say, not everybody should be obliged to look at oneself in the same mirror.

Women's language is unknown, but the masculine one is also because it is deformed by its uniform will to oppress. Women are working to deconstruct it. How?

There is no authentic masculine language. That is evident. Because from the moment that a pole of difference pretends to decree the universal, it says that its discourse is not sexualized. However, there are indications of sexual difference in this discourse that has pretensions to the universal. Therefore, what can we do? What I am trying to do is to discover the indices of sexual differences, to interpret and to show that the so-called universal discourse, whether it be philosophic, scientific, or literary is sexualized and mainly in a masculine way. It is necessary to unveil it, to interpret it, and at the same time to begin to speak a language which corresponds better to, and is in continuity with, our own pleasure, our own sensuality, our own creativity.

Do you know any masculine works which are engaged in the quest for a nonoppressive masculine discourse?

I would rather wait to answer. What I am able to say without hesitation is that when male theoreticians today employ women's discourse instead of using male discourse, that seems to me a very phallocratic gesture. It means: "We will change and we will speak a feminine discourse in order to remain the master of discourse." What I would want from men is that, finally, they would speak a masculine discourse and affirm that they are doing so.

In your work you speak about feminine autoeroticism. What role do you attribute to it?

It is important that women discover their autoeroticism and that this autoeroticism not imitate a masculine model, as it does in Freud's work. It is necessary that women discover their own autoeroticism, that they reveal themselves to each other and leave their rivalries, the hatreds which have been imposed on them as competitive merchandise in the marketplace. Accordingly, women will discover the positiveness of their homosexuality, in whatever form it will take. I would also say this about men. But I don't mean that women ought to renounce their heterosexuality, for that would lead to a new cloister in which we would be enclosed, constructed by our own hands. I am sorry when I see certain women falling into a sexual moralism, for example, aggressing against women who are heterosexual. I am sorry because in a way they endorse the existing order. But I am also able to say that the heterosexuality which is mandated is almost always pathological, if there isn't also for both sexes a happy autoeroticism and a happy homosexuality, whatever be the form. For me, these are two possibilities which ought to flourish in order for something as difficult and complex as heterosexuality to succeed.

What elements of Freud's theory can be retained in a new psychology of women?

I would say everything, on the condition that one goes beyond. All of Freud's work is to be understood as the work of an honest scientist. He said of women that which he was able to say in describing what he heard, with the ears that he had, which probably couldn't hear anything else. What Freud says about feminine desire is heard on the couch. But there are other things that are heard and the problem is that he stopped at a certain point, that is to say, that he normalized woman in her role, the condition that she had at a certain moment.

There is in Freud something else also. If psychoanalysis started with the hysterics, one sees Freud change his position toward them between his studies of hysteria where he listened to them for he had everything to learn, and the case of Dora, where, having constructed his system, he bent Dora to his interpretations. This seems to me very revealing. Thus he imposes his system and doesn't want to hear the famous debate of 1932 and what people like Karen Horney, Melanie Klein, Ernest Jones are telling him about sexuality. He doesn't want to hear because he prefers his system to what is said. Notably, he wants to save the Oedipus complex, which is the keystone of his system.

How would men be represented in a psychoanalysis constructed by women?

I feel like saying, as what men are without their feeling obliged to be something other than what they are. As accepting their sexuality without a categorical phallic imperative because that makes them and us suffer with their obligation to have an erection at the right moment. I think that it is the phallocratic system that they have endorsed which has been glued on their back. Historically, there was a division which was made, with women as guardians of the corporal and men of the sexual. I would hope that each would refind that which is body and that which is sex. Men are terribly separated from their bodies; they are sexual machines.

Simone de Beauvoir said that she admired your work very much but reproached you for not being shocking enough. What do you think of that?

I am glad that Simone de Beauvoir admired what I do because she was a woman who did a great deal, whom I admire for the direction and the risks she took. As for the second part of the statement, I do not understand it because I was excluded from Vincennes, put into quarantine from the analytic world (and I only give some examples). I also remember having a conference —in a progressive bookstore which the next day had a stone thrown through its window. It could be that Simone de Beauvoir did not totally identify the place from which I am shocking or maybe for her, shock is to produce shocking statements constantly. I do not say that I never speak shockingly but I think that there is a much more basic gesture to make, which consists not solely in making shocking statements or discourse but in saying from where we speak, that which permits us a certain type of discourse, that which changes deeply the position of the subject who masters the discourse.

Then too, to reconstruct a discourse in order to produce shocking statements does not interest me. One returns perhaps to the question of equality with difference. Probably and even surely, Simone de Beauvoir was much more interested in vindication of equality than I am.

Monique Wittig and other women writers have written utopias which illustrate a new consciousness of women. Do you have a utopian vision?

If to be utopian is to want a place that doesn't exist yet in some of its modalities, I am utopian. That said, I only speak of this place from the sensory and corporeal experience that I have of it. Therefore it is not a simple projection of I don't know what kind of dream; it is a place that already exists and that I wish could be developed culturally, socially, amorously.

What do you hope for in the future of women?

That they reenter culture and affirm their identity which is a special identity, that is, women should not be simply reproducers of the existent roles, they should also be cocreators of this world.

Monique Schneider passed her agrégation de philosophie in her early twenties and holds the Doctorat d'Etat de Philosophie. She now teaches philosophy at the Université de Paris VII and is director of research at the Centre National de la Recherche Scientifique.

SELECTED BIBLIOGRAPHY

De l'Exorcisme à la psychanalyse: Le Féminin expurgé. Paris: Retz, 1979.
La Parole et l'inceste. Paris: Aubier-Montaigne, 1980.
Freud et le plaisir. Paris: Denoël, 1980.
"Père, ne vois-tu pas . . . ?" Le Père, le maître, le spectre dans L'Interprétation des rêves. Paris: Denoël, 1985.

NINE

Monique Schneider

Paris, Summers 1985 and 1986

When we saw Monique Schneider for the second time—the first was at a conference, where we were smoked out by the French psychoanalytic intelligentsia—she was living in a middle-class neighborhood in spartan quarters (she has since moved). Her desk was a working desk, covered with books and papers. She is always in the middle of writing. Above the spare analytic couch was a picture of a lovely adolescent woman, who she told us was her daughter. With her functional furniture, Schneider seems indifferent to her immediate surroundings. But so intense, lucid, brilliant, and original were her responses to our questions, to which she listened with extraordinary concentration, that we felt ourselves plunged into an interior world of immense richness.

Schneider was one of the people who most welcomed our exchange, for in France, she claims, one asks her "above all to be more reasonable and to have less imagination." "The contact with you and the new world is very precious to me and allows me to feel less imprisoned."

What was your psychoanalytic training like?

My analytic training was diversified and somewhat contradictory. I wanted to be an analyst after reading Lacan's *Ecrits*. But in my philosophical training, for my thesis I worked on the connections between affect and the process of learning. And in my research I found that Lacan's reading of Freud was completely erroneous, that is, that the affect was situated at the outset in a too marginal way, so that to work on the problem of the role of affect in the process of achieving consciousness couldn't be done in the Lacanian perspective. Therefore, I was fascinated by Lacan but couldn't be his disciple. The whole Lacanian phenomenon appeared to be somewhat terrorist, even though it was very strong and fascinating, to the point that I felt like a heretic because in philosophical circles, Lacanian thinking was predominant. If one is a psychoanalyst, Lacan only occupies a part of the psychoanalytic field, but among those who are philosophers and interested in psychoanalysis, it is unthinkable not to be a Lacanian.

From the start I worked above all on Freud, reading his texts very closely, and I had two individual analyses with analysts from the Psychoanalytic Institute of Paris, a school totally opposed to Lacan; my second analyst had attended Lacan's seminars, however; therefore, Lacan's influence did pass into the Institute. It was at this juncture that I worked above all on my personal analysis. Afterward I didn't go through the usual institutional admissions and control procedures. I worked through captivating but very long and hard individual analyses. I agreed to be part of a school of psychoanalysts where there were both Lacanians and non-Lacanians. It was founded after the dissolution of the Ecole Freudienne. Certain dissident Lacanians are part of it. At the same time there was a whole influence of analysts trained by Conrad Stein at the Institute. He knew Lacan and enabled a transition to take place. Therefore, in a way Lacan has played a role from the beginning of the foundation of this school, which is a meeting place rather than a training institution. François Roustang and Serge Viderman are also part of it.

In the French psychoanalytic scene, I have a very marginal position. I cannot say that I have yet found a trend in which I feel at home. I go wherever I am invited but I am still in a phase of exploration and dissatisfaction. Very often I am asked to name my affiliation. I read Freud and other analysts. I like Ferenczi very much. But I don't belong to any school. This stuns people, for there is now a beehive of schools, above all the schools founded on Lacan's theory, but not the Lacan of the Freudian cause.

Who are your patients—men, women, your readers?

I have not been an analyst for a long time. At the beginning my patients were referred by the people at the Institute. Some asked to be treated free of charge. It is very different to get patients coming from an institute where they had an enormous "in-take." I think that there is a certain level of distress about life lived in anonymity. Patients come without knowing me, without reading me. They were given my address. It is a certain type of work and with them I do not listen in the same way. I work a lot with this first anonymous call for help, which also reveals an anonymous way of life. This is one of my main themes. The articulation of the fact of being born unique is for me a kind of grace, an election or the product of a long working through. Maintaining access to singularity is as important as opening oneself to the universal. It has become a philosophy.

There is a current in the thematics of Lacan which valorizes the passage from singularity to the universal as if salvation occurred through the universal. The problem that I am treating starts from the fact that the position of the self as singular is not given from the start, and I often feel that I am working not in the pre-Oedipal but in what I would call the prenatal. It is very important at the level of listening because I believe, for example, that patients need to be nurtured. Before a session they wonder if the analyst is going to be there. Even during the silences, there is this need to be carried and gestated. I think that it is very important not to demand that they be born; the important thing is the gift of birth.

We have to be happy that they are here. The experience of maternity is very close to the experience of being an analyst. Think of all the conditions necessary for a birth to take place: all this passage through silence, being carried, then being able to breathe. There are certain dark stages which could be lived negatively; not being able to speak is an attempt to abandon yourself to someone who exempts you from speaking your identity.

Generally, patients don't come because of my books. It's rather when I speak at conferences, which are less solitary than writing. There is a sort of gift of self which makes the sensitivity to listening more acute. It is a kind of meeting that I like a great deal, and I think that a certain number of people feel adopted at the moment that one speaks and listens. For me contact is made more by the spoken word than the written one. Sometimes they read me after. But very few of those who read me come to see me. I think that my books are very disquieting and arouse doubts about the value of the psychoanalytic process; they put too much into question. My writing can be appreciated by people who are skeptical about psychoanalysis, but it does not lead them to the couch. I am conscious of the risks inherent in the psychoanalytic process, of what there may be in it that is sacrificial, murdering. At certain levels of encounter I know that there are places where someone might miscarry. It is these high-risk places that I examine. There is an articulation of the theoretical work at all conferences. I speak about the themes on which I write, but the connection with the couch goes through the work, the listening, not the reading.

Does the psychoanalytic cure consist of an elimination of the toxic or a transformation of it?

A problem which I have questioned the most deeply since my earliest writing. In my first book, *From Exorcism to Psychoanalysis,* I dealt with analysts the way an ethnologist deals with primitive tribes, feeling that they suffered from a strange obsession: when something goes wrong, or someone goes wrong, some elements, which seem to be completely arbitrary and useless, have to be removed. I was comparing the analytic approach to the literary one, with the remembrance of things past: there is a whole literary desire to recover the past, to reappropriate certain rejected elements. Therefore I was fascinated with certain metaphors of readoption and assimilation. Lévi-Strauss tells us that in primitive tribes our Western methods of curing or of dealing with social justice would appear absurd. The primitive is cured and becomes stronger through anthropophagy, the incorporation of others and incorporation into the group. In contrast, on the Western model, one has the impression that salvation comes from what he calls vomiting men (the opposite of eating men). This seems to be an accurate way of describing what we call magic, the imaginary in our representation of the therapeutic work. In Freud, for example, the affect has to be neutralized, the transference has to be resolved, to get rid of certain toxic representations. The entire Freudian representation of the alien object seems mythical to me, as if in an irrational way the fact that someone is sick means the incorporation of a toxic element. Even sexuality is seen by him as toxic. As far as I am concerned, this representation of toxicity is based on cultural fantasies and I would like to rework things in a different way.

The concept of autotomy, which was taken up by Ferenczi, is important to me. He says that in the reaction to trauma, the psyche reacts in a way like animals that cripple themselves. For example, if an animal has a paw caught in a trap, it cuts off the paw and runs away. I have the impression that there is nothing toxic in this process. Where there is a psychic phenomenon centered on mutilation (I develop this more in my last book *Father, Don't You See?*), very often one wants to continue to reject this amputated part, but on condition that another person incarnate that part of us that we wanted to cut, to remove, not because it was toxic but because it was considered dangerous by others. Therefore I am very sensitive to all processes of mutilation and I have both an aural and visual representation of therapy which stems from the idea of autotomy, that is, the mutilation of parts of the body, of certain memories. And my wish would be to cure by readoption; it is a maternal image, this adoption of what has been rejected. And I think that it is fear very often which makes us see toxicity.

Doesn't this readoption of what has been rejected require a certain metamorphosis?

This process of readoption requires a metamorphosis of the self in a certain sense. One sees oneself as deprived, as discarded. This metaphor of rejection underlies the entire *Interpretation of Dreams.* The thrown away part comes back inexorably. If one feels like joining together with the torn off part, one of the first steps of the process is a form of metamorphosis, which consists of making the self a receptacle for others who in a certain way incarnate the possibility of the self which had previously been rejected. A first step in metamorphosis would involve a maternal adoption of the other and through the intermediary of the other the adoption of a part of the self. Both elements are necessary. I don't think that it is possible to have an immediate integration of the self. I think that there is a receptivity and that one works through the idea of rejection by admitting that outside of the self and outside of the part that has been rejected stands the other. It is after recognizing oneself in the other that readoption will take place. This reveals that the mechanisms which enable us psychologically to function as a parent start developing very early. Of course it's not real maternity, but I believe that if one isn't a mother as a little girl, one will never be one. As far as I am concerned, these elements of adoption of the other (Ferenczi also treats this), of the child adopting the parent, are necessary and constitute the first metamorphosis, which I would say is almost against nature.

How did you come to the equation inquisitor, exorcist, psychoanalyst?

The answer is personal. I encountered these ancient and medieval personages in analysis and before. I was led to my first analysis because of phantasms, a fascination with the devil, the feeling of having a familiarity with him. It was my childhood experience which resurfaced with my students at the beginning of my teaching career. And it was very strange because I was teaching Kant's categorical imperative and I spent my nights waiting for the devil. There came a moment when sleeping became impossible and I went to an analyst. But I didn't consider myself at all neurotic. During the night I had an acute awareness of everything which threatened destruction, the feeling that the floors could cave in. I knew that many people were dying. I felt that everybody that one thought stable and organized was threatened at every moment. And it is from that point that I contested the Freudian vision of cure as a passage to the reality principle. I believe that in order to be tranquil and sleep, one must have the great power of denial of reality, the power to close one's eyes and ears on a mountain of atrocities, on all the violence that occurs. Having been very sensitive and lucid not as far as the reality of the devil but with regard to a destructive force which took on a maximum intensity at night, I knew that no reasoning could convince me otherwise. I felt the threat, and the moment came when I could no longer face it. I then turned to my first psychoanalysis. A month later, all diabolical phantasms disappeared, but at the same time my analyst told me that I couldn't fantasize any more. Then I felt that from the moment that the devil was cast aside, a sort of exorcism had taken place but also that I was deprived of all my night. I had undergone a sort of liberating removal. I was more calm. I could succeed better in certain things, but without my inner self.

In my second analysis, the opposite phenomenon occurred. Instead of progressing from the beginning in relation to concrete reality, I had the impression of immersing myself into an imaginary fairyland and of recovering not exactly the experience of the devil, but all the internal rigor of a world of fascination, of terror, of night. And from that moment, I again dealt not with the mechanism of expulsion but on the contrary a sort of familiarity with the demonic world. It was as if I could be possessed again. I saw then that psychoanalysis could function in two diametrically opposed ways: either in the cathartic mode of expulsion and exorcism; or in a way whereby the analyst functions as a great sorcerer who leads you through the nocturnal labyrinth.

You seem to propose a new reading of Freud which puts in question the fundamental principles of psychoanalysis. What are the principles that you denounce? In which way is your reading of Freud original?

First, I reject the collecting of Freudian texts into a theoretical monument, even if it contains different levels. One period centers on one discovery; another centers on another. There is a way of reading Freud while trying to capitalize on the theroretical acquisition even if one admits that this is a constantly changing theory. In my reading of Freud, there is no monument and I emphasize the text itself. That is why I have been attacked for reading the text literally. From the moment that one emphasizes the text, the text structures itself according to the principles studied by Freud in his article on denial *(Die Verneinung)*. Freud shows that in all the processes of knowledge, there is a movement toward and a movement away. Some hypotheses are presented in both a furtive and sharp manner, with the possibility of being negated in the next moment. It is as if knowledge proceeds in steps which put the researcher at risk. It is like a war where one advances and then retreats. The construction, the rather theoretical steps, have to be studied in their movement, and not considered as immobile. If one admits that negating a proposition can lead to affirming it and being conscious of it, I believe that Freud should be studied in his moments of negation.

This seems very important for the whole study of women. In Freud the representation of women should not be accepted at face value, but has to be decoded, interpreted, seen in reverse. When he says that the woman is characterized by lack, that she doesn't have a penis, there is something there which for Freud is frightening. It is the opening. Therefore, characterizing the woman as lack represents for Freud a kind of escape from the temptation of falling into the abyss, of being sucked in by the woman, and we have to see what the phantasmatic negative of Freud's theorization is and transform some negative into positive images.

One of my principles of reading is to combine different levels of writing in Freud. There is theoretical writing, for example, in *The Interpretation of Dreams,* but there are also letters and the texts where Freud progresses in domains that he knows less about. This is in all of applied psychoanalysis, where he is himself a novice. I think that it is in his letters that Freud can move forward the least disguised, where he dares to express very violent and acute hypotheses with a sort of heedless daring. What interests me then is to see all the work of erasing, of restructuring in the different levels of writing. How is the dream going to transform experiences, how is the theory itself going to warp everything that is seen as terrifying in experience, and how is Freud receptive to the ideas of other cultures, for example, the terror of women's blood, which was so important in his letters? Freud is going to recover the importance of blood when speaking of the taboo of virginity, that is, while being interested in what he calls the primitive. In being receptive to another culture, Freud will express his own repression. And it is at this moment that there is a whole vision of femininity like a geyser of blood, blood seen as the vital element, the seat, the place of life.

This cannot be seen at all in the theoretical texts on femininity. It can be seen thanks to a process equivalent to denial, that is, displacement, the need to locate something in a strange place, far away and beyond what is more familiar to us in reality. My principle of reading is to reveal the phenomena of difference and reflection in very different texts so that one is not able to say that Freud's real position is found in such or such a spot. There is a back and forth game among completely different levels of writing or experience.

How could we deconstruct the Freudian sexual monism?

I have searched a long time for a representation of woman which could be opposed to the negative representation of Freud, and now more and more I am tending toward a dispersed, multi-faceted image of the feminine.

My initial approach, which some women hold against me, doesn't speak directly of what I see in women. I accept the detour of the master's unconscious, the viewpoint of men and men's fear. I place myself in the framework of an approach to women, not by saying, "I am a woman. I am going to tell you what a woman is." I can't. I believe in constantly distancing oneself in another's experience, and this other experience for me which is most fascinating is Freud's, to see precisely what in his experience represents at the same time a place of fascination, terror, and denial. I would place the force of negation in Freud in relation to the vision of femininity in male infancy. This is valid in a lot of masculine analyses. It seems that when a man needs to create a fossilized and simplified image of the feminine, it is very often in order to deny his own childhood experiences, as if a man who wants to appear as truly a man forbids himself to carry within him his own childhood.

For example, Viviane Forrester in *The Violence of Calm* emphasizes the importance of a strikingly traumatic experience in Freud's life, which is only briefly indicated in *The Interpretation of Dreams*. When he was two-and-a-half, Freud fell in the kitchen when trying to reach for something to eat. He cut himself. A doctor, Joseph Pur, had to come. It's surprising that this was not related by Freud but was told us by his personal physician, Max Shur, whose name ends like Dr. Pur's. The latter gave him several stitches. I was rereading the text of the *New Introductory Lectures on Psychoanalysis* on femininity. It seems to me that there is a connection between what is in the text about both the importance of pubic hair and women's weaving to hide the absence of sex, and the importance in Freud of the beard which hides the wound. The scar which Freud can feel, without acknowledging, is barely mentioned in his text. What is interesting is that after the appearance of cancer, he erases the passage which deals with the scar.

There is in Freud a whole system of representation of openings, blood, and wounds, which reveals his fear. He is afraid of rediscovering a mouth, lips, a wound in his own body. Therefore the connection in Freud between the traumatic and terrifying childhood experience and the vision of the feminine is very strong, as if he sees in the woman the injured child that he was. It seems to me that the doctor sutured the wound in the same way that Freud sutures the female sex, by saying simply, "There is no penis." That's not the essential point. There is an opening but this opening is too terrifying. That's why it doesn't exist. I think that this is one of the dimensions which has been rediscovered.

One could draw a map of the feminine zones in psychoanalytic writing. Curiously, what is part of the female body, the breasts, are not found in Freud's texts on women. The breast only exists for the infant's mouth. It is put in the singular. There are never breasts; this is very important because in saying breasts, one implies a hollow in between them, making us refind that opening that Freud was so afraid of, whereas if one says "breast," it is seen as phallic, an image of what men possess. If one gives the mother only one breast the way the cyclops had only one eye, she is made phallic and powerful. From this stems the theme of the rejection of the mother. With two breasts she possesses both a protuberance and a hollow like a sort of double womb. What is denied concerning woman, as if one had amputated her breasts from her in the barbaric operation performed by theory, one rediscovers in the mouth of the child. This brings problems to women on the maternal level because many women live, for example, as if their breasts don't belong to them.

Only in pornographic reviews is the breast vindicated, but in a provoking way, in a moment of rape. Otherwise the culture sees these elements of the woman's body as appropriated by the infant's psyche. One should study the psychoanalysis of the child to find, on the mode of fragmentation, on the level of fantasy, of split elements, a whole series of representations of portions of the body which are part of the woman.

Woman has been mutilated and one can only find her where she is not, and in multiple parts. I think that what Winnicott said about potential space can also refer to a certain type of feminine rapport centered on what is potential, on what is linked to connection with another, a type of communication and affirmation, not ostentation. For a child to be possible, one needs a certain type of femininity; yet it is only the assumption of it that makes the child possible. We don't ask ourselves what feeling of sweetness or power or fecundity the woman carries within her. There is a double distancing in Freud and then in the child who tries to find elsewhere the elements originally experienced as positive in the woman's body.

The endogenous casuality of masculine pleasure annihilates the woman. Are masculine-feminine pleasures condemned to be separated?

Pleasure in men isn't as predominant as they say. It is not certain that woman is always an object of pleasure. Men have a very great fear of pleasure. And the pleasure is perhaps accepted on condition of being localized and linked with woman seen as secondary, as situated outside; with the woman who is not necessarily the wife. And very often the amorous or erotic demand of the woman is perceived as terrifying. There is an important moment in Freud, which well indicates this mistrust of pleasure. It is when Freud says, "A man like me has nothing to do anymore with sexual excitation."* I think that his interpretation of Oedipus reveals a heroic character who wants mastery and not pleasure. I find that there is a false masculine discourse. In a man there is both a reclaiming of an aptitude for pleasure and the presentation of this aptitude as a victory over the woman. In reality there is a great flight with regard to the moment of pleasure. I find that there is a gap between the representation that a man has of pleasure and the experience that he has of it. On the level of representation, he sees pleasure as a conquest. On the level of experience, he sees pleasure more as a dispossession, an absence of mastery, and a fall. Therefore it seems to me that pleasure is experienced as the risk of feminization. In the structuring metaphors of *The Interpretation of Dreams,* the feminine is seen as an image of fluidity.

In the *Interpretation* I see sexual difference as in some way the difference between the structure which would be masculine, and the fluidity which is considered feminine.

Freud tells us that the father must "channel the power of the female sex." Woman is metaphorized as a power of inundation, irrigation, while the man is seen as a dike. Recently while working on the *Three Essays on the Theory of Sexuality,* I was a little surprised to note that if one were to study the metaphorical level—it is at this moment that a very close reading of the literary text seems important—one notices that we are in the presence of a system, a structure opposed to the one that Freud set up. Because on one side Freud says that the libido is essentially masculine but on the other, he compares the movement of the libido to that of a river, as if the libido incarnated this liquid and moving power that Freud in his usual oppositions places on the side of femininity.

After the formulation of the Oedipal theory and the effect of censure which went along with it, the libido is reclaimed as masculine in his official theoretical work. But on the level of the

*See the letter to Fleiss, dated 10/31/97.

metaphor we see a theoretical contradiction with the theory which is developed and used as a shield. Saying that the libido is masculine means that a man doesn't have to be afraid of the power of pleasure. But this power is translated into images whose themes are placed on the side of the feminine. For example, the libido is treated as a stream which irrigates the body. This vision of the libido is taken up by Ferenczi. I think that one of the interesting elements in Ferenczi, even if his texts are a little crazy, is the blurring of the traditional masculine/feminine polarities. In his text the psyche encounters a whole series of adventures where it undergoes a sort of drying up and then finds the equivalent of the primitive aquatic place. One feels that to get to the end of a masculine task, one has to go through feminine experiences. That is to say, in Ferenczi, there is a sort of dynamic where masculine and feminine are not two territories confronting each other but rather two territories which are impossible to divide.

It is from this point of view that I studied fairy tales. I am very interested in the Russian sorceress Baba Yaga, who uses her broom for a task which could be called antitheoretical; she erases the marks of her passage. She is a figure of the archaic feminine. Where we thought to put barriers and say, "Here is the masculine, there is the feminine," where one wants to create lines of cleavage, of division, the broom comes to erase all traces. Therefore I wouldn't work in the perspective of the difference because it is possible that the exclusive concern for difference could be reappropriated in a masculine finality.

Some men are very happy that there is a feminine discourse. For example, I was attacked for not having a feminine enough language in the sense that they feel I colonize their domain and invite them to think differently. But the exclusively feminine language could be heard as a charming song, something which would be beautiful but would leave intact official thinking. I think that women have been liberated by the discourse which tried to find the feminine specificity. That was necessary, but if one works with this hypothesis only, it can serve a masculine need of separating.

Can a neutral discourse be reached?

I don't really think that there is such a thing as a language shared by men and women. It's necessary to pinpoint how one can work with a certain distance in relation to the problematic of sexual difference without assuming a shared common language. It seems to me that criticizing the theme of sexual differentiation may help us to escape from the masculine trap, and here I am referring to W. Granoff's book *La Pensée et le féminin* (Thinking and the Feminine). Insisting on cutting and judging in order to give everyone his or her place is a defense against the feminine. But putting into question this process of cutting doesn't lead us to say that the two sexes are identical and that there is a common discourse. For example, Freud wanted a masculinity purified of all feminine elements. However, with such a masculinity, erection wouldn't even be thinkable. As Ferenczi shows in *Thalassa,* in sexual play, there is an identification of the partners. But this does not mean that the two partners are the same and that there is a common discourse.

If we return to the Freudian dualism which puts the masculine on the side of the stone, of the dike, of eternity, and which places the feminine on the side of change, of fluidity, of that which is born and dies, one would have to say that everything that moves is feminine. And I think that this leads us to a certain vision of masculine sexuality. Freud in his essay on the head of the Medusa presents erection as the fact of being rigid. And the purpose of the rigidity is to put to flight the negative spirit identified with the woman. It is not surprising that in *The Interpretation of Dreams,* one finds the image of erection in the evocations of the cemetery, funerals, and death.

Freud presents the erection the same way that the statue of the commander in *Don Giovanni* is presented. One might ask, how can the commander's statue make love? This doesn't pose any problem in the text on the head of the Medusa since the purpose of the erection is to put the female to flight.

My strategy is in a way to take seriously the Freudian duality in order to show how the encounter of the sexes would be totally impossible if one sex represented a purely masculine entity and the other a purely feminine one.

In certain civilizations the penile shaft allows the male sex to be presented as always erect, as if not moving. It is a way of masking the indecency which man disappropriates from his sex. It is surprising that this element of the man's body is presented as a sign of power. The sex is seen as a rod or as scepter, a vertical element; it is on the man's body. And this element, which is supposed to represent power, in reality functions in a way which a man cannot control. It's as if the scepter in the king's hand started to do tricks without the king having anything to do with it. There is an initial shame in the relation of a man to his sexual organ since sex is precisely that which does move. There is a great paradox here: making that which moves, that which is uncontrollable, the representation of omnipotence, from birth, in the masculine body.

Going back to the Freudian opposition, we must say that the masculine sex has to participate in this world of what is born and dies, of tumescence and detumescence. It has to participate in this supposedly feminine world of change, even for erection to be possible.

Therefore I think that each sexual or erotic encounter must be presented as a dynamic, bisexual phenomenon. This doesn't mean that the two sexes should be represented in the same person, juxtaposed side by side, as in Freud's first version of bisexuality. My view is different. I think rather there is a space in between. To become a man, to reach the end of masculine fulfillment, one has to pass through the supposedly feminine zone, and I think that the reverse is also true. People have spoken a great deal about the masquerade of femininity, as in J. Rivière's article. I think that there is also a masculine masquerade, wanting to have only the masculine in masculinity—when in reality there is an erasure of elements which are assumed to be feminine.

We can't only work in the perspective of ignoring the problematic of the difference. Amorous play, sexual play, I would even say paternity, are only possible if a sort of Winnicottian game takes place in the space that supposedly belongs to the other sex. This doesn't mean that the way a man traverses the feminine is exactly equivalent to the way a woman goes through something which is supposedly masculine. There is a difference but it is a difference of strategy. There aren't two continents, the masculine and the feminine, which are totally separated. There is a constant interplay between them.

If I am suspicious of the problematic of the difference that is upheld by men, it is because many analysts now like to speak about feminine discourse, of feminine *parole*. For example, if one has a somewhat attacking discourse, they say this doesn't belong to feminine discourse, as if feminine discourse should correspond to the charming chant which leaves limits unchanged. Because of this bias, feminine discourse remaining in the nebulous, in the flow, would be very well received by men as a diverting *parole* which creates the effect of removal from the ordinary but doesn't put into question the citadel in which one is sheltered. In order not to allow the walls to enclose us, it is necessary to problematize this masculine and feminine difference.

Is there a place for love in the Freudian theory of pleasure?

This is a question which leads us to examine the cracks in Freud's theory very closely. Because there is on one side all the reflection on sexuality which should result in genitality. This is what I call the *psychoanalytic catechism,* that stage at which the libido is supposed to become altruistic. This consists of being conscious of the other, as at the end of the *Three Essays on The Theory of Sexuality,* where Freud, introducing the theme of the transformations of puberty, writes that the sexual drive becomes altruistic in a way. It's an extremely optimistic vision, which assumes that sexuality carried to term would result in spiritual union. This would be paradisal. But on the other side, in *Group Psychology and the Analysis of the Ego* (chapter 8), for example, the amorous state is assimilated to a pathological, an annihilating one. The object has in a way absorbed the self. It is the happiest state, the most intense if one is lucky enough to encounter it, but at the same time the experience is dangerous, for it can destroy and lead one to madness. I must say that I love these radical texts.

What is the place of sexuality in these texts? One could do a different reading of them. One could start from the amorous state to show how through the sexual level one could reencounter childhood and the primitive situation of distress. The amorous state is defined in such a way that it comes very near the risk of death. Therefore, there is something like a submergence into love.

One might feel that the sexes come together in an experience of immersion, not of conquest. Therefore another reading of feminine sexuality and the female body could be drawn from this extremely dizzying vision of the amorous state, in which the feminine, the maternal, would constitute the place of immersion. This perspective continued by Ferenczi seems to me more interesting than everything that Freud wrote concerning genitality per se. The one in love is presented as able to become a criminal without remorse. There is an extraordinary emphasis, a certain romanticism. I find Ferenczi's text very rich and not at all dogmatic.

How do you define narcissism and what is its connection with love?

The theme of narcissism is extremely difficult to approach in Freud. I will limit myself to a little note which is taken from the essay on the two principles of psychic functioning. Here Freud gives a definition of narcissism which refers to the first relation with the mother. This is a fusional relationship that doesn't recognize any difference between external and internal and corresponds to the state in which the fetus within the mother's body doesn't recognize the difference between inside and outside.

I find this definition of narcissism richer than Freud's other definitions, where he assumes a fundamental egoism of the self, of the psychic being, which one leaves only through genitality when genitality finally becomes altruistic. I think that this supposed narcissism, which is based on the idea of self-sufficiency, is a myth, since narcissism from the beginning is only possible through maternal care.

Early infant narcissism is a way of negating initial distress. There is a beautiful quotation in *An Outline of Psychoanalysis,* where Freud speaks of distress. He shows very well that the first stage of infancy is absolutely not narcissistic. There is a sort of overture, a pretraumatic state. What Freud will later call the object has a very different status then. That is, the object is not simply what is going to fulfill the needs which will allow the narcissistic state to close in on itself. Freud doesn't speak of an object at that moment—he speaks of a well-informed person who comes to the aid of the child. What is later called an object is in reality posited as an active agent who not only will fulfill the child's needs but also interpret and read them. From that moment, one sees that all relationship to the self goes through the interpretation made by someone else, made by the mother concerning her child's needs. She has to interpret the child's cries. In such a perspective one cannot speak about an object, for the object corresponds to a need, while the other in such a case is presented as one who understands and helps, who knows which object she should bring.

There is a connection between this experience of initial distress, when we ask the other not only to fulfill us but also to make us understand what we need, and at the same time to bring us the desired object and to name that desire. This experience in which the other is placed not only as the one who satisfies but almost as the one who creates us is an extreme experience. The one who is going to awaken desire, to give us desire, to make us capable of desiring—this extreme experience of distress is activated again in the amorous state, when one falls in love.

If one connects it to initial distress, I don't see this amorous state as being narcissistic. I think that the amorous state appears in the analytic process at the moment when one brings trauma to the surface. Therefore, I don't see it as a constant in analysis. The call for help addressed to the analyst brings a radical dimension, the need to be loved unconditionally, and this need occurs when the patient in analysis is at the edge of the cliff, the abyss which is often bound to a question related to birth. Is it a good thing to have been born? Does one have the right to be? What is asked of the analyst is the authorization to live. Everything develops as if there were a connection between the amorous state and what I call the prenatal situation.

I see a lot of these connections in Racine's *Phèdre*. The violent amorous call, "Love me or kill me," is linked to the problematic of birth to the extent that Phaedra is presented from the beginning as the daughter of Minos and Pasiphae. Throughout the play, she is less the so-called amorous woman than the one who questions the conditions of her birth. She will ask Hippolytus the basic question: Can she or can she not live? The theme which is constantly reiterated is "to see the light." Is Phaedra permitted to see the light, or must she return to darkness? I think that one can connect the problematic of love and the problematic of birth to the problem of incest. Where there is incest, there is the feeling of the prohibition to be born. Therefore the amorous state itself doesn't express narcissistic desire but rather asks what the necessary conditions are to render narcissism possible.

The amorous demand can thus be seen as a request for birth. Immediately after *Phèdre,* Racine wrote religious plays, and there is in *Esther* a moment which strongly recalls the situation in *Phèdre.* At the beginning, Phaedra falls apart. Esther approaching Ahasuerus also falls apart and therefore mimes a sort of return to nothingness. What Ahasuerus tells her is not, "I love you," but "Live," and that seems very surprising to me. An a posteriori interpretation of Phaedra's demand to be loved is that it is a request to be born, what Ahasuerus will answer when he says, "Live."

In analysis the two problematics are worked through at the same time, that is, the process of being born and the amorous request. This explains the radicality of the amorous demand: it succeeds or it fails. One cannot be half-born. One exists or one doesn't.

Freud said that women are more narcissistic than men.

I don't think that women are more narcissistic than men. It's true that Freud was fascinated by the idea of the woman being narcissistic. But how should we understand Freud's own need to see woman as narcissistic? It seems that it is a defense against a radically different image. What I point out in *Père ne vois-tu pas?* (Father, Don't You See?) is that in *The Interpretation of Dreams* is a vision of woman diametrically opposed since woman is there defined by her endless power of bleeding. That is to say, at the extreme, she would be this wound bleeding to infinity without anything being able to stop it. This representation of woman is so insupportable that one needs to represent a situation that puts an end to this hemorrhaging. The mirror represents that in which the woman is able to recognize herself, and therefore recover her image and cure her wound. I think that not only in Freud but in culture in general there is a need to enclose the woman, to bind her in front of the mirror, to conjure up another image, in contrast to the image of woman as a spring, the hemorrhaging woman, who has a multiple being.

I think that the need to represent the woman as narcissistic essentially conjures up the image of the mother. In contemporary analysis one often refers to the mother as possessive, as wanting to guard the product inside her at any price. I am thinking of the myth of Demeter when she lost Kore. According to the contemporary reading, one might imagine Demeter fixed in her suffering and her claim. However, what the myth shows so effectively is very close to the Freudian amorous state, which in German is called *Verliebtheit,* where the prefix *ver* indicates at the same time the fact of going to the end and being lost. Demeter, who just lost her daughter, feels an antinarcissistic experience; she thinks she heard a cry at the moment when the earth opened and Kore disappeared. And each time she hears a cry, she thinks that her daughter is there, and that is what makes her go all over the world. There is here something beautiful concerning maternity which is not just limited to the womb. It implies in the maternal and in woman a sort of complicity with everything which is in the process of taking shape. Because the cry is not a word, it is not a form, it is the dawn, the beginning of language, and each time that something beyond the word emerges, Demeter has the feeling that it is Kore who reappears, and that makes the mother go all over the earth, in disarray, without adornment, a torch in each hand, looking for her daughter night and day. Looking for her daughter is looking for everything which is in the process of taking form; no mirror, no definite shape, can stop her.

It is important to see that in this myth one is not dealing with a relation of power as in the case of the myth of Oedipus. Demeter accepts a compromise. Her daughter will disappear in autumn and winter and reappear in spring and summer and be reborn in every bud that blossoms forth. Kore cannot be identified as a precise shape. She cannot be localized. And it is this terrifying power that woman experiences in the amorous and maternal which allows her to recognize something of herself in everything which is in the process of taking on a shape.

This experience has been dammed up—almost forbidden by culture. We are instead presented with repulsive images of the mother; in the French vocabulary concerning the housewife cooking, one hears a lot about a wall oven, a built-in sink, as if the woman were herself built in. The woman is enclosed in her kitchen as if in a prison. It seems to me that all the language of culture favors a woman who is at the same time enclosed and enclosing. However, the myth of Demeter shows something totally different, and the amorous state does also in its request for birth. It is true that maternity may be experienced by the woman as at the same time static and menacing. This is an essential dimension but women cannot live with this dimension alone.

Narcissism can reappear; so can a phallic position, that is, a localized power, a certain control over things, but both narcissism and the phallic position limit and make possible the other side, which is that of wandering and the radical absence of narcissism. I think that femininity and maternity can only be lived in a sort of equilibrium between two poles, one of them being narcissism, but narcissism perhaps introduced as a meeting point for a diametrically opposed experience.

In the masculine imagination, the sexual object and the instructress are not combined. In the feminine one, the seducer and the instructor coexist and are longed for by the woman who looks for this unity. How do you explain this difference?

One may say that some women wish to separate the two—it all depends on the figure of the father—and some at the same time want to combine them. What is true in your question is that the coexistence of the two feminine figures in men's representation is more difficult. Let's say that the joining of the instructress and seductress is not usual for men. They have to separate women or see them only one way at a time. In men's representation, the cleavage of the woman, it seems to me, is more irremediable.

What are the results of this instructor/seducer fusion in the feminine psyche?

I don't think that the fusion of instructor/seducer in the woman's psyche is always seen. It's a question of play as in Winnicott. The figures meet, then distance themselves to allow a certain freedom of movement. In the feminine psyche, there are splits as important as in the masculine universe, but it seems to me that they are socially and culturally less isolated and petrified. That is, even though women's representation of a man can be divided into instructor and seducer, this division is not going to be used in a strong way by culture, the way it is with regard to women. I think that on the level of the female imaginary, there are many splits and movements toward separation. But cultural petrification cuts and isolates the imaginary of man with reference to the woman's representation more. So that while there might be in men a split or mythic representation which could be restructured by experience, the culture imposes splits which go against this restructuring in each individual instance. We know that a "serious" man may have had affairs; it's even valorized. However, it is devalued in a woman as if at the cultural level, the ambiguity of masculine figures is permitted while the feminine figures are not supposed to be ambiguous. The real mother is pure, etc.

Is there in women's representation of men a split that corresponds to the virgin/whore dualism?

I have worked less on this question. I find it in analysis and also personally, however. I think that we can speak of a split and even of a fragmentation. That is, I don't know if there are only two images. There is at the same time a fragmentation not only in the representation that the woman has of the man but also in the representation that a man has of himself. But very often the man is not aware of his fragmentation. He presents himself in a phallic way when in reality he exists somewhere else, and it is somewhere else that he can be understood by a woman. There is in the woman a representation of the man as a seducer, the one who awakens her to sexuality and who is not exclusively the representative of law and power. There is a split between this man and the one who introduces power, which is only one of the representations of the father. There is a sort of official image of a father, which misshapes the perception of the father, and the man who initiates one into pleasure, Don Juan among others.

One is also able to find a mixed representation in fairy tales. I think that the wolf can represent the seducer: the little girl in the forest risks meeting the wolf who represents man in his otherness. One could also say that the wolf represents the archaic mother and the womb as well as the archaic father and that the masculine seductive figure is extremely bisexual or intersexual, that is, it reactivates not just feminine elements but I believe profoundly maternal ones.

I wonder about what seems very simplified in the masculine vision proposed by psychoanalysis and the fact that it is only interested in the penis—I was thinking of a passage in Michèle Montrelay's *L'Ombre et le nom* (The Shadow and the Name), where she says that the penis is the plaything of the sexual relation.

The sexual relation in which both partners would be only a vagina and a penis would be horrible. Both partners would be without a mouth or arms. Psychoanalysis doesn't speak about the mouth and the arms. Man is supposedly armless, as if mouth and hands were something feminine. At the same time, it is from the mouth that seduction comes. I think that in the image of the seducer, which can correspond to the whore, one finds all this hidden power of the shadow, which in the amorous state is experienced in the man as the power of enveloping, that is, as something equivalent to what the infant experienced with the mother in the womb. Man is not only phallic. I even think that he could not be tolerated as penetrating if he were not enveloping at the same time. Generally, psychoanalysis doesn't want to know anything about this enveloping power because it reactivates a sort of deep feminine and maternal identification.

At the end of his cure, Ferenczi had tender behavior toward his patients, which scandalized Freud. Even if the analyst doesn't have to act on the level of affective relations, it is certain that this image has to be found again. A man should allow opposing elements belonging to the two sexes to come into play inside him. He has multifaceted powers and when he expresses his feminine side, he has at the same time the sensitivity of a young girl and the enveloping care of the mother. There is in all experience an element of seduction and of affective encounter, and I think that official, cultural differences shade off.

Why didn't Freud deal with the seduction of the mother after dealing with the seduction of the father?

In *Freud et le plaisir* (Freud and Pleasure) I especially noticed the passage where Freud says, "in my case my father played no active role—my 'primary originator' [of neurosis] was an ugly, elderly but clever woman." The German version calls her simply "my progenitor" while the English and French versions add "of neurosis." ★ Instead of recognizing that the agent of seduction might be feminine, Freud thought it necessary to abandon the hypothesis of seduction. I believe that if Freud dared face himself as having been seduced, he would have had to question the status of his own sex. Considering what Freud said at the end of his life, that the child is the breast, this implies that the first identity of all children is feminine and maternal. If Freud had pursued the implication of the equation that he presents in the letter where he speaks about the seduction and says, "I am she" *(Ich bin sie),* he would have seen himself radically transformed into a woman and inverted the problems that he posed concerning women and the study of femininity. He wonders how the little girl who is at first a little boy metamorphoses herself into a little girl. The reverse problem might be posed this way: how is the little boy who is born as an offspring of the mother going to become a man? What does he have to give up? From this perspective, the access to identity poses problems, for the mother with whom one identifies is a place, a different element, a distinct form toward which one inclines.

She is less encountered in an act of vision than in a desire, an aspiration, a pleasure equivalent to sleep and to meeting again. There are very great difficulties both in tearing oneself away from this first identification and in recovering it in the sexual object of

★The edition that Schneider is referring to is Sigmund Freud, *The Origins of Psychoanalysis: Letters to Wilhelm Fliess.* (New York: Basic Books, 1954), (letter of 3/10/1897).

love. It is as if the man ought to see himself as a warrior, a conqueror, to give himself super-virile images which reassure him against the fear of a fundamental feminine identification. I think that it is this fundamental feminine identification which terrified Freud. He said on several occasions: "I don't like to be the mother in the transference."

The character Don Juan is always hidden by Oedipus and Hamlet, who introduce the whole process of memory. With them there is a development of the investigation, an education of the memory, which results in the death of a certain number of women. In contrast, Don Juan perhaps makes others suffer but he runs the greatest risk himself and ends up in the grave. There is a reverse connection to memory because, being pursued by women as well as fathers, men of law, he is seen as Orestes pursued by the furies, who represent memory. Don Juan is the antimemory. And psychoanalysis is founded on the rehabilitation of memory. The terrible words in *Hamlet* are said by the father, "Remember me." The father overwhelms the whole scene and the son's fidelity consists entirely in remembering the father, whereas on the cultural level, Don Juan falls into the grave and stays there.

Can the primitive mother, this sort of abyss in which one is engulfed, be seen in a way other than as the bringer of death, which is the way Oedipal patriarchy views her?

I think that the primitive mother brings death to the extent that she denies or renders useless visions of mastery, of conquest with which men want to identify. That is, she breaks, she destroys the image, she doesn't kill man; she kills an image that he wants to have of himself. It is significant enough that in the letter where Freud speaks of his mother's double, one always finds the problem of splitting, because there is the official mother, who belongs more to a representation of authority, and the nurse, who is much more carnal, who initiates one into pleasure. And Freud says clearly that this woman helped him to live and to go on living. Therefore, she is experienced as the source of life and I would even say as the antithesis of the representation of the mother who, in the dream of the Parcae,★ in *The Interpretation of Dreams,* rubs

★This dream is also called the *Knoedel.*

her hands together to let the dust fall to show that it's from dust that we come; we are made of dust. It was terrifying enough because it showed both birth and decomposition. And Freud said clearly that he had this idea that he owed nature a death. The French translation modifies this to "he owed a life to nature." Freud's text is severe.

One sees here two antithetical images, that of the official woman, the mother that the cultural verdict makes us see as a part of the phallic figure, as representing power, authority, the superego, the father, the element who cuts the thread of life. And to refuse her the strength of all her impalpable power, it is necessary to put another image at her side, one that is socially devalorized, that is, the servant, who carries with her the elements of darkness and seduction. Freud represents her as the image of life, whereas the lesson coming from the mother is a lesson of death. I believe that the cultural scene in placing a prohibition on the seductive mother also destroys the desire for maternity. Very often this isn't recognized because at the same time there is a great incentive to maternity; officially the mother is represented as untouchable, and, in reality, all possible dangers are put on her side in order to make the function of the father essential, so that the mother is the danger and the father the redeemer.

In reality, and very clearly in Freud, there is a sort of cleavage of maternal representations. The element of darkness as representing life, not bringing death, is recognized but devalorized, is put aside and expressly forgotten in the image of the nurse being locked up. And a little later—here also there is a difference in translation that I discovered recently in the English text: Strachey says, "I am burrowing in a dark tunnel and can see nothing else." ★ Freud himself says, "I am interred in a dark pit," and one sees him as a mole who is working intensely, and that was just after his nurse was locked up for robbery, as if Freud saw himself locked up, buried with her, put into the box/coffin with her. It was a call for help. I am often attacked for saying that there is something tragic in Freud, but I think that the official psychoana-

★ *The Origins of Psychoanalysis: Letters to Wilhelm Fliess,* p. 258.

lytic reading wants to embalm the master the way one embalms mummies and masks all wounds and calls for help.

How do you see the pre-Oedipal father? Is there a concept of the father that corresponds to the phallic mother? A sort of womb father?

I think that theory has dealt very little with the important dimension of experience of the pre-Oedipal father. This theme that you just indicated refers directly to the wolf. The wolf represents exactly this enveloping and carnal figure. It is also linked to the father's voice. Generally a masculine voice reveals a certain part of the body more, such as the hollow, the chest. One hears a deeper resonance in the masculine voice than in the feminine one as if the internal vaults of the body could become perceptible in the father's voice. Thus the child may experience this voice as an acoustic womb.

Do you see Freud's interpretation of the Oedipus myth as a genocide of the feminine?

Freud's reductionist view of the Oedipus legend treats only patricide and incest. He doesn't treat the two matricides, those of the Sphinx and Jocasta.

There is a link between Oedipus' wound, Freud's blood, and the meeting with the one-eyed doctor. What I didn't realize in my book *Freud and Pleasure* is that the doctor, whom Freud describes as an object of hate, intrudes on the child Freud's relationship with his nurse, who is an instructor in sexuality. Therefore, the memory of his wound is reactivated at the same time as the memory of the nurse. Here we have a good example of both feminine and masculine representations that intertwine, which originally came together in an experience of trauma. I believe that there is in Freud a sort of fall into emptiness. He said that he couldn't find the figure of the doctor again. It seems to me that in Freud the appearance of Oedipus puts an end to the trauma; at the same time this is an Oedipus who is deprived of his own sight, which is effectively the sight of the doctor.

Sight, which is rooted in a sort of bloody visual hole, is the sign of femininity, what Freud thought the feminine consisted of. Interestingly enough, however, there is both a denial of feminine maternal blood and an appropriation of it by men throughout myth and legend, as in Oedipus' blinding and Christ's crucifixion.

How do you see Antigone?

In Antigone there is tenderness for the brother, the unrecognized man, the male who is condemned, who is not a figure of mastery. The woman as sister can feel a great fidelity toward a masculine, close, familial but rejected figure. It seems to me that the complicity with the subversive face of the masculine may be important in Antigone's relation with her brother.

In connection with Oedipus, the figure of Antigone is immediate and fits so well that we don't see her. Antigone becomes so much the staff of Oedipus in his old age that she doesn't exist on her own. As in fairy tales, the king and his daughter, the princess, are only one character and she is the appendix of masculine power. Therefore I think that Antigone with regard to her father is effaced but she isn't in relation to her brother.

What bothers me in Antigone's representation, which in France and in the Greek view is noble and beautiful, is that she is a disquieting woman. I don't feel myself an accomplice of Antigone, who approaches men at the moment when they are dying or dead. She is valorized in order to give the woman a thirst for the suffering man who is going to die. Therefore she has been used culturally for ambiguous purposes. She's the opposite of the nurturer.

How do you interpret the Sphinx? Is she a representation of the primitive or the phallic mother?

I think the Sphinx is a place of encounter between different realms. We don't know if she is animal or human; above all, she is characterized by her song. I think she incarnates the archaic primitive mother very strongly. With reference to the phallic mother, I must say there are two possible meanings, according to whether you take *phallic* in the Freudian or Lacanian sense. In Freud's terms, she is fantasized by the child as bearing the equivalent of the masculine element, while in Lacanian terms, *phallic* signifies lack. At the same time, it is all that one can imagine: the void, everything. I see this concept as much too large because I believe that when we speak of the interior darkness, of the hollow, we aren't as precise as in defining the masculine sex. Moreover, we don't mean *lack* in the visual sense. This is why the concept of the phallic mother is extremely ambiguous when taken in the Lacanian sense. One uses everything which in the feminine and the maternal does not correspond to the geometric, determined, circumscribed figure; all that which doesn't enter into this logic of the circumscribed of the line is assimilated to lack. However, there is a whole series of registers, for example, touch, which do not correspond to linear logic, to precise representation, but which are not the incarnation of lack. From this point of view, the phallic concept applied to the mother or the woman in Lacan is a concept which poses problems for me because I would prefer to work on an intermediary level.

Now then, if one takes *phallic* in the Freudian sense, one could say along with Marie Delcourt, who is essentially a Hellenist, that according to the legends and the drawings she studied, the Sphinx is entirely on the side of the primitive mother. But Sophocles transforms her because there are denial and cultural lies about the Sphinx. In reality she acted through her song. Sophocles wrote: "The bitch has bewitched us with her songs." And Marie Delcourt says that she is thirsty for blood and love. How can one resolve a song? If she really sings, will Oedipus be able to give an answer to her song? One cannot answer a song. Therefore this figure was transformed into a representation that was effectively phallic in the Freudian sense, that is, into an examiner who asks questions. We see how this appearance of the phallic mother allows the man, the writer, to master his terror, to ignore everything about the primitive figure. I think that in many couples very often the woman is seen as the spokesperson of conscience but the man doesn't want to hear her voice. It is this phallic, authoritative superego which is imposed by force on the voice of the woman. The man doesn't have to listen to the voice of the woman, just as he doesn't have to listen to the voice of the sirens.

Do you attribute Freud's silence on menstruation and menopause to his denial of feminine blood?

There is an almost total absence of thought on menstruation and menopause in psychoanalysis. In the phallic perspective, if the woman is simply a man deprived of a penis, all her internal cycle is ignored and also the problem of menopause. This silence, this blank which replaces the red, is rooted in Freud's prehistory, in the wound and fear of blood. In the case of Emma, Freud almost fainted at the sight of blood. To the extent that it was traumatic for him, female blood could not be seen as connected to female sexuality. As is often the case in Freud, however, one cannot talk about an absolute. What would interest me would be to study the Freudian theoretical topography, that is, to see how certain themes, which were left blank in the official theoretical level, reappear, either when Freud speaks about literature or about the primitive.

As a psychoanalyst, Freud ignored female blood, but in speaking about primitive cultures, he does consider defloration and menstruation. He states that they see female blood as the seat of life and menstruation as the result of a phantom spirit's bite—the young girl is seen as possessed by a spirit. Therefore, there is a very rich imagery, which is abandoned again to the dark continent and is ignored among the civilized.

This forgetfulness is not unique to Freud. One finds it in culture in general. In a Hungarian film, whose title I have forgotten, at the moment of the first sexual encounter when the boy tries to penetrate the girl, she confesses that it is her first time. The man withdraws immediately and says, "I could have imagined anything but that," as if it were absolutely impossible. In another case, after the young man prepares the place for the amorous encounter, the young girl confesses her fear, to which he exclaims, "You aren't a virgin?" When the young girl confesses that she is, the man pushes her away saying: "Forget it." The act of defloration does not interest some men. Among the primitives, it was sometimes carried out by priests. It was thus possible to imagine defloration as a civic action. This shameful vision of defloration contrasts with that of the preceding century when we had the idea that the most important thing a woman had to offer in marriage was virginity and that it was the husband alone who should deflower her.

Now we have reached a totally opposed view where defloration must not exist. I know a patient who paid a drunkard to come to her place to initiate her because she was ashamed to be with a man and still be a virgin. Virginity has become inadmissible. Another patient ruptured her eardrum when she lost her virginity. The patient came very much afraid and said that because of a cold she had ruptured her eardrum. I tried to suggest that there might have been a certain anxiety concerning defloration but that was an almost inadmissible theme—as if I had suspected her of having old-fashioned ideas the way her grandmother did. The fear couldn't be expressed, even the dizziness linked to the experience of defloration was inexpressible. This had to be worked out in a very subtle way on the analytic level. I treated the experience as if it were an integral destruction of the self which left the body open. This is to give a certain dramatization for the woman to be able to admit that defloration could be a strong experience, that one might love the fear into which one is plunged. But one feels that a modern woman must present herself as deprived of a hymen.

Therefore we see that everything which deals with the female cycle—initiation, defloration, menstruation, and menopause are forbidden, in the sense that one does not consider woman, but rather a masculine image supposedly in contact with eternity. Therefore, one takes something from this masculine image to make a woman out of it. One stays in a kind of eternal masculine and negates the connection to time, to change in the body, and also to blood. It seems to me that the connection to blood must be rediscovered in the sense of a vital blood which cannot be treated in a familiar or banal mode. Freud failed in the face of the feminine and was not able to theorize on it.

Why are so many women psychoanalysts interested in Lacan while Derrida and others accuse him of phallocentrism?

Derrida puts into question phallocentrism, which he calls phallogocentrism. With Derrida, there is an emphasis on dissemination, which is the title of one of his books in which one can see the representation of a connection to the world, to the Other, which is extremely close to what one is able to recover in a dimension of femininity. But although certain analysts are seduced by Derrida, Lacan's influence on psychoanalysts is much stronger than his.

Phallocentrism is welcome because it is inscribed in the whole Greco-Roman culture, which rules the French intellectual scene. (In that sense, it's very different from the Anglo-Saxon world.) It had precedents in the Greek period, in a certain type of music which was founded on mastery and harmony. What reappeared with the inquisitors in the struggle against the devil had already been prepared for in the Greek theater in the struggle against so-called lycanthropic music. The word *lycanthropy* reappears in the Middle Ages and the sixteenth and seventeenth centuries to characterize the order represented by the devil, who is seen as a wolf who can possess certain men who become wolf-men. In the same way, people think that the sorceress is inhabited by the devil. What is the devil's place of choice? Inside the body. There is in all of Greco-Roman thought a tradition which places the demonic in the woman, inside the womb. And to conquer the devil, the inquisitors had a solution: to burn the sorceress. What is interesting to me is the medical interpretation which takes place in the seventeenth century when the medical doctors say, "It is not the devil who inhabits the possessed, it's the womb which is full of vapors, humors, liquid elements which rise up to the brain and produce the imagination." Therefore what will have to be purged, cleared, is the womb; something must be destroyed in the imaginary of the female body. It is the whole inside which is supposed to be filled with liquid and evaporating elements.

When Freud speaks, he doesn't even need to say that we should be suspicious of the womb. In some theoretical texts, the womb has disappeared since woman is characterized by the fact that she doesn't have a penis. Therefore if one takes a man and castrates him, according to the Freudian imaginary we should end up with a woman. A castrated man is not a woman, but this is what French psychoanalysis ignores for the most part, and the notion of the phallus for me is extremely bothersome and ambiguous because it places under the sign of lack what is seen in the imaginary under the sign of an uncontrollable internal abundance. As

Freud said, in dreams or in poems—that means with irony—it
was a question of "damming up the power of the female sex."★
But this power is seen as indefinite, as repeated and uncontrollable. I think that there is a break between the unconscious, which
attributes an immeasurable power at the internal visceral level to
the woman, and the conscious interpretation which simply ignores all this power. And I think that Freud performs on the
female body the equivalent of what the doctor did to his body at
the level of the jaw when he was a child. In the same way Freud
sutured the edges of what he had experienced as a female wound.

It should be possible to come back to what Freud perceived as
the interior of the female body, to take out the stitches to make
the opening appear again, an opening which is not a wound but
could be fantasized in a very different way as the entrance to an
interior world, creating life. It would be the threshold in a sense.
This metaphor of the threshold to represent female space is totally
absent in the Lacanian problematic.

I very much like the notion of the dark continent used by Freud
to designate femininity. But if we take the metaphor seriously we
see effectively that a whole part of femininity is experienced by
man as well as woman. She doesn't control what happens in her
uterus and her womb, either. She is able to know the threshold,
the entrance, and to have a certain connection with herself in
autoerotism, but she cannot see what her sexuality represents on
the anatomical level the way a man can contemplate his penis.
There is a part unknown to the woman herself, a continent which
is dark even for her. It is surprising enough that we were able to
ignore this dark continent to the point of nonawareness of the
female being. It is a way of translating something else, the interior
of the female body.

A patient recently asked why he was so afraid of women and
added, "What is there in this fear?" And I said, "What is there
inside, inside the woman?" He answered, "It's a bomb, a factory
for making children." That's surprising. From the outset, what
sprang forth as menacing was the power to create. This is the
opposite of the phallus seen as the signifier of lack.

★Max Schur, *Freud Living and Dying*. New York: International Universities
Press, 1972.

To the extent that there is a phallic state, as Freud outlines it (in which the phallus is the signifier of lack), woman can see herself as a man without a penis, but this is only one vision among others. The fault of psychoanalysis, part Freudian and part Lacanian, has been to strengthen this state, this figure among others, in giving it an absolute value and in continuing this kind of inquisitorial purge, the destruction of the womb. The womb has been destroyed so well that no one speaks of it any more.

Do you think that literature reproduces the sexual monism? Does philosophy? Religion?

It seems certain to me taken all together that the theme of sexual monism is the principal tendency in philosophy and religion also. I believe that the different cultural disciplines have a specific and original position and one can't speak of culture in general. It's literature which goes the furthest in the domain of exploration. That means that literature doesn't need to attach itself to a credo the way certain analysts feel obliged to recreate Lacan's work, for example. A writer doesn't have to redo the work of another writer. There is an improvisation in the act of writing, a relative freedom which allows literature to be the instrument which can best explore a multiplicity of representations. A man's doubt concerning his virility, all his hatred with regard to femininity— all that is taboo in psychoanalysis but can be said in literature. Alain Roger, who wrote *The Misogynist,* shows all the ferocity of man toward woman, all the images of the fear of woman. Therefore, I would say that in examining literature more, one could understand the reasons for the analytic block. It is for literature to analyze analysis.

In the other disciplines, there are new ramifications. For example, philosophy can present itself as following the system, a rationality wanting to annex everything in an integral universe consecrating monism. Derrida is not into sexual monism. He doesn't pretend to deal with a philosophy of the sexes, but let us say that he mixes the tracks concerning the vision that the thinking man may have of himself. On an intellectual level, he is a figure similar to the one of Baba Yaga in the fairy tales.

I also think that in the Jewish tradition, there is a philosopher who depends a lot on the Bible: Emmanuel Levinas, who proposes a vision of the alterity of the woman which opens up ways which are totally different from that of monism. What's interesting also is that he presents a philosophy in which the mouth and the connection to the mother take first place. What is denied by a number of philosophers is of first importance for him. The essential is not representation. One doesn't represent things; one lives them, is nurtured by them. He proposes as a term the *elemental* as an all-encompassing element which seems to me extremely womblike. One doesn't represent the song; it is. One is surrounded and lives through it. He speaks of the possibility of living as if in the entrails of being. In philosophy, to my knowledge, there are overtures to the extent that there is a sort of breach occurring in the great rationalist tradition. Even the fact of putting aside philosophy makes philosophy in France more marginalized and able to explore the points more.

Therefore it seems to me that psychoanalysis, instead of being a reference system, now constitutes a reductional impact in certain fields, and that psychoanalysis would gain in opening itself up to different disciplines. Freud freed himself a great deal from different repressions when he worked with creative figures, in his fascination with Leonardo da Vinci, for example. There is also his great closeness to Goethe. It seems to me that the alleviation of repression in psychoanalysis comes in connection with creative activity which doesn't feel the necessity of being in a state of uninterrupted erection. There is an essential mobility in it.

The religious level is extremely ambiguous and it's necessary to be more precise. In the Old Testament, the religious man, that is, man in his connection with God is absolutely not presented as having to be 100 percent masculine. On the contrary, it's very surprising but being a man or a woman in connection with God, is to be the spouse. Therefore the man is feminized in connection with God even if this feminization is presented as taking place without being theorized about. I wonder, however, about the importance that a decline of religious power could have since the mystics, even if they are men, allow a great deal of femininity in their writing about the power of worship and ecstasy, and live as women in relation to God. There is therefore a *parole féminine* and *masculine* at the same time which reaches not every domain of religion but certainly the domain of mysticism and prayer. This allowed the human being in general to live more easily by mixing up the sexual division whereas rationalism expresses an unbridled masculinity. That is, the prohibition of feminine positions which are not necessarily recognized as feminine but are, however, experienced as feminine. The prohibition of the feminine position has been reinforced with the putting aside of a certain type of religious discourse. And I wonder about the possible connection between the fall of a certain type of religious discourse which had nothing of the heroic (in connection with God there is nothing to conquer) and the necessity for women to discover a feminine connection to the extent that certain images have been taken up again and put in the forefront by feminism.

What is the keystone that women have to remove to liberate themselves?

There is no keystone to be removed for liberation. The keystone is a representation coming from the masculine imaginary to fill up the feminine void. We have to find a link in woman which is connected to that which is germinative, that which seeks to take on a form. I believe that the womb isn't only a place, it is the place from which another existence takes its form. One of the representations of the woman, the sorceress, makes explicit this existence that is impossible to confine to one form or place. The sorceress is the image which is able to be found everywhere, to which we cannot assign a residence.

There are two ways to approach femininity. There is a whole movement after cultural fragmentation, in which it is normal that the woman try to begin again, to put herself together, to seek what is specific in her. In a way she has been obeying a certain cultural arrangement which has a great tendency to stress feminine narcissism and to imprison the woman in a confrontation with power. Therefore the search for a specific feminine identity might lead again to a prison, where the experience remains essentially narcissistic.

This is only a moment of reparation, but a necessary one, that is, we must define the feminine, beginning with alternative phases like inhaling/exhaling. This restorative reassembling is necessary after a cultural crumbling, but in order for the woman to take up her place again, she has to begin with the different elements of her body, with a multitude of figures: the sister, the wife, the courtesan, the mother. The woman has to try to fight the theme of unity, of one figure bringing things together, to work in a sort of multiplicity.

The title of one of my articles was "Mère innombrable" ("Innumerable Mother"). Even in maternity, I had the feeling that there was a multiplying of figures, one giving birth to the other. My daughter as a child asked me: "Mama, will I have big breasts like you one day?" I saw myself as a small prehistoric statue where one has the impression that the woman is like a bunch of grapes. There is something of a passage from the unformed and the multiple which is able to be recovered by women first; so that there wouldn't be a single way of acting which is the right way of being a woman, but rather a power of improvisation which will ultimately link different feminine elements, where not everything converges around the penis, the phallic element.

England

Juliet Mitchell, one of Britain's best-known feminist thinkers, was born in New Zealand but has lived in London since she was four years old. She was a lecturer in English literature at the universities of Leeds and Reading and has often been a visiting professor in foreign countries. Now a practicing psychoanalyst, her publications range from literary criticism to political theory, feminism, and psychoanalysis.

SELECTED BIBLIOGRAPHY

Woman's Estate. New York: Vintage, 1971.
Psychoanalysis and Feminism. New York: Random House, 1975.
(Edited with Jacqueline Rose). *Feminine Sexuality: Jaques Lacan and the Ecole Freudienne*. New York: Norton, 1982.
Women: The Longest Revolution. New York: Pantheon, 1984.
The Selected Melanie Klein. Harmondsworth: Penguin, 1986.

TEN

Juliet Mitchell

London, Summer 1986

Juliet Mitchell lives in a row house in the outskirts of London on a street that reminds one of the French provinces, with its whitish houses and red chimneys. Granted it was a sunny day, there seemed to be a permanently bright feeling inside, aided perhaps by Mitchell's incredibly blue eyes. We sat upstairs on a large sofa with deep pillows. Downstairs the big dining room table reminded one of a French country kitchen. A profusion of Raggedy Ann-type dolls lay on the front parlor floor, for some lucky member of the household, Mitchell's young daughter. Nothing pretentious here. Just warmth, space, comfort.

First of all, we would like to ask you why you became an analyst.

There are two levels at which one could answer the question of why one becomes an analyst: the level of a conscious intellectual interest and career decision and then looking back, the level of all the less conscious determinants. I first got interested in Freud in an explicit way in the States at the beginning of the women's movement when I found that feminists were so antagonistic to Freud; it was de rigueur to have an attack on Freud in everybody's major book in the early seventies and after.

In England, it just wasn't an issue. We didn't have everybody going into therapy. Nobody would bother to attack psychoanalysis. So I was very struck by the American feminist attack on Freud. I thought well, there must be something here that matters. I became more and more interested in psychoanalysis, and there was a point at which I thought I could get no further by reading alone.

Retrospectively, I can see an interest in the formative effect of infancy and childhood was already with me by the time I was eleven. Then when I was teaching literature in my twenties, I was particularly interested in the psychological aspects of fictional characters—the emphasis on psychological growth and development and the crucial place of childhood in the English eighteenth- and nineteenth-century novel.

Where did you do your psychoanalytic training? What school do you place yourself in?

There is only one place in England to train for treating adults and that's the British Institute of Psychoanalysis. I trained in what we call the Independent or Middle Group. Klein came to this country in the twenties. Freud and the refugees came again in the thirties, and during the war, discussion was divided in this country initially between the Anna Freudians and the Kleinians. The Middle Group emerged later.

Was your analyst male or female? Does it make a difference for the transference?

My analyst was Enid Balint. By definition, it doesn't make a difference whether the analyst is male or female because you transfer the significant figures of your past onto the present, not the significant figures of the present onto the past. And if it's your father that's the significant figure at any given time, then that's who you're going to see or hear in the chair behind you. But having said that, it's not as simple as that because, of course, we are not only in what we might call the "past historical" transference situation. One comes into a room, one goes out of the room, one knows the gender and characteristics and age of the person behind one. In that sense, you could say that we are in two places at once. We are both in the past historical transference and in the present historical transference. And the part of us that's not in the past historical transference of course knows the sex, the gender of the analyst, and that's likely to have a bearing on what comes up first and where. Women may bring up things sooner with a woman analyst than they might with a man analyst. I think it also has bearing when one is in a maternal transference. If there is a woman there, it may alter the nature of the transference.

Enid Balint has a paper on a woman analyst with a woman patient which is very much about this question: through having a woman analyst a woman can feel what it is that she wants in relation to her mother. And probably in that sense the woman analyst is like a trigger, something that introduces earlier on that sort of possibility. Both Freud and Lacan thought that women analysts were probably ultimately better analysts because of the easier possibility of a maternal transference and the centrality of that relationship. They also thought that because femininity was the mystery, that women therefore had the clue to it, which isn't necessarily true.

Do you have more women than men patients? Do you find that your countertransference differs depending on whether the patient is male or female?

I have more women than men patients at the moment. But that's by chance. I no longer notice a generic difference in the counter-transference with a male and a female patient. I mean, different things come up with different patients. I think I did at the beginning, when I was training. There is a rule in the English Institute that you start with a patient of the opposite sex from yourself because it's supposed to be easier to handle a heterosexual trans-

ference than a homosexual transference. I don't think that's particularly true. In some ways it is easier but it is also more dangerous
in a way to analyze somebody of the same sex as oneself when
one is very new to it because it is easier to make identifications
with somebody who in some sense has had a comparable history
to oneself. There's all the more need therefore to pull out from
the identifications and to be able to look at them. It's harder to
make an identification with someone who has had an opposite
history from oneself, but on the other hand it's easier to look at
the identifications when you make them. I think what you're
doing is moving in and out of identifications that you're looking
at, in order to understand.

When one is a young analyst, and I'm still a young analyst—
Anna Freud and other people have said that one starts to be an
analyst after ten years—but when you are really new to it, I think
that it is easier to make those identifications with people of the
same sex, but it is also more difficult to withdraw from them.
You have to be very careful.

**Obviously, you were very influenced by the women's
movement; in fact, you said that a lot of your reading of
Freud stemmed from what you saw happening in the feminist movement. How would you say that the movement
has influenced your theory?**

I became interested in the question of women and the question of
femininity before the women's movement. I first started to write
about women in 1962, and the only thing really on the scene then
were a few books that have disappeared now and Simone de
Beauvoir. I was enormously impressed, in a sense somewhat
negatively, by *The Second Sex*. (I first read it when I was eighteen.) I learned to respect it much more later. I thought it was a
great book, but I took a critical relationship to it because I think
one doubts until one finds one's own feet. I almost don't want to
remember the things I didn't like about it. It felt very French; it
didn't feel at all appropriate to an Anglo-Saxon situation. I was
very much a part of the New Left. We were, indeed, as a group,
very Sartrean and phenomenological, but actually I never found
myself to be entirely absorbed by that.

I was already in a sense interested in psychoanalysis even though I didn't formulate it as such until several years later. And of course, psychoanalysis is exactly what de Beauvoir was hostile to. I talked with her subsequently and we still continued to disagree about psychoanalysis, and yet I find our positions in some senses close, but what we attribute things to is fundamentally different.

The Mandarins, which I also read when I was about eighteen, was the first great novel for me, after reading *Wuthering Heights* at ten or eleven, that I felt as a woman I could identify with. My eleven-year-old self—and I forgive her—could identify with Cathy Earnshaw. I wanted to be her and then I moved on to Anne, in *The Mandarins.* It was an important novel by a woman writing about women's experiences. I had no problem then, at that age, identifying completely with *The Mandarins.* I would now. I've moved the other way around. I am now taking a more critical distance from *The Mandarins* and appreciate *The Second Sex* more than I did earlier.

To have these sorts of points of identification, Cathy and then Anne, I suppose is very interesting, but they are pretty ghastly people in some ways, both of them.

But they are heroines of women writers.

But I've never identified with Maggie Tulliver, or all those nice sorts of positive heroines.

Perhaps psychoanalysis can help us understand those identifications. How would you say that psychoanalysis has affected feminism?

Psychoanalysis has had an enormous effect on feminism: the practice of psychoanalysis as well as the theory. A lot of feminists went into psychoanalysis here who wouldn't have done so in a previous generation, and I think analytic experiences changed individual people's lives. On the theoretical level, it's given one of the greatest, most important tools for understanding questions of sexual difference in different arts, in ideology, and in the representation of women.

Its influence has not been on the level of a political movement, but on an intellectual level; on the level of the concepts of what constitutes sexual difference, it has been extremely important.

How would you say that feminism has affected psychoanalysis?

Amongst my colleagues here, it's the presence of the feminist movement, the presence of the feminists on the couch if not as colleagues, which has made psychoanalysis aware of the question of the nature of sexual difference in a way that wasn't true fifteen years ago. There was nothing much written about psychological questions of femininity and masculinity even ten years ago.

It's a resurrection of an old and central question and one that is in some ways *the* question of psychoanalysis if you ask me, but I think there was a sort of diminution in the awareness of the problem of sexual difference as a conceptual center point in psychoanalysis, and feminism has made many psychoanalysts re-ask questions about sexual difference.

What would Freud say if he were alive today?

He would say, "Here we go again." It has all happened before.

What are some of the major differences that you see in England and in France?

There is a much stronger orientation toward object relations in England. That's really the British tradition, both Kleinian and non-Kleinian, Independent and Kleinian. There is always the question of the relationship between two or more people and taking that back to some starting points. The relationship that a person has to the fantasized object is crucial. Everybody of course accepts the notion of drives and instincts. But there isn't a drive without an object in this country. I think that's the initial difference. From that spring many other differences.

Another major difference is the very strong orientation towards clinical work here. It's an old story to say that French are theorists and British are clinicians. And hopefully, the polarity is not as great as it once was. It's a polarity that I deplore because I think you cannot think theoretically if you don't think clinically as well, and you can't work clinically without working theoretically. If you're writing clinical papers you have to have some theoretical hypothesis which you may then knock down, and similarly, the other way around, if you think theoretically, you have to think through your practice. So, hopefully, the distinction is one that will lessen, but there's definitely a very strong clinical tradition in this country, a strong experiential tradition.

And when we train here, the emphasis is, first of all, on one's own analysis, which is absolutely crucial, the major component of the training. And second, the amount of clinical experience that one has. The difference between here and the States is of course that we always have had a lot of lay analysts. We have always had a lot of women analysts, and the two possibly go together because one didn't have to come through the medical schools during a time when medical schools discriminated harshly against women. The analytical tradition here did not discriminate against women. So there has not been the orientation to medicine and the orientation to a patriarchal tradition as there has been in America.

If you were to rewrite your book *Psychoanalysis and Feminism,* is there any major point that you would change?

I would have to reread it, which I haven't done, but of course it would be a different book. There's a section of it which gets left out of most people's minds, which is on Reich and Laing. I'm actually quite interested in them because I came out of the New Left tradition, which was very Laingian if it was oriented to any form of psychoanalysis: Laingian, Sartrean and/or Reichian, which is the anarchist tradition, not the New Left. Reich and Laing were enormously important figures. I suspect that Reich is going to become important again. (Unfortunately, Laing's later work isn't as good as his early work.) If I were to rewrite that book in the eighties, they would not be the people I would be thinking about, although I might think about them again in the nineties. The feminists I would talk about would not be Germaine Greer and Kate Millett. The whole mass of other literature that feminism has produced on psychoanalysis is now much more complex than that.

The book was published in 1974, so I must have written it in 1972 or thereabouts. Some fifteen years later, a lot of water has flowed under two different bridges: both psychoanalysis and feminism; it would be a different book.

I had decided at that time if I wasn't accepted for training as a psychoanalyst after I'd done the book, I would go into anthropology. I was very interested in kinship, an anthropology of sexual difference. And I think that the book in a sense uses psychoanalysis in an anthropological direction, which I have since dropped. I am interested in it, but I don't know any more about it than I did then. But I was really very interested in the work of Lévi-Strauss and of the sort of people that went into Michelle Rosaldo's wonderful collection.

And I think that's the sort of area I would have gone into. The book was on an apex, which could have gone in either direction, into the clinical work of psychoanalysis or practical work in anthropology. I took the former path.

In your essay "Femininity, Narrative and Psychoanalysis," you write, "If language is phallocentric, what is a woman patient doing when she is speaking? What is a woman analyst doing when she is listening and speaking back?" Well, I ask you, what is she doing?

Those questions are addressed to a debate about whether there is one language or two languages. Is there a male language and a female language, a feminine language and a masculine language, or is there only one which we both speak? It's a highly complex question. But I think—and I don't want to be dogmatic about it—that there are different histories to the way the two genders use language; therefore, after the formation of language or during the formation of language there may well be different idioms and different ways in which a girl and a boy will come to speak, not grossly different, but there will be variations which could be sex-linked. So there is a different history to the use of language. But there isn't a different formation to language between the sexes. Language and sexual division—the psychological divisions between the sexes—come at the same time. You speak in a structured sense when you know there are two sexes. Though you have words, you don't speak before that, that is, you don't use words that relate to each other.

So that sexual division—the assumption of psychological sexual difference—and the assumption of language go together, and in that sense the acknowledgment of sexual difference is the same for both sexes. In its formation, there isn't a difference in language for the two sexes; in its history—and that will vary in different societies, in different social classes, in different ethnic groups—there may well be a history of difference between usages of language. We have to separate out these two questions.

Now, in an analytical situation, what you're essentially doing is trying to listen to the manifestations of a latent unconscious content, and I think you will get, so to speak, that history and that formation in the unconscious, which also has a history; it also has a prehistory if you like, which is not sexually divided in any absolute way, and a history which is. And the language that you are listening to will reflect therefore that double pattern of similarity and difference.

So, again, I think that we have, if you like, one voice shared between the sexes, which may be dominantly male, because of the nature of language in the culture, and that we have a sort of subvoice which actually may be feminine, an idiom which will be heard differently by a man and a woman.

Do you believe as some of the French writers do that there is or should be an *écriture féminine*?

I think that we are caught in a very serious dilemma if we think there is a feminine writing, an *écriture féminine*. The French feminists are talking about an original language which has to do with the relationship of bodies to each other, which has to do with the woman's body. What I am talking about is a masculine and feminine language which has a different history of the usage of language. Most writers who write about the *écriture féminine* are talking about the formation of language, not the history of language.

I think that there is a feminine history of language, but not a feminine formation of language. There is something called body language, but that's precisely not what we mean by language; it's something else. It's definitely a form of communication. But it's previous to the assumption of the psychological meaning of sexual difference. Though the baby boy and girl pre-Oedipally, pre-language, may be characteristically different, in the essence of a symbolized sexual difference, they are not meaningfully feminine or masculine. They may be proleptically so; they are going to be that, but they are not that yet.

So then we take it that you would not agree with Kristeva that this early pre-Oedipal "language" or nonlanguage—what she calls semiotics—is feminine.

This early pre-Oedipal "language" or nonlanguage, the shadows and images within the *kore* that Kristeva talks about, the sounds of the gurgles and the noises, can become structures of language which will become identified with the masculine or the feminine. But they are not in themselves such.

As for the very early phonemic structures that precede language, I think there are all sorts of structures that precede the representation of the symbolization of sexual difference. Now, these presymbolized forms, if you like, in a pre-Oedipal period, will become the content of femininity and masculinity after what I see as Freud's emphasis on the significance of the castration complex as the mark of what symbolizes sexual difference. I think that Melanie Klein's work which charts sexual difference or even more perhaps Winnicott's interest in the area of bisexuality and creativity are proleptically forms for what would become the content of femininity and would become the content of masculinity, post-Oedipally, postcastration complex.

But sexual difference in that early period has not yet been symbolized. Freud did not chart what he called this earliest dark continent. I think other people have started to. But what Klein, what Winnicott, what Balint, what many British analysts with their orientation toward object relations really started importantly to do, was to map those sorts of shadowy forms, those phonemic utterances, those body images, those fantastical contents, a sort of Kleinian fantasy world that is pre-Oedipal in the Freudian pre-Oedipal sense, not in the Kleinian one. Now, to me, those forms have not yet taken up positions of a symbolized difference between the sexes.

To be reductive about it, let me say that Melanie Klein gives a sort of language, sometimes jargon, to the fantasy of the infant, for example, the good breast and bad breast. Now the good breast and bad breast can also have, in her terminology, a penis within the breast which can be devouring, or it can be good, it can be nutritional. I think those are powerful ways of imposing a perception on what we imagine the baby is imagining, which we can glimpse from the fantasies of patients. Later the forms of sexual difference will take up those earlier forms. Klein is right to put them in terms of what will become acknowledged as sexual difference.

They are, of course, not yet a penis or a breast to the baby. Prochronistically, they are that; they are ahead of their time. And in that we are always retrospective human beings, we're always using our history; then these early forms are proleptically sexually defined, but they are not yet symbolized as such. They will become the content of what is subsequently symbolized as sexual difference.

In this sense I'm incredibly eclectic. I find Klein and Winnicott and the whole tradition of object-relations theory, on which I have been brought up so to speak as an analyst, not only immensely important clinically—it's how I work clinically—but also important theoretically and how I think theoretically through my clinical material, but I then go to the fundamental structure that Freud first proposed, which is the significance of the castration complex. And that's where my interest in Lacan comes in because he returned to that. Klein and the object-relations people used a different Freud to be creative and to explore another area. But they tend to forget the importance of the castration complex.

If the privileged phallus is simply a metaphor as Lacan implies, why didn't he suggest how another system of symbolization might work? How would you go about constructing an alternate symbolic universe and what might that universe be like? Or do we not need it? If Freud and Lacan were right about castration, then maybe we shouldn't try to construct another universe.

I am not enough of a linguist or enough of a logician, but I suspect that there's something impossible about the question, not just simply that we cannot fantasize a future. Of course we can and I think millennarian visions are extremely important because, like that early pre-Oedipal period, they give shape to what then comes later with a revolutionary change. Imagining the future matters. I don't think it's unimportant as a political policy, but when I say there is something impossible about the question, I mean on another level. I mean at the level of imagining a different metaphor.

A metaphor refers to something. If we say the phallus is the penis, we know that we can talk about, for example, the phallic woman, the phallic mother, and the phallic breast. We know that it can be something else, but ultimately, originally, indeed, it is attached to the penis, and historically this is the way we have symbolized sexual difference.

You can't wish away the content of the metaphor. You can't wish away the whole of a history that has attached phallus to penis and literally to that concrete organ, the penis, and has seen it as that. There is a relationship which may ultimately be arbitrary, but in history it is not arbitrary at all.

And this has to do with the necessity for human society as such to differentiate between the sexes, and this is where I think feminism gets into real difficulties because there is a relationship between the symbolization of sexual difference and language as such. The only ultimate point about sexual difference is exactly that difference, and it is actually the nature of structural difference and what object is so to speak selected to structure difference that is important. You can't have a random number of multiple differences. One thing is needed to differentiate the two sexes. Even though we know there are intersex groups in some cultures, there are always dominantly two sexes and that has to do with the nature of language. So we couldn't say that brown hair could be the mark that differentiates us, and curly hair and straight hair couldn't be used to organize society because curly hair and straight hair are not attached to language in the same way that something selected to symbolize sexual difference is attached to language.

Enid Balint has been a training analyst since 1963 at the British Institute of Psychoanalysis, where she also served as director from 1970 to 1974. She maintains a private practice and serves as a consultant at the Institute of Marital Studies, Tavistock Institute of Human Relations.

SELECTED BIBLIOGRAPHY

Psychotherapeutic Techniques in Medicine, coauthored with M. Balint. London: Tavistock, 1961.
Focal Psychotherapy: An Example of Applied Psychoanalysis, coauthored with M. Balint and P. Ornstein. London: Tavistock, 1971.
"Fair Shares and Mutual Concern." *International Journal of Psycho-Analysis* (1972): 53–61.
Six Minutes for the Patient, coedited with J. S. Norell. London: Tavistock, 1973.

ELEVEN

Enid Balint

London, July 1986

At the time that this interview took place—she has since moved —Dr. Balint lived in a magnificent house outside of London. But it wasn't inside that we spoke. Rather it was in a kind of enclosed gazebo across a garden path, an idyllic outdoor study with books, papers, a heater for warmth, and birdsong that we spent a most pleasant afternoon. A woman of great humanity, Dr. Balint conveys a sense of valuing all that is most important in life.

Why did you become an analyst?

I can give you a rational reason. It made good sense at the time. During the war I worked with people in the London area in the Family Welfare Association, and they needed to set up special bureaus to help people who had trouble during the war, so I worked with people in crisis situations. I realized during that experience that however much there is a crisis, there is also always an underlying problem, sometimes showing up between the husbands and wives at that time. And so after the war, I decided I really must learn more about it, and I got to know some other people just out of the army who were starting the Tavistock Institute of Human Relations—a part of the Tavistock Clinic.

Having got in with this group, I wanted to start some kind of research into the difficulties between husbands and wives. Of course, that was what I had been seeing in my work during the war. And in order to get into that, I realized I needed to understand the unconscious. So I started an analysis along with the people I was working with at the Tavistock, and became a psychoanalyst after the war. It seemed it was the only way to get an understanding of why people behave the way they do, why they loved and hated one another, why they chose each other as husband and wife, and what went wrong. I started training in order to help these people and also, of course, to understand myself better. If I hadn't needed it myself, I wouldn't have gone into that at all. I think we are all wanting to find out about ourselves.

Who was your analyst?

Well, I started with a marvelous man named John Rickman, whom you may not have heard of although he wrote very good papers, and then after less than two years, he had a sudden heart attack and died. It was a terrible disaster for me early in the analysis. Then I went to Donald Winnicott, a wonderful experience, and I had the rest of my analysis with him.

What was Winnicott like as an analyst? Joyce McDougall says he was absolutely fantastic to listen to. But she didn't have him as an analyst, I don't think.

Well, I think quite a lot has been written lately by various people about their experience of him as an analyst, but their experience was different. I'll tell you what mine was. I think that the special thing about Donald Winnicott was that he really listened and understood what one would say in a very simple, direct, unjargonlike way, right from the start. He was not interested in the superficial. He wasn't, I don't think, very interested in the Oedipus complex, except insofar as it was taken for granted, but he didn't work in that kind of area. He worked in a very intense and caring way with the most primitive parts of oneself and one's relation with one's body. It was a remarkable experience working with him.

Some years after the analysis, I saw him constantly and did some work with him with children. He was a direct, simple, straightforward analyst in the sense that he sat behind the couch, and he commented when he wanted to and didn't when he didn't want to. The analysis with him was very different from the one I had with John Rickman before. (I can't say whether that was because I had suffered this tremendous loss in losing my first analyst.) Winnicott was interested in the most primitive parts of my organization, my relation with my body, much more than with my relationship with the external world.

There are many women today who say that they would go only to a woman analyst because they feel they could not express themselves as freely, particularly in relation to the body, with a man analyst. Obviously you didn't feel that way.

Not at all, no. There was no hindrance of that kind with Winnicott. He was a remarkable man. Sometimes I think people only know him by his later writings. His early writings were very proper psychoanalytic papers. In the later years, he also continued to write those papers, but people picked up on the squiggle, for example, which was a way of describing how Winnicott worked with children. He got them to draw something on a bit of paper and he added some more and so on. It was called the squiggle technique, and that's been, I think, overemphasized by a lot of people. He was a very serious analyst and his papers written in the sixties and later were quite remarkable papers, which were mostly about the infant-mother relationship. He had an enormous insight and was also a great clinician.

Do you think Winnicott was helpful to mothers in his concept of the good enough mother, the idea that one didn't have to be perfect?

I think he was. It's very interesting, that question. I've seen quite a lot of mothers, and naturally I've been very influenced by Winnicott's thinking about that. I had my own children and grandchildren, but I think he was a very great help to a lot of mothers and made them feel it's all right sometimes *not* to be "good enough." I'm talking about his being of great use after the war, and in the fifties and sixties.

More recently, I have had mothers tell me that he gives them great anxiety. I am not really quite sure why, but I've spoken to quite a few recently who have read Winnicott and have been very troubled by him and have come to me to ask whether they ought, for instance, to be there all the time with their babies. He didn't think that. He felt that if the mother was a good mother in the sense of being really tuned in to her baby part of the time, that's much, much better than most mothers do by being with their children all the time. It was the quality of the relationship and the understanding, which didn't have to be a twenty-four-hour day thing, which some people have turned it into.

I think that it's very bad when the mothers are under pressure not to leave their babies at all. In my experience, that just isn't right for an awful lot of mothers or babies. The quality of relationship is what matters, not the quantity.

My writing, my thinking, has been very influenced by Winnicott, obviously. But it so happens that I have worked with a lot of quite ill patients and recently have been interested in very primitive forms of communication that I have found on the couch from my patients, which I think has taught me quite a lot about difficulties in very early communication. I have come across some very intelligent and highly successful (in many ways) adults that I'm analyzing who have problems, and had problems when they were quite young in relating to their mothers, mothers and fathers, probably. And I have found the ideas expressed by Frances Tustin, who spent her life working with autistic children, very useful to me, following on Winnicott's and my own observations in relation to difficulties of communication between a mother and child, which lead to failure in the adult's capacity to love, or to make adult relationships of a meaningful kind.

How do these failures in communication manifest themselves in the very early stage?

I've come across these failures by patients coming to me because even though they may be extremely talented in their specialty, they have no real relationships in the external world, with their husbands, with their wives, even with their colleagues. And I found this very puzzling for a long time. And their particular kind of relationship with me is puzzling, not the kind of thing I could put down to any particular, described defense mechanism. It isn't in any way schizophrenic or even schizoid; it isn't muddled or confused. There is no difficulty in their ability to express themselves well. Their thinking processes are quite normal, but they are still not really relating either to me, though they seem to be sometimes, or to other people in their environment.

I found it difficult to describe this, but recently I have been able to do so; I think this is about very early disappointments, probably in their mothers' lives. There must have been some relationship at some stage for these people, perhaps quite a good one, for a very brief time, and then a too sudden disappointment, a too sudden disappearance of the object, and therefore withdrawal by the infant, who, as an adult, can't risk making proper relationships with any object, except under duress and then perhaps only in a very excited, ecstatic way, usually to withdraw again. I see it as the mother's problem, where the baby was not real to her.

I think Winnicott wrote about this a bit, when he spoke about subjective and objective objects.

How can this be overcome through the analysis?

Well, it's terribly difficult to describe. You have to be able to tolerate not being a real object, a real person to a patient, for a long time, which is really trying. I mean, you hear what he or she says to you and you respond, perhaps, but you know at the end of the session that you're not really in touch with that patient. Of course, you can interpret that. But I think it takes the ability to tolerate not being properly related to, and to go along with rather unintegrated material, for quite a long period.

When the bits and pieces that the patient gives you get integrated, and the patient begins to build, you become a real person, but he may be broken down again, and you're disappointed, and then he builds it up again. It's a question of integrating, disintegrating, integrating again, until relationships begin to be formed. And they can be quite easily shattered again; you see this in the transference.

Do you have more male than female patients?

I think I've had about an equal quantity. At the moment I have more women than men, and I've written more about women than I have about men, because I've followed up threads which interested me about women. I wrote "What Does a Woman Want?" and quite a lot of other papers, and I've been asked to put together a book.

Does your sex affect the transference of the patient, and does the sex of the patient affect your countertransference?

I think that's where one has to watch it, in how the sex of the patient affects one's countertransference. Maybe for the first six months or a year, one's sex does affect the patient. But once you really get into the world of the patient, I don't think it makes any difference.

My reactions to a man are probably different from those to a woman, and I have to watch that, not because of genital sexuality, but because I suppose in some way women are more familiar always. I had daughters and not sons. I don't know whether that has added to my feeling of greater ease with women, but this usually passes after perhaps the first couple of years. Analysis goes on a long time. And I think I feel just as comfortable with my men patients after a time.

I'm sure there are differences and I do watch myself, but I've never made a systematic study of it.

This also raises the question of why a man would choose to come to a woman analyst. To be sure you hear someone's terrific and you don't consider sex—

Oh, they do. They all come because they want a woman to start with; there's no doubt. When they come to you, whether they're men or women, they come because they want a woman. That nearly always is the case.

What are some of their reasons?

They say, to begin with, that they find women easier to talk to. They couldn't possibly talk to a man. One of my present male patients had seen two other women analysts before he came to me. When he came to me, I said, "I think it would be better if you went to a man." He wouldn't.

He was a very talented man, but seemed very ill, very disorganized, rather disintegrated. I like working with this kind of patient, probably more than the ordinary neurotic. In the end, I did take him on, after about six months; he waited until I changed my mind. I can see now why he wanted to come to a woman. There are no strong men in his world. (There are no real women either, really.) I don't think he'd have been able to work with a man.

I have three or four candidates in analysis because I am a training analyst, and they came because they were sent; they didn't come because they wanted a man or a woman. They could have gone to either. But as for the people who are noncandidates, the men who came said they couldn't talk to their fathers. There's no particular reason why I shouldn't have said, "Well, you better go to a man so that you learn how to." But I don't think that's particularly sensible. I work with people I think I would like to work with. It boils down to the analyst making the choice, I think.

I'm going to ask a question that might be somewhat stereotyped. We were talking about failures in communication. Do you see a sexual differentiation, that is, do you find that these failures in communication are more prevalent among men than among women?

So far, I haven't found that with the patients I have. It depends on the early relationships—on the mother's feelings about *sex*— not on whether they are men or women. If we are talking about the genital sexual behavior of men and women, whether it's more difficult for a man to tell me about his sexual difficulties than a woman or vice versa, I would say it's more difficult for a woman.

Why?

It is rather odd, and this is only guesswork. It could just be the women I've analyzed, or it could be something in myself as a woman, not women analysts in general. But I think the women, when they started, thought of me as a well-married, conventional woman who would disapprove of their perversions and abnormalities. This is rather a hindrance—to be seen as a conventional woman. And it took some time for them to get over that, which of course they did.

I don't think the men saw me like that. This is a hunch. It may not be true. But I think the men came as do all patients, with an enormous desire to tell me about their problems. Consciously or subconsciously the drive is tremendous. It seemed easier for the men patients to tell me than the women, to start with. But once women made a good relationship with me, got over that, then perhaps I got further with them. They had a more relaxed, easier relationship with me, but it took some years. It was quicker with the men. But perhaps I didn't go as far with the men.

Do you think that the women's movement has influenced your practice, your theory, psychoanalytic theory in general?

I have analyzed feminists, I have analyzed people in the women's movement, and this seems to be an awful thing to put on record, but I am often more sorry for the men. I think the men have had a harder time about this—in a way which has not helped the women. The men have been quite badly hurt, hit—I was going to use the jargon "castrated"—by the women's movement. And I think that some of the women have thought it right that that should be so. I haven't found it helpful.

For the men. But what about for the women?

No, I wasn't meaning for the men. I haven't found it helpful for the women, the women I analyzed. I'm not generalizing; I'm not talking about it as a kind of social issue. That is a different matter, but the feminist women I find have a very complicated history; all sorts of paradoxical things have turned up. I know what they say about status and what's imposed on them is true. But so many other factors come in, also. And I have found that one's got to be able to analyze the paradoxical nature of all of their relationships and hostility, which is sometimes terribly damaging to themselves. I find this, as an analyst, a very difficult thing to talk about. In the personality of a woman there is much put into her by the environment but also by her mother's unconscious. She may be helped and freed in some ways by the movement, but she is scarred in others.

You think that she would not respond to the imposition of the ideas, if there weren't something in her that was very receptive?

No, she wouldn't. I agree.

Would she attach herself perhaps to another kind of movement or another problem?

Absolutely. I do think they're in a transitional period about this and at the moment it's very difficult to talk with any certainty because in my analytic lifetime of thirty years, the mood has changed a very great deal and feminists thirty years ago were very different from the feminists today. The search for real femininity that is *not* imposed on them, their own choice, let's say, is very sincere, very moving, and I think the men are left out of this, left with different problems, of course, their own choice, their own perverse activities, their own feeling of being endangered by women, which indeed they are. If they're endangered, then the women are too. And if they are less, the women are less, too.

Could you say something about the differences between thirty years ago and today on the analytic scene, which obviously has been affected by this social movement?

Yes, it has been. It's just very difficult to say what I feel, and not contradict myself in the next sentence. A patient I worked with twenty years ago who wanted a child and not a husband didn't think she could have it. The analysis was a long time ago. I am thinking of her particularly because she was a good example. She was not one of a group then. She felt isolated, miserable, an outcast. To begin with, she thought I wouldn't understand her, but actually she worked very well with me. We had a rather long, useful analysis. She did actually have two children and did try to accept a man.

A husband?

Well, she wouldn't marry him.

A partner?

A partner, yes. By the end of the analysis, she did. She found it very difficult to let her children, as young babies, small children, have a father. She could accept a husband, but she couldn't let her children have a father. One of the problems that I see in this room is that some women find it very difficult to have the same man as father to their children and their own husband.

Well, that leads me to a question about splitting the sexual object. Do you think that women split the sexual object in the way that has been traditionally attributed to men? Obviously, what you just said would indicate yes.

Yes, I do. I think it's far more acceptable now. Perhaps it's been changing in the last twenty, thirty years. I think until recently, women have been expected and expected themselves, also, to have their husbands as the fathers of their children, and I have had several patients who come along for an analysis, with a problem of quite a different nature, but what has cropped up during the analysis was that they didn't in fact let their husbands father their children or they have had lovers for sexual partners. They may have kept their husbands as the fathers of their children and were very fond of their husbands, but they kept their sexual lives separate. They might have had intercourse with their husbands, but it didn't interest them, whereas with their lovers it did interest them very much.

And how do you account for that split psychoanalytically? Is it comparable to Freud's depiction of the split into the

madonna/whore? He didn't use those terms, of course, but talked about the degradation of the sexual object.

I think it is a bit comparable, but in the case of the patient that I am thinking of who primarily demonstrated this, her mother had no relation with her father, who lived abroad. I think I ought to put it this way: there's been a historical reason for it in the patients that I have analyzed; this already existed in their mothers, or in their mothers and fathers. Why it existed in them I don't know, but they were acting out their mothers' histories, or their mothers' and fathers' histories. (This might also be true of the men.) It didn't come as a kind of madonna/whore division. It came much more as the nice man, who was not sexually exciting or is that the same thing? Whereas the other men were also quite nice, but were sexually exciting.

I don't think I can see the contrast quite so clearly as depicted by Freud. But it was always my patients that were acting out or completing their parents' history who did this. They thought that they were joining the function of the father and the husband, but were not really doing so and came to the analysis to find out about other problems. They were not aware that this was the problem until they came to analysis.

So a different history would have enabled them to make an integration?

In the end, after analysis, they did actually. The one I'm thinking of did make an integration, but I'm not sure it was entirely a satisfactory one. In due course one of them left her husband and the other one got the lover. In the transference this was acted out. I mean, there was a very genital sexual relationship with me in the transference. It didn't have to be analyzed outside even though I'm a woman with women—it was analyzed in the transference.

How often do you see your patients in analysis?

I used to see them five times a week, or four. The past year and a half, I've stopped seeing anyone five times, so I take patients four times a week now, and even sometimes three. I have for various reasons sometimes tried to see people twice a week, but I don't like that; I don't find I can manage it. Too much gets built up and

I can't really keep the continuity going. I see occasional people once a week, who come from far away, see them perhaps twice the same day, but I can't do the same kind of work. However, I had one patient coming from Florence, for about eight years, and I think the work was comparable to an analysis, but I'm much happier seeing people many times a week, which I know is different in other countries.

Well, it's an economic problem elsewhere, and probably here as well. It's not that the people don't want to see an analyst more often, it's that they are not able to, financially.
So people tell me.

I'm not sure what an average fee is here.
Here, it's probably between twenty and twenty-five pounds.

Maybe you are just very kind.
No, I don't think so. I should say twenty-five would be the average.

Let me get back to splitting. In the female imagination can the seducer and the instructor coexist more readily than in the male imagination? The tutor and the lover are one. At least, that's the way it has been depicted in literature. One figure initiates the woman into sexual experience and all other experiences. Of course, there are social reasons for this, but are there psychological reasons as well, having to do with the separation/individuation process and turning to the father as the teacher?
At first thought, I'm rather doubtful about it. But I'm not sure. I don't think I do see women as the people who get seduced any more than the men, really. I think women are just as much seducers as seduced. It is often shared.

But can a single male figure function in a dual capacity for women in ways that a woman cannot function for a male? I grant you that, in Europe, there is the tradition of the young boy being initiated sexually and taught by older women,

but it's a rite of passage that he goes through, whereas at least until recently the woman very often would turn to one man for everything. True, this is a part of the social structure, but aren't there psychological reasons for this fusion being satisfying to women? Nonetheless, you've just spoken about patients who split the husband/lover.

I'm not sure that it is satisfying for a great number of women any more than it is for men. I've had quite a number of men in marriages who really want the one woman once they have got over the trauma of recognizing that one woman is not just the Madonna but also the seducer, and they accept the woman they love as a seducer, which I think is part of the analytic process. A lot of men—let me talk about Englishmen, although I'm sure this is true of others as well—want there to be one woman.

I wonder if that's a recent change. Another difference between literary treatment and reality is that very often in love literature the triangle consists of two men and a woman. For example, in *Tristan and Isolde,* Isolde is married. In *The Sorrows of Werther,* the heroine is betrothed to another man. This seems like the Oedipal constellation in adult life. But in reality, at least until recently, more often it was the triangle of two women and one married man, who was turning elsewhere for his sexual satisfaction, and, of course, you describe this as happening with women too. But there seems to be a preponderance of the former kind of triangle in literature as opposed to reality.

I think it's an important question and I'll now think about it. And what's your suggestion? That there is some psychological reason for the fact that the little girl turns away from her mother to her father, who then becomes the instructor?

A related question is whether women are more capable than men of reconciling tender and erotic feelings? This is connected to the question of splitting, whether that split between the virgin and the whore still exists in the male imagination, and if so, why does it persist? Is it rooted in the Oedipal period, or does it perhaps relate to something earlier? You said in the piece "What Does a Woman Want?" that perhaps more important in a relationship between men and women than the Oedipal theory is the pre-Oedipal one, the relationship to the mother.

I think that, yes. I think also that the whore and the virgin myth still exists. Or can we say the witch mother and the safe one?

How can we get rid of it? Or maybe we shouldn't?

Maybe we shouldn't. This is another question I would like to think about. How dominant is it? How important is it to the patients I have now got on my couch? Do they need to split?

You mentioned the Englishmen a couple of moments ago, who want one woman after they can get over this feeling of sexuality being associated with the whore.

Yes. They want it and they adore it. I am thinking of one particular man whose seven- or eight-year analysis is now finished. One always does have to work with narcissism. This is the central part of the analysis of any patient, but certainly in men, in their relation to their women partners.

Are men more narcissistic than women? Unlike what Freud says?

I often wonder. It's easier for me to find it in men. It's much more hidden and therefore difficult to get at, but when you get at it, it's astonishing. It's such a shock with men; it's unexpected. Male narcissism is very important and must be analyzed before one can do anything else. I think men would be delighted at being able to see their wives or one woman as the seductress, as a dangerous person, as a virgin, no, as a virgin and a seducer. But this is linked with their ability to tolerate their narcissism or to overcome it.

Is there love beyond narcissism? Freud's theory of love really seems to be rooted in narcissism, both the anaclitic and the narcissistic type. Is there something beyond this that we could be aiming for?

I think the early relationship to the mother, which is primitive, a part object relation, comes before narcissism, the state of primitive concern, really.

So you feel there is an initial state of concern, which may be covered over by narcissism.
Or is covered over by aggression or hatred and jealousy and envy and the lot. If you observe infants, you can see it. In certain phases of the analysis you see it; it's there, but it's quite quiet. I mean, there's no scream about it, and very quickly it gets covered perhaps by aggression and hostility. One finishes the hour, and it goes but it can come back again. Most analysts don't think this. Michael was a great believer in primary love. I prefer to think of it as primary concern. I think it's prenarcissist.

Why do so many women analysts marry male analysts? Why are there so many couples, so many famous couples?
I was married to one. Now, I'm married to a nonanalyst. I suppose, it's the easiest thing to do. At least, you think it's going to be. One thinks that one can talk about things that interest one, such as the unconscious, which is the worst thing to do with a husband. One does it for comradeship. Of course, when I got married to Michael, he was a famous analyst and I was a beginner, so it was an obvious thing for me to want to do. He knew everything. I knew nothing.

Seducer and instructor?
Yes, you're right. Absolutely. He was.

That occurs so often in women's relationships. It does not happen the other way.
You are right. I hadn't thought of a seducer and instructor, but he was. But can I be a seducer and an instructor? I am not sure. I think I was to him too!

Hanna Segal was born in Poland and attended secondary schools in Warsaw and Geneva. Her medical studies were interrupted by World War II, but she qualified at the Polish Medical School in Edinburgh in 1943. In 1946–47 she qualified as a psychoanalyst. Melanie Klein was her training analyst and Joan Rivière and Paula Heimann her first supervisors. A few years later she became a child analyst, and in 1951–52, she became a training analyst of the British Psychoanalytical Society, where she has also served as president. She is a fellow of the Royal College of Psychiatry as well, and has been a visiting professor for the Freud Memorial Chair, at University College, London.

SELECTED BIBLIOGRAPHY

Introduction to the Work of Melanie Klein. London: Heinemann, 1964.
Melanie Klein. Modern Masters series. London: Heinemann, 1979.
The Work of Hanna Segal. Northvale, N.J.: Jason Aronson, 1981. In addition, Dr. Segal has published many papers, mainly in the *International Journal of Psychoanalysis*.

TWELVE

Hanna Segal

London, Summer 1986

Hanna Segal lives in an apartment house on a tree-lined street in a suburb of London. A woman of great presence, she seemed as solid and dependable as the imposing pieces of seventeenth-century furniture in her living room. An admirer of Freud, as well as the great disciple of Melanie Klein, Dr. Segal was the only woman participant along with four men—Sir Clive Moser, Harold Blum, Anthony Storr, and Peter Gay—in the ceremony for the opening of the Freud Museum at Camden Hall. There she appeared in a flowered dress, and one was quick to notice her warm smile.

The first question we wanted to ask you is why you became an analyst.

I wanted to be an analyst from the time I was sixteen. There was very little Freud translated into Polish or French, which was my second language, but as an adolescent, I read all there was, and was extremely attracted by what I read. I also, accidentally, when I was quite a small child, met Mrs. Sokolnicka, a friend of my mother, who lived in Paris, and was, I think, the first psychoanalyst and representative of Freud in France. What I remember about her is that she had six black cats, which fascinated me. I don't think she inspired me to be a psychoanalyst because she was a very neurotic woman herself. But we did have some interesting conversations when I was thirteen or fourteen.

Later on, I didn't really know what to do. I thought of studying literature or art history. I was very interested in art, but I also had quite a severe social conscience and I thought that art was too academic and too abstract, so I thought of studying sociology and psychology to do something in prison administration. But my father gave me very wise advice. He said, "If you want to reform something, never be dependent on a salary. Find yourself a profession which makes you completely independent."

So then I started toying with the idea of medicine as an independent profession of social use, and somehow I turned back to my first love, being an analyst, whereby you can combine intellectual and cultural interests with a profession which is "useful."

It's rather interesting that you mention your father as having been very encouraging to you. That's often the case with successful women.

I had a very neglected early childhood, which was then common in well-off intellectual families. From the time I became a sort of intelligent human being, however, my father was a great inspiration and very facilitating in whatever I wanted to do. He himself had an interest in art which he gave up to become a lawyer. His father was a lawyer and my father was supposed to take over from him. In 1905, when the students were on strike against the Russian authorities, he went to Paris and wrote an extremely authoritative book on French sculpture of the nineteenth century, which in 1939 when I was in Poland was still a classic book of reference. But as for a profession, he settled down to being a lawyer as his father wanted him to. Later on he emigrated to Geneva and became a journalist.

When I was in my second year of medicine, I met Bychowsky, who later became a well-known analyst in America. He was a lecturer in neurology and one of the few psychoanalysts in Poland, and I asked him how one set out to be an analyst. He said, "You go to Vienna." Well, I had no wish to go to Vienna. Then the war broke out when I was in my third year of medicine, and I went to Paris, where my parents lived. When it was clear that I would have to stay in France, I rang R. Latergue, who was the only French analyst I knew of, because of his book on Baudelaire, with the same question: "How does one set out to be a psychoanalyst?"

Fortunately for me, he was leaving Paris that day. I say "fortunately" because he was a disastrous psychoanalyst, and also, I believe, the only French psychoanalyst who was excluded from the Society for suspicion of collaboration with the Germans.

So that was that. Then in 1940 I left France to come here. I resumed my medical studies in Edinburgh, and I rang Dr. Fairbairn and asked, "How does one set out to become a psychoanalyst?" Now, Fairbairn was enormously helpful. He explained to me about having to go to London for formal training, and he told me about the differences between Melanie Klein and Anna Freud at that time, though he didn't tell me about the quarrels, and he was the first to give me a Klein book to read. I remember he gave me Anna Freud's *Mechanisms of Defense* and Mrs. Klein's *Psychoanalysis of Children*.

He was also very helpful in that I was in Edinburgh on a scholarship of two pounds a week; he could not take me on because his fee was one pound a session. But he said that he had a friend, Dr. Matthew, who had been analyzed by Mrs. Klein and who also came to Edinburgh during the war, and Dr. Matthew took me on at a nominal fee. So I had a year of analysis then. And after having read much more in psychoanalytic literature, the international journals, and other publications of Klein, I came to London extremely determined to have analysis with Mrs. Klein —and somehow, that's what I got.

What was it like having Melanie Klein as an analyst?

There was an enormous stability with her, which I think is crucial in a psychoanalytical setting: a stability in the number of sessions per week and the length of the sessions, and, I think, a kind of interested detachment. In contrast to her writings, particularly the early ones, where she emphasizes the negative, in fact, the sessions in analysis were very evenly balanced. I think the reason why she appeared negative in her writings is that aggression, projection, persecution were so much ignored, and they were so much her own discovery that she was emphasizing them enormously. This is corrected in her later writings. From about the time of her publication of the work on depression, her description becomes much more even.

What do you think about the Grosskurth biography, which, after all, is the one that's going to be read in the United States?

From my point of view, it is very disappointing because although she did a great deal of research and had access to a lot of material which wasn't known, such as a year's correspondence to Mrs. Klein from her mother and brother, I think that she distorts a lot, first of all in the use that she makes of the letters. She says that Mrs. Klein's beloved brother was a morphine and a cocaine addict. I've read the letters. There is not a shred of evidence for this, except in one letter which says that after an operation, he was in such pain that he had to take a shot of morphine. Addicts don't usually say that. That's her evidence for his morphine addiction. Her evidence for his cocaine addiction is that he spent a lot of money on cigars—often cigars were cocaine cigars—that cocaine was used for treating morphine addiction, which she never proves he had, and that a contemporary graphologist told her that his handwriting is like that of a cocaine addict. And this is, later on in the biography, presented not as her guesses but as absolute fact.

The biography also presents Mrs. Klein's relationship to her brother as some kind of mad idealization. Now, obviously, this young man was very disturbed. From his teens he knew he would die of a prognosticated heart attack. Grosskurth makes it out that he died of self-destructiveness and addiction. Klein's simple sentence that she often wished or thought if he were alive now some cure might be found is treated as a denial of this destructiveness. But he had been told by the doctors from early on that he would die, that his heart would not last, so he didn't die, as she implies, because of self-destructiveness.

There is also some distortion of facts. But the main thing from my point of view is this. The book states, I think quite correctly, that Mrs. Klein had been pretty neurotic and difficult as a young woman. What Grosskurth doesn't seem to understand is that after her two analyses and a great deal of painful self-analysis, by the time she came to London, Mrs. Klein was a different woman. If you met her socially—and all of my friends say so—you were immediately impressed with this person of quite a different caliber from the other people in the room. There was a greatness about Klein and, in her later years, a sort of dignity, which Grosskurth has really missed. She also missed the sense of humor. In her account, Klein becomes—and some American reviews pick this up—totally humorless, but she was, in fact, a very humorous person. I told Grosskurth that one of my colleagues, not a Kleinian, said that the thing she remembers best about Mrs. Klein was her extraordinary laughter. She had a spontaneous, infectious laugh which was extremely attractive, and the last thing that one would say about her was that she was humorless.

It is true that she could be very fierce, but only in the area of defending her ideas if she thought they were attacked. One thing which people say was awful, and it was pretty bad, was her blowing up at Jones for bringing the Freuds here. It seems to be appalling, but she thought Anna would be such a threat to her ideas that they might not survive. She could be fierce and self-centered in those ways, but only in relation to the protection of her work. Otherwise, she was an extremely warm and kindly person in a very human way. She was very pleasant company and a very good friend.

Could you tell us something about the disagreement between Klein and Anna Freud?

It has been so well documented that I don't know if it's useful for me to go into it.

Basically, Hug-Helmuth, who was the first pioneer, didn't believe that children under seven could be analyzed. She and Anna Freud thought that psychoanalysis should be a kind of educative procedure because a child's superego was so weak the analyst had also to be a superego. They thought too that there are reassuring procedures that you can use to sort of seduce a child to make the child accept you as an ally before you can analyze him or her. Klein contended that psychoanalytical technique could be used with children. She introduced play therapy for children since they don't communicate mainly verbally, but in play, and she set up this technique in which children have small toys and painting materials and also, of course, are encouraged to talk. But she also analyzed nonspeaking children; she presents the first autistic child ever analyzed, who began to speak when treatment progressed.

I was amused by the size of the toys that Melanie Klein used when we saw them at the Institute the other day. They are so tiny! How could she work with them? How could children work with them?

Winnicott, in his typical Winnicottian way, once said, "The greatness of Klein was not in inventing play therapy. Anybody could have done that. Her greatness was in using such little toys, because they're so suitable for the child's expression of fantasy. They are so tiny and malleable." Now I don't believe that anybody could have invented play therapy, but I see Winnicott's point. First of all, the important thing about the toys she used is that they don't dictate any play. They are little figures, little animals; they give free play to fantasy. But the other thing is that being so small, it's almost as if they belong more to the internal world than the external one and allow the child to manipulate them. When I trained as a child analyst, we were always looking for these little, little toys, but of course they don't exist any more.

Mrs. Klein felt that one cannot establish an analytic technique without an analytic setting, and an analytic setting means the analyst has an analytic attitude that is neither educative nor reassuring. Anna Freud said that children don't develop transference, and Klein disagreed. That was the basic argument. Then when she started analyzing small children, she came to the conclusion that, far from their not having a superego, it's the other way around. The more primitive the stage of development, the more savage and primitive the superego. The way of reaching the child's anxiety is by analyzing that in the transference. According to the classical Freudian technique, the superego appears more or less in the latency period at the end of the Oedipus complex, but she observed a savage anal and oral superego in children; her youngest patient was two-and-three-quarter years old. She also described children between two and three, where there was already an Oedipus complex with a long history. So all the data for her changed. Of course, technique and theory always have a mutual effect on each other; for example, Freud used free association to get at the truth, and the new truth affected his technique.

I think that now, at least in this country, many Freudians are very much closer to our theory and they all take small children for analysis, although there are still very considerable technical differences. But these are more discussable because the basic principles of analytic setting and of analyzing the transference have been established. This is not so in America, at least in the cases that were presented to me. What was presented to me as analysis, I wouldn't even accept as psychotherapy. I remember a young man having a marvelous, tremendously cooperative child in treatment and not taking up transference at all. It was before a holiday. The child made paintings of drowning and wrote poems about being left alone in the desert, and the young man didn't say a word about the holiday and the transference. To me, it was heartbreaking.

Would you tell us something about your supervising analysts, Joan Rivière and Paula Heimann?

Joan Rivière, my first supervising analyst, was a most fascinating personality and is tremendously underrated; not only was she the first translator of Freud into English, I think, but her contribution to psychoanalytic thought was also very significant. Early on Mrs. Klein didn't write well, but Joan Rivière writes really beautifully. She wrote the introduction to *New Developments in Psychoanalysis* and a big paper on infantile anxieties, which she presented in Vienna in exchange lectures. She also made quite a number of original contributions.

I recently reread her papers because they are being published in France. She was the first one before Mrs. Klein to bring out the importance of jealousy as a defense against envy. Her paper on jealousy is quite an original contribution, as is her paper on the negative therapeutic reaction.

As a person, she was formidable. She was about six feet tall, very beautiful, rather severe and snappish; she couldn't stand fools. People were in awe of her, but I loved her. We got on very well. She introduced me to Henry James, and as I had no money at all at the time for buying books, she gave me the freedom of the library. Unlike Mrs. Klein, who was humorous and funny, she had a very sharp wit, like a rapier. I remember one incident. I said once that my husband was a socialist and she said, "Ugh, that religion of younger siblings." She was a very powerful and very intriguing personality. Now when I read Jones' biography and other works, where she appears very neurotic with an erotic transference to her analyst, I cannot fit this Joan Rivière with the one I knew. She was also behind this formidable mask a rather shy person. But she was extremely intelligent, very cultured, and tremendously involved with analysis.

Toward the end of Mrs. Klein's life, there was a coolness between them, I think partly because Joan Rivière didn't like movements and there were so many people around Klein, it became a movement. She was a more retiring person. What else there was I don't know, but Sherry Turkle makes the mistake of saying in one of her reviews that Joan Rivière turned against Mrs. Klein. That wasn't so. Mrs. Rivière did continue as a Kleinian analyst. Toward the end of her life, Rivière went into supervision with Rosenfeld to learn about new techniques. And she left the residue of her estate to the Melanie Klein Trust. So she was not a pupil who left Kleinian work, even though there was a coolness between her and Mrs. Klein at the end.

Paula Heimann was my second supervisor. I liked her, but she had nothing like the intellectual stature of Joan Rivière. I treated her more as a sort of good chum very soon after supervision. She was also extremely aggressive, not to her friends but to her enemies. I think some of the reputation the Kleinians got about being tough and aggressive may have actually come because of Paula Heimann's aggressiveness when she was a Kleinian. She became even more aggressive to Klein when she turned against her.

I would like to say something about women analysts, because Freud is presented as being so phallocentric and paternalistic, and that in a way is certainly true. He admitted he understood very little about women's psychology, and he paid very little attention to the mother's role. In Freud's notes on the Rat Man—I think in the first consultation—the Rat Man talks all the time about his mother. But all of Freud's case study is about the father. I think Freud's theory that little girls think they have got the penis and then discover they don't is bunko. On the other hand, Freud was the first to treat women as human beings in the sense that he gave a proper place to female sexuality. He didn't consider them asexual beings.

And even more important, I think, psychoanalysis is the first organized profession in which from the beginning women were treated exactly the same as the men. From the beginning of the psychoanalytical movement, women were extremely important. People sometimes ask if women are more talented as psychoanalysts than men because they are more turned inwards. I don't think so. There wasn't a lack of talent in Freud's time or today among men—Abraham, Ferenczi, Bion, to name just a few. But it is true that from the beginning they were given a chance, absolutely on equal terms, which I think allowed for a development of women in psychoanalysis.

So we take it that you don't believe in penis envy, or do you think that both sexes have it?

I think that both sexes have both breast envy and penis envy. Certainly little girls have penis envy, but if it acquires pathological proportions, it's usually because there's a transfer from the primitive breast envy.

Do you think that there is a difference between the way that the little boy and the little girl view the very early mother, the pre-Oedipal mother?

I think that early in infancy the baby boy and the baby girl probably don't view the mother differently, but as soon as an early idea of the sexes enters, difference develops. Even though both the little boy and the little girl have an interest in penetrating the mother's body, I think the evolution must be different. Certainly very often when I watch babies, I say, "It's a little boy, isn't it?" I don't know how I know, but I know. I think that there's an innate knowledge of our anatomical function and that through reality testing and reality sensing, the little boy must be aware very soon that the mother is complementary to him. I think it's a matter of inborn reality, a sense about one's composition. That's why I have never accepted the theory that homosexuality is just as normal as heterosexuality, only it happens to be different. I think that there is some reality sense and some innate idea about the parental couple and creative sexuality which is attacked by homosexuality. You ask me whether it is a perversion. I don't know if I'd use the term perversion for it, but then what's in a term? Freud called it an inversion, so what? But in fact, all homosexuals that I have analyzed did have a perverse personality structure.

In the United States there's a great deal of talk about eliminating gender differences as far as possible. What do you think of this?

I am very much in favor of little boys and little girls not being pushed into femininity and masculinity and being given the possibility of having the same toys and developing their interests in the same way. After all, we are basically bisexual, not in the sexual, homosexual sense, but in that both sexes have an internalized father as well as mother. For true independence we should be able to sublimate, as it were, in both directions, but I would have thought that with a reasonable background, with a reasonable sexual relation between the parents, even if one reached complete gender equality, this is not the same as being exactly identical.

There are certain areas which are supposed to be more masculine, like mathematics or science. I don't think this is so. Since women have been allowed to study science, quite a number of them got the Nobel prize for scientific research. But it's one of those things girls are steered away from. And in the other direction, certainly the greatest chefs are men though cooking is supposed to be "female." I'm for equal opportunities and encouragement to develop one's identity in whatever way, but I would assume that with a good internal personality structure, the sexual development would be in keeping with one's talents. You do get people who mistake their talents and spend their life trying to be, say, good painters when they haven't got any talent in that direction at all. For me that would be like the homosexual spending his life trying to do something which he is just not built to do.

Mrs. Klein thought that what she called the epistemophilic instinct starts in relation to the mother's breast and body; then symbolization carries the interest to all explorations. I don't know if it's an instinct or a drive which can be associated with love or hatred, but it will be the basis of our epistemophilic interest in the world.

In fact, Bion developed that idea in an interesting way by saying that there are links between the subject and the object: loving, hating, and knowing.

Do you think that there are differences between the epistemophylic instinct or drive in boys and girls, which stem from their different relationship to the mother's body?

I would think that the drives in boys and girls are identical, but maybe they're more likely to be squashed in girls socially and also internally since the exploration in fantasy of the mother's body can be felt as very destructive. I think that reparative ideas are easier for the boy in that in sexual intercourse he can give the mother children, whereas the little girl does not have that easy route. So that may account for some differences. I am sure that sociological factors are very important for the role assigned to men, but then sociological factors come from psychological ones as well.

The reparation directly to mother's body is easier in fantasy for the little boy. He doesn't have to give up the mother. He can make reparation directly to a woman. The little girl has to make reparation more to her internal mother by identification. After all, the man gives the baby to the woman, who also represents Mother, whereas the little girl does her reparation, which is in conflict and in rivalry as well, by becoming like the mother and having the baby. But both sexes have ways open to reparation. My men patients always complain that it's so much easier for women; they're not so envious. They know they'll become like Mother. And all the women say it's so much easier for males; they can keep Mother.

One theory holds that men are more creative artistically because they can't have children. It could be that men have to compensate more, while some women seem to be satisfied with having children as the main reparative activity, but by no means all.

What would happen should reproductive technology bring us to the point that all reproduction would be ex utero? Or what if reproduction were possible through parthenogenesis?

I can't imagine a more boring world than producing ourselves mother-daughter, mother-daughter, should reproductive technology bring us to that point.

Well, then what do you think would happen to the development of the little boy or the little girl if there were more equal sharing of parenting?

Here I speak from my own experience, with my husband but particularly my two married sons. They have only boys—I don't know what would happen to girls—but they certainly benefit from having two parents who share the child-rearing tasks. Then again, I don't think that they're identical. When I watch my sons handling the children, they do so very differently from mothers. It's when Father becomes nothing but a substitute mother that you get confusion in the child's mind. But if the relationship between the parents is unambiguously that of a man and a woman and the man remains a man, his handling of the children is different, and they turn to Mother and Father for different things. So again I say, equal but not identical.

Anyway, it can't be identical. I think small babies should be breastfed and that's something a man can't do. But I think we simply don't know enough about these issues yet to generalize. Maybe when the social conditions are better for women and when children are less forced into stereotyped roles, we will all have a clearer view of how parenting or gender affects the development of sublimations.

What do you think of the increased number of single parents — parents deliberately choosing to have babies alone?

People deliberately choosing to have babies alone is disastrous. A mother who happens to lose her husband in the war or through divorce or desertion is quite a different thing because it means that, in her mind, she has a concept of masculinity. A woman who chooses to have a child alone is so narcissistic. She wants to be omnipotent. I once read a letter in the papers that horrified me by a lesbian who said that she couldn't tolerate the sight of the male body, but that she had a lovely little boy through artificial insemination and that he is a joy. Now, what is going to happen to this boy in adolescence with the mother who can't bear the sight of a male body?

In her description of the mother, to my knowledge, Klein does not say anything about the envy or the gratitude of the mother for the child. That is, everything is described from the child's point of view. Are the paranoid-schizoid and depressive positions of the child divorced from the mother's feelings?

According to Melanie Klein, the paranoid-schizoid and depressive positions of the child can't be divorced from the mother at all, and certainly mothers can be very envious of their babies for being babies. And they certainly have gratitude for all the joys that the baby gives. Klein doesn't go much into the external factors, but, for instance, envy becomes very strong in infants, not so much with bad mothers as with the narcissistic ones, mothers who always present themselves as perfect with nothing wrong with them, the mothers who won't allow the baby any virtues because they have them all. Klein does make a general theoretical point that in every stage of development, the reaction of the mother is decisive.

If one looks at envy not from the point of view of the experience of the baby, but rather if one analyzes the child in the mother, one would see that it is the child part of the mother from whom the envy comes.

Nonetheless, the Kleinian approach to the mother is much more positive than is that of the French analysts, who constantly depict the primitive mother, the archaic, dangerous mother.

The Kleinian approach is more positive than that of the French analysts, where Mother is always the bad mother. I think that comes from not seeing the child's projections. The infant often experiences the mother as bad through projection. The infant wants to get inside Mother and is devouring, is possessive. That gets projected onto the mother, causing the child anxiety. Now it's true also that some mothers are possessive, but the idea of the controlling, possessive mother has become a stereotype. Some mothers are and some aren't. Some, for instance, are frustrating rather than possessive. And some are quite good.

Would you comment on your postscript of 1980 to the book *The Work of Hanna Segal*, in which you say that you would now emphasize the role of idealization stemming from the paranoic schizoid position more in artistic creation.

I still think it correct to say that artistic creation has to do with the resolving of depressive anxieties, but formerly I had underestimated the role of idealization. If idealization is too great, then the work of art doesn't live. It becomes pretty and perfect, it doesn't contain any conflict and resolution; nevertheless, there should be somewhere an idealization of beauty and the seeking of it. This is not an original idea of mine. I take it from Adrian Stokes, who says that art has this aspect of pulling you to another world, which he calls envelopment, at the same time that one wants to recreate the real mother and family and the external world. I suppose that art is like a successful love affair. When there's too much idealization it breaks down, but if there's none, it may not take off at all.

Is there anything in the Kleinian theory that you reject?

If there is one view of Mrs. Klein that I reject, it's that on countertransference. Like Freud, she recognized only that aspect of the countertransference which is the analyst's neurosis, which was Freud's original view. She never agreed with the view that countertransference feelings may be due to the patient's projective identification and thus be an important source of information. It is strange that she didn't see that it is her work on projective identification that gives the best support to that view. I also think that in her theory she does not elaborate enough on the role of severe or neglecting parents.

What about the early father?

People say that Mrs. Klein is all mother, but in fact she introduces the father much earlier than Freud. From the depressive position onward the father plays a fundamental role. And even before that. But I think that while Freud didn't say much about early infancy or about women, there is only so much one man can do in one lifetime. Well, the same with Mrs. Klein. There are some things that she hasn't done enough with. But there is a limit to what one woman can do in one lifetime.

Dinora Pines received her medical degree from the Royal Free Hospital in London and was a consultant dermatologist as well as a general practitioner before becoming a psychoanalyst. She is now a training analyst and supervisor of the British Psycho-Analytical Society and a member of the editorial board of the *International Review of Psycho-Analysis*.

BIBLIOGRAPHAL NOTE

Dr. Pines has published articles on pregnancy, abortion, motherhood, skin communication, and working with women survivors of the Holocaust in such journals as the *British Journal of Medical Psychology, International Journal of Psycho-Analysis,* and *Bulletin of the European Federation of Psychoanalysis*.

THIRTEEN

Dinora Pines

London, Summer 1986

Dinora Pines lives in a lovely house in Hampstead Gardens, where Aldous Huxley used to live. It has a marvelous sweep of parlor and dining room and two gardens—in the front and back. There is an impressive library in the room with the psychoanalytic couch—a rather Spartan one compared to some of the French ones that we've seen, but firm for the back. Light streams through the large bay windows on the many plants in rooms full of spirit and cosiness. Dr. Pines too is full of warmth and graciousness.

Why did you become an analyst when you were originally a dermatologist?

I became an analyst because I was interested in the psychosomatic expression of psychic pain. I got rather bored looking at spots and giving out ointments. I found that if one talked with patients it was a most interesting experience and somehow the symptoms that they were presenting tended to clear up.

It so happened that I was working in a woman's hospital where I had been the senior resident in dermatology, and the parallel senior resident in psychiatry was Hilda Abraham, Karl Abraham's daughter. We used to refer each other patients and she used to say to me, "You seem to be able to make people talk." Gradually I became more and more interested in that aspect of dermatology, and with her encouragement I joined some seminars; and again with her encouragement and that of the analyst who conducted the seminars, I applied for my entry at the Institute and was accepted.

Most of the people we interviewed talked about past influences—childhood experiences, saying: "I had problems or I wanted to make reparations to my mother or grandmother." But you are talking about something that happened in your adult life. Do you think that this was reinforced by anything in your early background?

I am sure and I am quite willing to talk about it. I was born in Russia and came with my parents to England at an early age. Both my parents were doctors. My mother, being a very Russian type of personality, was enormously attached to her family, her home, and her country, and became extremely depressed at being in voluntary exile. I am quite sure that both I and my brother, who is also an analyst, were deeply influenced by her depression and our attempt to deal with it and to help her with it. That in a way became not only something we learned during childhood but something that developed a skill—if I dare call it a skill—some sort of capacity to help people to talk about their suffering which then became translated and sublimated into a professional choice. I suppose many people would have looked at spots and not done anything about it. Because I had that specific experience I could recognize aspects of the patient's personality that needed to be expressed and shared with somebody else.

It was by chance that I became a dermatologist. I happened to be quite a good student at medical school and the dermatologist was very pleased with my work. And as soon as I qualified, she invited me to join her staff. This fitted very well with my life because I got married, had two children, and I could therefore work part-time as a dermatologist as I was bringing up my family. It so happened that there were two hospitals at that time totally devoted to women patients, staffed with women doctors. I was on the staff of both, which gave me a fairly accurate vision of what women have to deal with in their lives. And in particular what aroused my interest was the way they expressed pain and suffering through their skin.

Do you think that men do that as well, or are women particularly prone to express their problems psychosomatically?

Men do that a great deal too. But in my view, a woman is much more aware of her body because of her periods, because of the use that a woman has to make of her body; in many ways women therefore have an alternative choice as to whether to verbalize their feelings or to express themselves through their bodies if verbalization is blocked.

Who would you say were your important influences when you turned to psychoanalysis?

Well, of course, my friend Hilda Abraham was very much behind me. Not knowing very much about working in the British Society, I naturally chose to do my training in the B group of the Society, the B group being the group that was around Anna Freud. My analyst also belonged to this group. These two women were the first influence in my psychoanalytical life. Enid Balint had also become someone that I very much admired and respected. And I have very much appreciated her approach to psychic pain and suffering. So I would say that there were three women.

In what psychoanalytic school would you place yourself, if any?

Well I have stayed loyal to the B group, which is the classical Freudian group; in fact, I was chairman of it at one stage. But I would say that I am not as classical as some of my colleagues because I do find other people, other groups of ideas, extremely interesting. I do think about them and use them in my own way when I think it is appropriate. What one would say of this generation of women analysts is that we all are very open-minded to other people's ideas and use what we find most helpful and most applicable.

Are your patients primarily women?

No, but I happened to have started writing about women, and in fact my men patients complain bitterly and think it is time I do some writing about men. I began to write about women because of my long experience with women and physical pain. That has always been something that I understood more.

Do you think that women are more prone to depression than men?

Well it is interesting that you asked that question because a friend of mine is just laboring with that. She is writing a paper on it, so we have talked about it. I would find it very difficult to generalize. I have seen depressed men, of course. But I do think that women are influenced by the stages of the life cycles in which they are. One can very much find a woman who has a postpartum depression, a woman who has a postmenopausal depression, or who is depressed. I had a patient who had an ectopic pregnancy which she mourned, as if there were a baby who would come to term and die at birth. I think that these are events that influence a great deal every aspect of depression that might be there. So I would say that my experience is that women are more liable to depression at certain stages of the life cycle which their bodies have to adapt to.

The body is something which Americans—particularly the feminists in large measure—have tried to ignore. But going back to the patients, how do you find that their sex influences your countertransference, or doesn't it?

Well I suppose it does to some extent but not very much. I think that there are of course masculine eroticized transferences, which coming to a female analyst highlights, but the same can happen with a woman who has a homosexual transference. There is a subtle difference, but not a great one. One has to be very sure of one's sexual identity in any countertransference.

How do you see yourself in relation to feminism? Would you call yourself a feminist, or do you reject the term?

My parents were quite feminist in the sense that my mother before me had been a doctor and was a highly educated woman. And there was no question in my parents' mind that I would receive the same education as my brother did. From that point of view it has never been an acute question for me. In my choice of profession, when I was a young doctor applying for jobs, I definitely did think that there were prejudices against me because everybody was asking: "Are you going to try to have children?" And when they heard that I certainly was, then I didn't get the consultant jobs that I was well qualified for and would have got otherwise. I found that quite difficult, but I came out of the hospital when I had my children and worked independently in general practice, just to keep me going as a dermatologist. And certainly I didn't encounter any prejudice, nor would I have done so in women's hospitals. So my own life has not been particularly affected by feminism.

In my own Society as well, as a psychoanalyst, I find that there is no prejudice against women; we are treated as equals. I happen to be chairman of admissions at the Institute.

Would you say that feminism has influenced your theory?

Well, I would say that if I look back at my patients, the ones I first started to write about, there have been big changes in their external lives, but I don't think that the internal world has changed very much. Perhaps the next generation will show more changes. There have been enormous changes for women, for instance, the introduction of contraception. When I started as a doctor, abortion was a major problem if the patients didn't have enough contraceptive experience or contraceptives good enough to enable them to have a sexual life without fear. So all that has changed a great deal, but I wouldn't say that that was feminism particularly; it is technology. I also think that the influence of new technologies is interesting. The whole prospect of infertility is now modified because there are so many new techniques. Infertility in my experience is one of the most painful symptoms in a woman patient who wants to have children, and the choices now are so much better.

I think that women feel more secure now in the capacity to own their bodies, but I am talking about a certain section of the population whom I see as an analyst. If I went into a working-class environment, I wouldn't be giving the same answers. In a fairly liberal, well-educated society, which most of my patients come from, women are not as desperate to be married. Divorce is much more frequent. Perhaps these are aspects that feminism has influenced, but the internal world is what we have to deal with, and I cannot say it has made too much difference with that.

Is there anything in the Freudian scenario that you feel should be rejected?

That is a very dicey question. Freud himself was the first one to say that it was the dark continent that he didn't understand.

I wonder what he would say today.

I think he would change a great deal because even in his last work, "Analysis Terminable and Interminable," he was radically changing his ideas. But living in the culture in which he lived, his ideas were very much that of a woman being passive; it was more phallocratic than we would regard it today. There is his famous quotation of the Mycenian civilization arising behind the Greek civilization, however. He was aware of the pre-Oedipal phases, but only briefly, I think, because his main focus was on the Oedipal phase. Today we are more aware of the influence of the mother and of the earliest foundations of the woman's relation to her own body, which is founded on the way in which the mother handles her own body and that of her baby. Now these ideas were not yet described by Freud.

In the society in which he lived, women were very restricted in what they could do. Anna O., one of the first patients, was a social worker. However, most of Freud's patients were not working, except for those who became his trainees, like Helene Deutsch.

Do you agree with Freud that women are more narcissistic than men?

No, I certainly don't, and I wouldn't say that little boys are less narcissistic than little girls. I think that little boys are very interested in what they wear, how they look, just as little girls are.

What about the formation of the superego? Freud says that men have a more strongly developed superego because of the castration complex. Since little girls perceive themselves as already being castrated and not having much to lose, they don't develop a strong moral sense.

I don't think that most people today would agree with that. In fact, I think it is rather strange that he says this when it is the women who carry the rituals, the traditions of the family. The mothers are often stricter than the fathers with their children, nor would I say what he does about the castration complex.

Melanie Klein believes that the achievements of civilization represent a sublimation of the child's early relation to the mother. Do art, culture, religion depend on one's response to the mother's body? Obviously the little girl's experience of the mother's body is going to be different from the little boy's. Could you describe that? How is this going to affect the later development of the sexes, their achievement of knowledge, and their contribution to culture?

What I dislike about the question is that I do not believe that this is as simple as all that. I don't think that it all begins with the mother's body or ends there. Human beings are much more complicated and there are far more influences: envy, curiosity, wanting to know, to learn, to achieve the adventures of the mind. If you take music, for instance, I have always been rather impressed by the way babies in utero respond to music. My son was very sensitive to ballet; he used to kick like mad at certain beats, and he still takes an enormous pleasure in that type of music. I have a patient who is a singer, her husband a conductor, and she sang in an opera toward the end of her pregnancy, which he conducted, and for her it was an ecstatic experience because the baby joined in by moving in her womb and the three of them formed a trio. You can say that this begins with the mother's body but that is too simplistic.

One of the questions which is receiving a great deal of interest in the United States right now and probably in England too is: What if there were more equal parenting by the mother and father? How would this affect the development of the little girl and the little boy?

A lot of experiment about this is being done at the moment, and I am not very competent to answer. But it appears that the father and the mother are two mothers at the beginning of the infant's life and that the father begins to emerge as a masculine person later on. I don't have clinical evidence of the difference it makes because most of my patients were born into families where fathers did not take those roles, nor did my own father take that role. I can certainly talk about the experience of having an absent father during the war and the influence that has on children.

That is important because many women are choosing to be single mothers today.

The experience that is missing very much for the little girl whose father is unavailable physically and emotionally during a war is that first step of turning to the father away from the mother; the first tremendous experience of the little girl being able to excite her father is crucial for the little girl's development. Because how is she going to feel that her body is sexually exciting if this is not established at the beginning of her life with her father? I have seen with women patients whose fathers were absent that they don't have the same sense of security in their own capacity to be successfully seductive. This very early stage is tremendously important to the little girl's development in terms of her capacity to believe in her sexual attractiveness. I don't think that the mother can do that. The mother can make the little girl believe that she has a good body, that she is satisfied by it and she can be someone who can enjoy her own body, but I think that the father is needed to start the next step.

Should the new reproductive techniques be available to people who want to be single parents? With a woman who is fertile, there is not much of a problem. All she needs is male sperm and she can inseminate herself. But there are cases of homosexual men who choose to be genetic fathers and raise their children alone. You seem to feel that it is best for the child to have both parents available.

If it is a good marriage, I would say it is the best situation without reservations. If it is a bad marriage, then it is a very bad situation for the child. The problem for single-parent families is that the mother of a child becomes so enmeshed in forming a couple that it is very difficult for them to separate when it is the appropriate time. I am thinking of a very intelligent professional woman who became pregnant by a man who didn't marry her. She decided to go on with the pregnancy, and had a boy who looked exactly like the man who abandoned her, which was an enormous problem, making her feel very ambivalent to him. This child is now an adolescent, and should be able to leave but he is not able to do so because they are still enmeshed in that unique relationship in which none of them seeks other partners. This can be a great problem. It is also necessary to face the fact that parenting a child is one of the most difficult tasks in the world and if there is no one to turn to, the mother can hate the child for the demands he or she makes on her all the time.

What do you think of communal child rearing, children brought up in groups? There is something of an experimental situation on the kibbutz in Israel, but that is not as radical as a group of women bringing up several children together. It is an unorthodox way but do you think it can work?

It makes me think of Arab women whose children are brought up in a harem. It must work to a certain extent. I have not had experience of patients being brought up in that way. I have been to Israel and I think that the kibbutzim have had to modify the child rearing not because of the children's demands, but because of the mothers' demands. The mothers have found it too painful to be separated from the children and not have more of a hand in bringing them up, so that more and more time is spent with the children.

The pressure *has* been for more contact with the children; one theory holds that because the values of Israeli society are so male-dominant, there are few rewards for women except those of motherhood. That is one possible reason for the shift toward greater family life.

It could be but I think it comes much more from the maternal emotional pull because of the bonding. After all, mothers don't have to give the baby immediately into the children's home. They found the separation very painful. It is because of this internal pressure that there are modifications now.

There are thinkers in the United States like Shulamith Firestone, who feel that only if reproduction were taken out of the body entirely, which some biologists think is going to be a possibility not too far in the future, will women be truly liberated. We could say that Simone de Beauvoir implied the same thing in *The Second Sex,* where she writes about pregnancy and childbirth as an enslavement to the species. Obviously, you don't feel that way about pregnancy and childbirth.

I don't at all. You see de Beauvoir never had a child, so whatever she said may have revealed enslavement to the mother. The fantasies of every woman around this creature which is growing inside her—and I think there is enormous pleasure in feeling the baby—this feeling of creating a new life is an exalting experience if you enjoy being pregnant, and many women do. It would be an enormous deprivation to many women to miss all that. Even giving birth and delivering a child into the world. Today when fathers help, it is as a couple they deliver a child. The bonds between the father and the baby are so much more intense now than they used to be.

What would be the ramifications of such a system of reproduction for psychology? Have you done any thinking about this?

I have one patient now who is going to start an in vitro fertilization because she is infertile, but it is not the same and it can't be the same. It becomes a scientific procedure or technology rather than a capacity to feel oneself able to conceive naturally. That is something very precious that a woman can do, and to put it all into technology is a deprivation of the feminine aspect.

The Warnock Committee in England is very much against surrogacy. This is not the official position in the United States. But what do you think of a woman who would be willing to carry a child for another woman and then give it up?
Well I think that in the mind, it is easy for a woman to think that she can do it. But once it is a real baby and not an idea? An interesting report came out from three women who have been surrogate mothers. One woman felt desperate every time the child's birthday came around and felt deprived as if she were the child that didn't get the card on those occasions. So she was left out and she said that she spends a lot of time thinking of this baby, wishing that she had it with her. Another one said that it didn't matter at all, it was the best way she had to earn money, and that was what she was going to do. But the third one was suffering from depression after having given the baby away. So I think that when it is an idea it is fine, but the reality of feeling the baby moving inside you and then giving birth to it and losing it is very painful.

What about the psychology of the child who discovers that she was carried by someone who was not her genetic mother (but rather received an embryo transfer) or was carried by someone who was her genetic mother who then gave her up for adoption? How will the child feel?
It is very difficult to say. It can only be a conjecture on my part. I have never had a patient like that, but I have had people who were adopted as children in analysis, and I think that one thing that one cannot get over is: "My mother didn't love me. . . ." I think these children are always testing people as if to say, "I am terrible, awful. I do all the worst things but you have got to love

me just the same." This is such a wound that one's own mother "didn't care enough to keep me."

Do you think that these children are always testing the adoptive parents?

Yes and always somewhere there is a fantasy of the ideal parent whom they lost and whom they always look for, and who will always love them more than the adoptive parents. I think it is a great demand.

You spoke of the satisfaction of so many women in being pregnant. How does this affect the psychological status of the postmenopausal woman? Obviously it is going to be different depending on the individual. But how does the society see her? And how can we do something about the double standard of aging, which I am sure you have in England too?

Being an older woman myself, I am speaking very subjectively of course. Most people think that the menopause is enormously painful. My experience is that for many it is not.

Margaret Mead thought it was a period of great strength, energy.

With menopause, women are more aware of their sexuality because it is not linked any more to childbearing, and they can recover much more sexual pleasure, sexual vigor. It is almost like a second wave, a second adolescence in which women can enjoy their body, where the sexuality means more because it affirms their sense of keeping their attraction. For other women, it is enormously painful even though they may have enough children. I think there is always in the mind another child that could be born, and it is painful when that hope has to be given up. But for a lot of women, there is liberation and the capacity to become more energetic, and if one wants to talk about masculine and feminine, a woman who becomes menopausal and has passed that *rite de passage* can then use more masculine aspects of herself like returning to a professional life, using her mind, being free of child care and child rearing. That may be very stimulating to some women who waited a long time to do it. But to other women, it is like coming to an end; they are not needed anymore. Being needed is to my mind more precious to women than to men. I think women need to be needed.

Is this need the result of social conditioning, or is it biological?

I don't think it is biological; it is emotional. Women who rear children have learned to be needed and like being needed. And when mothers are not needed any more, are discarded, they have to go through mourning at that stage. And then they have to separate and look for their own life. I wrote a paper about Holocaust victims, about women who reach this stage of life and who had avoided mourning by living through the children. When the children separated, then they had to face the destruction of their inner world and it became a very painful period for them. However, it may be a great liberation not to have to worry about having a baby. It is marvelous for some women to be free to enjoy their own lives.

How does a woman who is aging deal with not having a sexual partner available?

It is very painful, because I don't think that a woman—if she is alive herself—as she ages loses any of her sexual drive or even the feeling in her mind that she is still a sexually desirable woman. It is only by observing the reactions of others that she adapts to the fact that time has passed on. In most lively older women there is a young woman to the day of her death, still available for sexual adventures, for sexual encounters, whether she is married or not.

A very old analyst once said, "In her internal world, a woman remains a prostitute." I think that has a certain truth. However good the marriage is, there may be aspects of the woman that are unfulfilled, and although she may not act on them, there may be fantasies about other men or other sexual encounters.

What you just said—that in every woman there is a prostitute—would be a surprising statement to many people.

It is not my statement; it is a quotation. But I think there's a certain truth in it.

Traditionally it was felt that the man was more prone to split the sexual object than was the woman, while the woman seemed more capable of reconciling tender and erotic feelings. Do you think that's true, or do women split those feelings also, turning to different kinds of men, whether in fantasy or in reality, to satisfy them?

I think it depends on how strong the maternal feelings are that the woman has toward the sexual partner. If there are maternal feelings, tenderness, and love, as well as adult sexuality, and they are combined, it can be very difficult if the woman is excessively maternal for her husband to retain his capacity to be her adult sexual partner, because something in him responds to the maternal aspects and this may arouse primitive anxieties about intercourse. It depends on the type of woman. I find it very difficult to generalize.

For some women, erotic feelings are not as important as the tender ones. Perhaps not so much today, when there is so much talk about orgasm, but my experience is that many of the older women have enjoyed sexuality in terms of giving affection and loving, bodily feelings, not necessarily culminating in orgasm. I believe some people could find sexuality an exciting—I was going to say—game, but it's not; it's an exciting encounter in which aggression is provoked and survived. I think it's a very different sort of sexuality.

Some analysts have said that the lover is a narcissist with an object.

I suppose there's some truth in that. Yes. But that's not love; that's sexuality. That's what I am trying to distinguish, there can be sexuality between a man and a woman which has very little to do with love, which has to do with one's own power to seduce, to control, to escape danger, or to make it dangerous, whichever way. And the partner, I'm not going to use the word "lover," is used for that game. It's not to give and receive pleasure and love. I think that one has to make this distinction.

Is this related to Freud's theory of narcissistic love in any way?

I would say that what I'm talking about belongs to the narcissistic pleasure of the woman who uses her partner this way. As for the anaclitic type, there are women that rescue the object as they would wish to be rescued themselves.

The rescue of the object that Freud talks about refers only to the male rescuing the fallen woman.

But the woman can also do that.

How would it work, if the woman were to do the rescuing? Do you mean that the woman would reform the man?

That's right. Consider a situation in which a woman uses a man to be successful herself. She perhaps is too intimidated by the world and he is somehow unable to be successful. In this situation, the woman uses the man as an object. Or consider men who complain about their mothers and when their wives or girlfriends try to do better—try to rescue the man—they only fall into a disaster themselves. I think there are many ways to seek an object.

What is the best way?

I wish I knew.

There's no single way, but how would you as an analyst define a mature object relation?

I think a mature object relationship is one in which you don't have to use the object in order to gain something for yourself, as if it were yourself. It's a capacity to be nice to the other person and to expect the other to be nice to you. Whether that's love, I don't know. But it's sharing life, sharing interests, sharing bodies, sharing children in a way in which one can be separate and yet united. Struggle, interdependence, independence, that goes on in every human being. I don't know the answer to that. I think there are many solutions.

Do you think that the split between the virgin and the whore still exists today in the male imagination?

Yes, very much so. It is grounded in the boy child's view of his mother and the problem of the mother being the father's sexual partner, not just the child's mother. I have a patient who watched the Royal wedding between Prince Charles and Lady Di. What he picked up was the Queen was on her own all the time. And that even when she was looking happy at seeing the happy couple off, there was no husband around her.

Like the Virgin Mary.

That's right. So he saw it that way and it's what he wanted to see. What, my mummy and daddy? No, they can't be a united couple. I think there's always a split.

But this is more of a problem for the man than the woman, isn't it?

Yes, in response to the way in which you have put the question.

Does the woman have the same problem as the man? It wouldn't seem so.

Not about the man, but about herself. I would like to emphasize that the woman's attitude toward her own sexuality very much depends on her mother's attitude toward it, and that therefore a young girl may think, "If I am seductive, am I being like a whore? My mother would say I am." Or if she is not too openly seductive, because her mother said she should not be, there is an enormous envy of other women who can be free themselves and the feeling of pain and longing for something that is so strongly inhibited.

As an analyst, do you have any advice for mothers and how they should treat their daughters and their sexuality?

The less inhibition the better. Children will grow up well if they're not interfered with too much. Mothers who have the really distinct superegoish ideas about what a child should or should not do, particularly in the early stages when the body is involved, really make it difficult for children later. The attitudes toward their own body begin with the first contact with the mother and are carried on up until adult sexuality is established. I think it's how the mother deals with the girl baby's body and the products of her body that leave a stamp for the rest of her life.

In the French analysts, the image of the pre–Oedipal mother as a dangerous, primitive, all–engulfing figure, is pervasive. Some of the French analysts' descriptions of the mother really sound like a form of neomisogyny. Is there anything equivalent in English theory about the pre–Oedipal mother?

I wonder if this primitive, engulfing mother is also a projection of the child's wish to engulf the mother, to be the only object of the mother's life and even to swallow her up and put her inside, because she is a good thing, not just a bad thing. It seems to me that that's very much so. My grandson said to me recently, "Do you know what I am going to do with you? I'm going to eat you all up and put you inside me." So I thought that was very sweet; actually, it wasn't meant sadistically at all, it meant—

That you are good enough to eat.

Yes, good enough to eat and I'd like to have you always. So don't go away. I'll just eat you up. This has something to do with separation, doesn't it? Now, I do think that there are enormous primitive terrors—archaic terrors about the mother in all children, particularly girl children, who, after all, are a threat to the mother—mirror, mirror on the wall, who's the fairest of us all— but it seems that this engulfing mother is only one side of the mother and the other side is the all–loving one. But the all–loving one draws a very narrow line between eating someone up and not allowing them an identity at all, loving them and wanting to give them everything. And the child perceives this according to her internal world.

Would you tell us more about the internal world?

I think the prime difficulty for every little girl and every woman is how to separate herself from her mother, how to be a different person from her mother, how to be like her and yet not like her. This separation and individuation from the mother goes on throughout a woman's life. It's particularly difficult when the woman becomes pregnant, because she is becoming like her mother. And the whole problem then goes on as to who is going to engulf her. And that can be projected onto the fetus.

I live in a French village quite a lot of the year. Watching child-rearing customs there, mothers are much more controlling than English mothers. And family ties are much more strict and retained much longer than they are in England. So that I think when French analysts write about this engulfing mother, it's part of their own childhood experience.

The United States

Marianne Eckardt was born in Berlin and came to the United States in 1933 to join her mother, Karen Horney. She graduated from the University of Chicago Medical School and had a psychiatric residency at the Payne Whitney Clinic in New York. She was trained as an analyst at the American Institute of Psychoanalysis in New York and has been in private practice in Washington, D.C. and New York since 1941. She is a past president of the American Academy of Psychoanalysis and is currently associate clinical professor in psychiatry at the Division of Psychoanalysis, Department of Psychiatry, New York Medical College, in Valhalla, New York.

BIBLIOGRAPHICAL NOTE

Dr. Eckardt has published numerous papers in the major psychoanalytic journals on dreams, the history of psychoanalysis, the history of organizational schisms, changes in theory and technique, and the contributions of the neo-Freudian group, particularly those of Erich Fromm.

FOURTEEN

Marianne Eckardt

New York, Winter 1987

We interviewed Marianne Eckardt on a freezing cold evening in mid-winter in her apartment, which has a beautiful view of the Manhattan skyline. Though the large leather sofa and chairs looked inviting, as did the cheese spread set before us, Dr. Eckardt seemed initially resistant to our questions, perhaps because she feared that we would make her look like a feminist ideologue. Later however, her willingness to give of herself, her integrity, her probity, her wide knowledge of the psychoanalytic theories that she addressed, her reminiscences of her mother, Karen Horney, and her ease in accepting the differences in their personalities, gave the interview a rich and broad perspective.

Why did you become an analyst?

I became an analyst accidentally. I finished medical school at the University of Chicago. At that time it was still a young university, and during my clinical years they had as yet no psychiatric department and no psychiatric lecturer. Then I interned there, but again I was not blessed with a single bit of knowledge about psychiatry. At the same time I realized that people would expect me to know something about psychiatry, so I obtained a two-year residency at Payne Whitney, and, once there, I began to be analyzed. If my training at Chicago had been more complete, I don't know whether I would have gone into psychiatric training.

Why did you decide to become a doctor?

I really did not decide. This is totally different from my mother (Karen Horney), who was very self-determined. She decided to be a doctor when she was fourteen years old, when women weren't even admitted to medical school. They were just opening a Gymnasium for girls at that point. It was her father who had to be persuaded. He said she should just help her mother in the house. Her father was finally brought around with the help of her mother and brother, but they had to sign a contract that after she graduated from high school, he would not have to be responsible for her any more.

It was certainly taken for granted that I would go to high school. I was studying in Germany at that time, in Berlin, where one automatically could go to the university, which at that time was still a state university. I graduated at seventeen. One then studied to become a teacher or chose economics, law, or medicine. It seemed to me there weren't that many choices, so I chose medicine.

It was again one of those things. I can only assure you that while I have become fairly decisive over the years, up to a certain point, I would describe what I did as sliding into things.

My mother came here in 1932 because Franz Alexander invited her to codirect the newly formed Chicago Psychoanalytic Institute. I hadn't quite finished my premedical studies in Germany at that time, so I stayed until 1933.

Would you call your mother a feminist?

She was not a feminist. It is important to understand the sequence of her writing. She wrote on penis envy and addressed other questions of feminine psychology early in her career, which was in the 1920s. But by the beginning of the thirties she began to develop her theories on character neurosis and she was no longer interested in feminine psychology whatsoever. It never reappeared.

Her book *Feminine Psychology* is a collection of papers that was not published until 1967. She died in 1952. In many of these early papers her ideas are still rooted in Freudian libidinal theories. Her very first paper, in 1922, on penis envy, did not as yet talk about cultural factors. It was not until 1926 that she expressed the challenging idea that the whole question of human psychology was written from a male point of view and by male analysts. It was in this paper ("Flight from Womanhood") that Horney first said that it was the privileged position of men in the society that women envied. In other words, it was her first awareness that cultural factors could play an important role.

In the twenties, she also wrote papers on men's envy and fear of women, but from the early thirties on, she was interested in constructing a nonlibidinal theory of neurotic development. She wanted to arrive at a theory of how neuroses emerged and how they cramped people's spontaneity and their potential for realizing their own selves. That's where self-realization came in. It was a theory that applied to both men and women. So in that sense she really never was a feminist.

She was not actively interested in promoting sociopolitical factors that would aid the emancipation of women, nor did she particularly write on the plight of women caught in the prejudices of the society.

Now, in her adolescent years she certainly had to battle male prejudice. When she was seventeen—we know this from her diaries—she was very interested in feminist writing. But it never took the form of any ideological or political direction. She was fascinated by it and it strengthened her confidence to pursue her own path, in a way, her own destiny.

She had the ability to decipher the male and female roles in society. Her view of penis envy was in a sense original. She placed it with the Oedipus complex, didn't she?

For her, penis envy is a metaphor for envying the male position and wishing to have male power or male ability or male status. She was not interested in the developmental stages of the child; she just accepted penis envy as a label applied to women who very much envied men.

In her papers about womb envy, she shows that it's not only women who envy men; there are also men who envy women's ability to have children and be creative. She was using metaphors for personality traits because that was the Freudian language that was employed. But as her ideas progressed, she became more interested in characterology.

But her description of the penis and womb in terms of metaphor is precisely what a number of feminists are saying today, and this is why I find it rather extraordinary that they do not reach out to your mother as a kind of heroine.★ A lot of what she had to say, in 1926 for example, about the little girl being aware of the sensations of her vagina, other people presented much later, as if for the first time. Some people give credit to Bettelheim for the concept of womb envy. It's rather interesting how people say something first, as your mother did, then it is forgotten. Or other people start making a great deal about it later, without acknowledging the earlier source.

Now, in France, analysts are talking about male narcissism as the reason for the theory of penis envy. Your mother was saying this in the 1920s.

Yes, she was talking about male narcissism in one of her papers ("The Dread of Woman") on the distrust between the sexes. She says in very clear terms that the man continuously has to prove

★Such books as Susan T. Quinn's *A Mind of Her Own: The Life of Karen Horney* (New York: Summit Books, 1987) and Marcia Westcott's *The Feminist Legacy of Karen Horney* (New Haven: Yale University Press, 1987), which appeared after this interview, do see Horney as an avant garde feminist.

his ability in sexual intercourse and the woman can just allow it to happen. He has to prove his manhood.

In "The Dread of Woman" she talks mainly about men's fear of women's sexuality and the attempt to control that sexuality by forcing women into passive roles, in part through the examples of mythology. All of this is exciting in connection with what is going on now in women's theory. It surprises us that Horney isn't the big figure today. Do you think that this has something to do with her style, which is a beautiful style, but a tentative, modest one? It's not authoritarian.

No, I think it has to do with the fact that these early papers on feminine psychology were her beginning steps into a different direction. These early impressive papers have been greatly appreciated by later feminist writers. But she herself emphasized the determining role of cultural factors in neurotic development. This was then new and challenging to the libido theory. She did not emphasize a new theory of the psychology of women.

What is important to you as far as women are concerned?

In my practice I am continuously seeing women who have not really found their own voices or who still suffer from the old stereotype that women are to be housewives, are not to be successful, and are not to assert themselves. We all still meet them in practice. But the basic problems I see in men are not that different from the ones that I see in women. Differences have to do with different cultural background. There is a tremendous amount of variety. I certainly see sensitive men, very good in interpersonal relationships, who suffer from continuously being misunderstood by their women, and I see the same thing in women as far as men are concerned. True, it's a little more often that women feel completely misunderstood by men. Men are often impatient about intimate talk and revealing emotions. Those things exist, they are part of a culture. But on the other hand, in practice, I deal with individuals and thus uniqueness, so, in principle, I do not care to generalize about characteristics of the sexes.

In France we found that the analysts largely feel that you can't eliminate gender roles without causing psychosis. In this country, on the contrary, the more radical analysts ask why there shouldn't be total freedom for men and women to choose what they want to be, what they want to do.

This does not make sense to me. There is no culture which has not assigned roles to males and females. In spite of all our society's diversity and chaos, we still have the tradition of assigned roles. There is no society that exists or could exist without patterns, and patterns refer also to above and below. There are different roles, but I don't see women as always just having been helpless and submissive as if they didn't have their position of strength, whether within the home or behind the scenes.

I don't quite see how differentiated roles will ever be eliminated. We are concerned about having equal pay for equal work, we don't want women to be harassed as sexual objects in their positions, we want them to get into political roles. There is no reason why we can't strive toward changing the society because it will change anyway. But societies will always have some sort of stratification.

There *are* biological differences. One is very much aware of this when you see men and women in their thirties. If the women haven't married because they've been in a long relationship and then broke up because the men didn't want to commit themselves, suddenly at thirty-five, they get panicky about finding relationships so that they can still have some children. Then they meet a man who already has two or three children, and he isn't that interested in having a second brood. These are issues that definitely have to do with biology.

This is a very widespread problem. How do you advise your patients to deal with it?

I am very sympathetic to this particular issue, and I definitely want my patients to be realistic and not dream that the man they are attached to will come around and be very happy to have a child with them even though he is very adamant that he does not want to have any more children. If they continue the relationship, the women should be aware that they have to take the risk that either it may not happen, or that they will have to get pregnant without the willingness of the man. They do a lot of wishful thinking and dream that love will make him come around. Some of them succeed and do have a child, and that's fine, but they have to be realistic and not just assume that this will happen.

What do you think about women becoming single mothers?

That is also very much up and coming. There are many women who are determined to be single mothers, and some of those that I have met have been very realistic about their earning powers, about their need for help, and about what it means to have a job and come home and take care of the child. And again, I'm very much in favor of this if that's what they want to do, but I inquire very carefully about all the practical issues that I know will arise. I do not neglect the pragmatic issues in my therapeutic inquiry.

What about the effects on the child?

I don't think that's a problem, especially with day care and kindergarten. It's important that the mother has friends, and that the child gets exposed to both other children and other adults. But there's no question in my mind that children can be very healthy under many diverse circumstances.

What would you advise the mother to tell a child whose father was never her husband?

That depends on the child's relationship to the mother and the child's comprehension; it also depends on the culture. If the child meets children of other single mothers, it becomes a cultural fact of existence. Then there is no problem.

When my daughter had divorced her first husband and I asked what her daughter was feeling about it, she said, "Oh, there's not a family on the block that isn't divorced, so she is just experiencing exactly what everybody else is." You cannot predict and you cannot advise on the basis of supposedly cultural norms these days.

Do you feel that psychoanalysis has a role to play in women's liberation?

I think psychoanalysis in the past very much overestimated its role in changing the culture. It will continue to have an important role in helping individual women create a more satisfying life for themselves, in marriage and outside of marriage. It will also continue to enrich the other behavioral sciences, as it is enriched by them. There are good books on women's role in society and books on women's support groups, but they are not necessarily informed by psychoanalytic theory.

Do you think that feminism has to be against men?

In a paper that I wrote in response to a paper by Dr. Jean Baker Miller ("The Development of Women's Sense of Self"), I said, "I have preference for an approach that recognizes that men, too, have been cast into stereotypes in the past which had its disadvantages, for an approach that deemphasizes gender differences and addresses the need for creativity in mutual living arrangements, an approach that respects uniqueness of inclination in either sex within our communality, that also respects the need for individual space and privacy as well as connection, an approach that acknowledges the basic difficult and often tragic nature of our existence and aims at strengthening our creative ability to tap the resources of both men and women."

I have not been very active in many of the panels on feminist issues because they very easily veer toward the anti-men stand, or they do not include men and I think they should. What I see in my children and in their friends is the creative way in which these very intelligent couples where both have jobs in academia, work things out and share household chores, children's chores, living arrangements. You can't generalize, but certainly in the younger people, in their thirties and forties, you see a great deal of change away from stereotyped assumptions. But life is not easy. For it is hard to juggle the demands of good parenting, good relationships, the demands of professional growth and advancement, and the demands for private or creative time. Modern living even without prejudices poses many a challenge and demands ingenuity.

In a sense the term *feminism* sounds as if it's against the interpersonal theory and that may be one of the problems. We were wondering if you would define interpersonal in contrast to libido theory, since it has been so influential. Even the changes you're talking about right now seem to owe much to interpersonal theory.

As a concept it arose within the neo-Freudian circle, especially as it was used by Sullivan, and it was also somewhat used by Horney. They jettisoned the libido theory, which is intrapsychic, a matter of libidinal forces that struggle and run into the Oedipal conflicts with mother and father, having very little to do with their personalities, and then resolve themselves in one form or another or not. The cultural theories evolved in the thirties and the forties, when the neo-Freudian group supported by anthropologists emphasized that it's partly your own constitution that you bring into the world, but it is also the influences from the culture and family in particular that are important. The family is the mediator of the culture so that the environment and the role of the mother and the father and their personalities have a tremendous influence.

The word *interpersonal* as used by Sullivan is a very specific and complex one. Sullivan worked with schizophrenics; what he saw of their pathology was organized on the basis of anxiety. Anxiety was the instigator of a self-dynamism, as he calls it, a self-development that starts with the child being aware of the anxiety in the mother, which gives him a sense of discomfort or dyseuphoria. Sullivan says there are two kinds of satisfactions: the satisfactions that come from being nurtured, from being fed and being warm —the physical needs—and the satisfactions that relate to the child's security needs. Anxiety relates to these security needs. The anxiety over parental approval or disapproval is so great, according to Sullivan, that all pathology is basically a pathology of interpersonal relationships.

For Horney, the theory was different. Children who grow up in difficult environments suffer basic anxiety and develop three different types of defensive structure, which may reveal psychopathology. One is to move toward people, to try and please them so that somehow the child's anxiety is appeased. But it's just pleasing in order to relieve the anxiety. Or children can decide that people are really hostile, so they are going to fight them. They gain security by being aggressive and idealizing power. The third way is to move away from people, which is basically a kind of withdrawing and detachment. The security comes from non-involvement.

But the problem, she says, is that no matter what mechanism we develop, we also have a need for people, as well as for self-assertion. If we develop a subservient manner, we may still be very ambitious, so that conflicts arise. Then we may try to find various solutions for these conflicts, which lead to vicious circles. Her great contribution is the description of neurotic character, of character neuroses, which are classic. She is accused of neglecting early trauma. She explicitly says that neuroses do all arise out of early trauma, but as she pictures or dramatizes the development, it's as if the particular mode that the child develops, the style of life, as Adler would say, becomes almost independent of the original trauma.

The whole neo-Freudian group defined psychopathology in terms of neurotic character structure. They assumed an ideal norm of personality and an ideal society, so that stress in coping was equated with being neurotic. These are generalizations that arise with either/or dichotomies of any theory. Every theory high-lights one or related aspects of our existence, gives it or them a pivotal and dramatized role in the structural drama of the theory. But highlighting also casts shadows and obscures. This is the nature of theory faced with the interacting multidimensionality of our existence.

The word *interpersonal,* however, has had a very important life of its own. It means that you look at the interpersonal relation-ships of early childhood and know that they're important. They played a role in the particular development the child took. This focus on early interrelationships has at times placed too much blame on mothers. The world has always been difficult, and there are some children that have coped marvelously and some that have not because the child has its own creative force and shapes its own coping habits. They are influenced but not determined by the mother.

What do you see as the major difference between the inter-personal school and its various manifestations in object relations theory?

Theoretically, they come from somewhat different places, but fundamentally they go in the same direction. Object relations theory arose from Melanie Klein but I find her theory hard to comprehend. Her followers, Fairbairn, Guntrip, and Winnicott, people in England that I highly respect, give Melanie Klein credit for developing the theory of object relationships, the emphasis being that the child internalizes the good and bad aspects of various people around him. Fundamentally this is also interpersonal relationship, but the theory is phrased differently. I have had a great deal of difficulty reading about object relationships because I don't like the term. I don't want to be an object of somebody else. *Object* comes from the Freudian terminology relating to the object being invested with energy. Then its meaning changed. People borrow terms because they want to remain within the psychoanalytic tradition.

The problem of living with different theories is that you have to understand the theory and then retranslate whatever is useful into your own terminology. Nobody can use the theory the way it's handed to us. It's not meaningful. If you're a good clinician, you'll see the uniqueness of the person. Every patient is a challenge. I don't know of any patient that fits a pigeonhole. If I think that a patient is exactly what So-and-so describes, I very soon discover that this is not so.

In that regard, what do you think of such categories as neurotic and borderline? Do you think that we now have a borderline personality of our time as opposed to an earlier neurotic personality of our time? How would you define borderline?

They used to be classified more under the psychopathic, near the schizophrenic. As for current categories, I don't want to define borderlines, but certainly they are people without a very solid ego organization who very often have an acting out style and need a different therapeutic approach. What has been good about having a lot of books and papers written about borderlines is that they permitted more orthodox Freudians to use different parameters of therapy. New, dynamic concepts of this new category of patients allowed therapists to feel free to justify confronting the patient, being aggressive with and setting limits to the patient, and doing all sorts of things which they could not justify when treating neurotic patients according to the rules.

Do you think that our society has become more psychopathic?

No, hardly. I don't find labeling my patients as neurotic in one form or another very helpful because most of them struggled in very ingenious ways against difficult circumstances, but the very ways in which they struggled later stood in their way to further development. That's just the happenstance of existence.

What percentage of your patients are women?

Most of the time I'd say two-thirds. The only thing that has changed much in the way people come to me is that there are many more women these last ten or fifteen years that very specifically ask for a woman, and if I don't have any time, they want to be referred to another woman.

In earlier days they would say, "I'd like to work with you," but they had no particular sex preference. Now they feel, rightly or wrongly, whether it's the time or the culture, that they may be better understood by a woman.

What would you say are the central questions in psychoanalysis today?

Psychoanalysis is at the moment in a precarious position. Far fewer medical students go into psychiatry today. Of the psychiatry students, a far smaller percentage than ever go into psychotherapy or psychoanalytic training, so that all institutes have fewer M.D. candidate applicants. There is a tremendous shift from

M.D. therapists now to Ph.D. therapists because they have more training facilities.

So the field is shifting and there are thousands of therapists and therapies vying with each other. The Freudian theories are also coming more under critical attack. But psychoanalysis will remain; I don't think it's going to go under. In many ways as clinicians we're becoming wiser. We have to weigh many more options in our own minds and make more clinical decisions. We cannot rely on either a theoretical system or on any particular technique because there's no technique that's going to guarantee results and there's no technique that's always right. I do believe that one has to have thorough training, and then have a lot of experience.

What do you think we should dispense with in Freud, concerning women?

Freud's discoveries began this whole fountain of investigations. I do not believe that one should blame Freud for the fact that his theory needed expansion and revision. I see him as the genius who gave life to our field that then evolved.

I think Freud has to be read as part of the history of our field. He aimed at a universal biological theory. He wanted to be the Darwin of psychology and was very deterministically minded.

But I don't think he had anything to say about women. Just forget it. Somewhere he was very much rooted in the Victorian era and also in male chauvinism. Whatever he says about female psychology can be dismissed. I don't even feel that this ought to be emphasized because I think he made so many contributions that were of tremendous value. The question of his theory of the castration complex played a great role because it was out of the boy seeing the girl having no penis and being afraid that he could be castrated that his superego arose, which really meant the civilizing force. The castration theory was conceived as a part of Freud's imagining how the male could develop into a civilized human being. He just simply wasn't interested in the female.

Your mother says that the theory of feminine psychology as described in traditional psychoanalysis, whether it's true

or not, is the image of the little boy, never mind the adult male.

Well, it's the way Freud thought the little boy saw the girl. It all has to do with boys and men. The woman was just something to be used in the construction.

Yours is such a tolerant point of view. The problem is that when someone is a genius we expect him to be right on everything, and that's part of the reason for the attack on Freud.

Well, I regret this because I think we should appreciate what he did give us, the concept of the unconscious and the mechanism of dreams and their interpretation. Everybody works with dreams, not the way he used dream interpretation, but as part of something that is going on underneath our structured consciousness. New ideas can develop out of a bad part of a theory.

There are women theorists today who consider themselves feminists who accept the theory of castration, like Juliet Mitchell in England.

I sometimes see theory building as an art product. I have a certain admiration for a structure that is ingeniously conceived, and certainly Freud's structure had a fantastic impact on literature, on our time. Today there is criticism that he didn't report his patients truthfully. All sorts of facts are being discovered. I can only say, so what? He started something that just took off like wildfire and we are still part of it.

Do you think that the society is now allowing women to develop the self? To express their anger?

I have not been very much in favor of the concept of self-realization divorced from the idea that self-realization also means an improvement in interpersonal relationship. And I don't like the word particularly because it suggests that we have a self to realize. Knowing one's self refers to a much more subtle process of knowing what we feel and giving validity to what we feel, and being creative about it. Emphasizing the benefits of expressing anger can be an oversimplified notion. Anger is a sign that something is wrong, but we do not necessarily know what. Anger is an indication that we aren't sure about what we're feeling in the first place and secondly that we have not thought very much about what we might want to do about whatever the disturbance.

In her book *Toward a New Psychology of Women*, Jean Baker Miller says that women are the carriers of the problems of the culture, that whatever the culture can't solve gets projected onto women. One major question we have is how are we going to get away from that if the father is still seen primarily as the person who fosters the individuation of the child and the mother is seen somehow as standing in the way of that development? Do we have to have that kind of split? In the new arrangements of the couples you were talking about, with their creative solutions to problems, will the mothers still represent that engulfing, protecting force that keeps the child from moving out? Will the father still represent the excitement of that outside world, or do you think that's going to change?

I think it has already changed, because among most of the young people that I know well, both the men and the women have an active professional life and share the chores and delights of in-the-family affairs as well as those out in the world. I don't see that there is a tendency for mothers in any way to represent a force that is against individuation, because they have a life of their own, and children hear about the excitement of their life being brought into the home, just as they hear about the father's exciting life outside being brought into the home.

I'm now talking about the middle class. Most of the younger women want to keep developing professional skills, partly so that they have an earning capacity but also to develop their own particular inclinations.

You have spoken a good deal about younger women, young mothers. What about the older woman? By older, let's say, anyone postmenopausal. This is a category that's neglected in the psychoanalytic literature. How can we change the

double standard of aging, the stereotypes pertaining to the supposed demise of sexual interest in older women?

These are cultural stereotypes. Masters and Johnson wrote that sexuality is very much in the life of the older woman, especially if an active sexual life is continued. Menopause is being made less of because I think it is very much less of a problem. What is much more of a problem is that if women in their fifties have been divorced or widowed, their chances of remarriage are very small, and so they have to create a life that is active and fulfilling even though they are single, and some are able to do that very well and others who are not initiators and who are not venturesome about their own lives find it difficult.

That is why new lifestyles and women connecting with other women and making good friendships have become very important.

Dorothy Dinnerstein is Distinguished Professor of Psychology at Rutgers University, Newark. She has written numerous journal articles about experimental studies on perception and memory. Her current work-in-progress is entitled "Sentience and Survival," an exploration of human passivity and denial in the face of current threats to life on earth. Her *Mermaid and the Minotaur* is a psychoanalytically oriented analysis of the uses of gender.

SELECTED BIBLIOGRAPHY

The Mermaid and the Minotaur: Sexual Arrangements and Human Malaise.
New York: Harper and Row, 1976.

FIFTEEN

Dorothy Dinnerstein

New Jersey, Winter 1986

Dorothy Dinnerstein lives in a gingerbread house in New Jersey. Her study, full of yellow-pad paper, covered with manuscript— no computers for her, not even a typewriter—was bathed in yellow sunlight. An old velvet couch facing a fireplace sat in the living room. We did not. We chose the large dining room, with its big round table around which we sipped endless cups of tea in Chinese ceramic cups. We were immediately taken by the quality of Dinnerstein's presence. Besides charm, she has an honesty, an openness that most adults learn to hide, fearing that it makes them vulnerable. Yet it was from these sources that her strength seemed to come. Although Dinnerstein is not an analyst, we wanted to interview her because of the great influence of her book

The Mermaid and the Minotaur: Sexual Arrangements and Human Malaise.

Your book *The Mermaid and the Minotaur* had such a great influence. How come you did not continue writing about women?

Well, I am a slow worker and must use my time carefully. I said what I most urgently had to say about our uses of gender. I'm working now on the question of why people cannot think about what they need to think about if the world is going to survive. And, of course, what we do with gender is part of that question. *I am interested in feminism only insofar as it bears on that question.*

I talked about this in *Mermaid,* and it was a serious disappointment to me that so many readers failed to connect with this central feature of my argument. People were very much interested in what I said about personal life, but most simply ignored what I said about outgrowing normal psychopathology in time to stop ourselves from killing nature.

And yet, a number of feminists are very involved with the ecology and peace movements.

Those are the feminists I identify with.

How did psychoanalysis influence your work?

Psychoanalysis has deeply affected my perception of the way people use gender. But I drew upon psychoanalytic thought as an amateur, in an unsystematic way. For example, I was influenced by some central features of Melanie Klein's point of view, while finding other parts of it absurd. And I was influenced by my own analysis with somebody I would describe as eclectic.

Of course I read some of the feminist criticisms of Freud. But I found them aridly polemical. Even when accurate, they seemed to me a waste of energy. To be iconoclastic toward the classic figures feels to me childish. I don't like polemic, anyway. I am appalled to see it developing among feminists. The way women have traditionally talked—putting their points of view together gently, to make consensus, instead of confronting each other head on, each side trying to be invulnerable—has always seemed to me an expression of female strength. As they enter the public ideological realm women are under pressure to adopt male language, which has been the prevailing language until now. But I do think that we're working on a language of our own which is less warlike, more open. Sarah Ruddick and Carol Gilligan, for instance, explore the ways in which women have learned to communicate as a result of their traditional nurturant responsibilities: listening to what the other person has to say and framing what they have to say in terms that would make as much sense as possible to the other. I think this is an immeasurably useful human skill.

Did you ever think about being an analyst yourself?
No, I didn't.

Why not? Sounds like you'd be a good one.
I treasure my amateur status in interaction with others. I like to feel that I don't know exactly what's happening between me and the other person and that it's not my responsibility really to understand it.

You said you were indebted to psychoanalysis for your theory and yet your theory about gender arrangements really is quite dazzling. And we were wondering how you came to it.
Melanie Klein's book *Envy and Gratitude* helped me think. It emphasized the enormous importance of the pre-Oedipal period. Then, examining my own experience, in psychoanalysis, I got a deep personal sense of what kind of figure the early mother is. And how the father is then used in the effort to come to terms with the problems of the first relation, which is essentially dyadic. You begin in a couple with your mother. Then after a while it becomes a triangle with your father.

I loved my father and I loved my little brother. I love men. I cannot see them as these terrible oppressors that most feminists have described them as being. I don't think that men are the cause of the suffering of women. I think we suffer together. And certainly, if I were born again, I would prefer to be born again a woman. I think it's a much more fortunate fate. The possibility of real androgyny is much more available for a woman under traditional conditions than for a man: as a woman you identify with the earliest person that you encounter, who treats you as an extension of herself, a "little me." And so there's that base in human solidarity. As a boy, you're immediately different from the first parent; that parent sees you as someone excitingly strange. But when you're a new baby what you need is continuity.

Is a reason for some people's antipathy toward feminism the result of associating it with militance, with being antimale?

Probably. But that's a shallow basis for antipathy. I think that a certain amount of militance is necessary. You can't change existing arrangements without fighting against entrenched interests. Men fight hard to maintain their privileges. Although these privileges are not good for them, they don't know that. So while we may feel that they shouldn't be fighting, they understandably feel that they should. There *is* something ugly about traditional man, but also about traditional woman. It's a distortion of the animal to be organized around gender in the way we are: the way we walk and the way we dress! Both sexes! And so I can't say that I've always been affectionate, loving, or forgiving toward men: I am angered by the ugly way that they fight to maintain what they think is valuable privilege. But they are our brothers, and they are in at least as much trouble—I think *more* trouble—than we are.

French analysts tend to describe the pre-Oedipal mother in two major ways: either as the dangerous, primitive mother who threatens to engulf us or else as a more structured phallic mother that seems less forbidding. You don't say very much about the phallic mother, and we were wondering if you consider it a myth that exists less in experience than in theory.

The child can perceive the mother as dangerous and overwhelming, but that means that the child fears being engulfed, not that the mother wants to engulf the child. It can simply be that the mother is the biggest reality. (I remember dreams of mine that certainly revealed a fear of being buried in the mother.) It's such an *enterprise* to become a separate creature: one fears doing it, and fears that one can't do it, that one will drown.

I can't connect with the nature of a phallic mother. My experience was very matter of fact about the way boys are different from girls. They had this little thing hanging there that didn't seem to me like anything special. I understood that you could pee standing up with this thing, and that seemed very nice. But on the other hand, a girl's body seemed nicer to me because it didn't have these dangling parts. I thought I was the only really nice looking person in the family because my brother and my father had these dangling pee-pees and my mother had these dangling breasts, and I had just a perfectly compact symmetrical body. And I'm sure many girls feel like that.

Why is the phallus so central in traditional symbolic systems? You do say something about this in *Mermaid*.

What I said is that it seems those systems are male-created. Certainly his penis is very important to a man. It's a delicate and vulnerable and feeling part of the body. Of course he'd treasure it, be concerned about it. It's a water toy, to begin with. I can see that it matters a lot to men that they have it. But I don't believe that it is such a grief necessarily to women *not* to have it, unless they very early connect it with privilege.

Do you think that we could replace this phallocentric symbolization with another kind of symbolization, and what might it be?

There is an Italian expression that people use for girls, meaning "little purse." Very early a little girl is lovingly informed that she is a container for something wonderful. That's an example of how girls' bodies can be celebrated.

Do you think we should make a deliberate attempt to do so?

Probably it will happen spontaneously as the relations between the genders change. It is more true in some cultures than others that generative powers in women are celebrated from the beginning. My grandmother used to call me "mamala," little mother. Reconstructionist Jews are creating ways now to celebrate crucial times in the girl's development the way crucial times in boys' development are celebrated, so a ritual for solemnizing the first menstruation is one of the things that has been worked on. To the extent that rituals are necessary, we need more of them for solemnizing the passages in a female life. In general, we need more emphasis on the peculiar resources that women have all along contributed to the human situation. Are you familiar with Sarah Ruddick's work? And Carol Gilligan's? And Nancy Chodorow's?

We want to ask you how you place yourself in relation to other writers, particularly Nancy Chodorow.

She arrived at many of the same conclusions that I did. I think the big difference between us is that she was more interested in the way the family structure reproduces itself than I am. And I was more interested in the implications for normal psychopathology: for assaults on nature; for the perpetuation of exploitative and coercive economic and political forms, and how those are held in place by our uses of gender; and in what makes people willing to destroy the Earth. Our biggest love should be the natural realm in which we evolved.

Does the Earth symbolize the mother?

The Earth is also our father. It's our parent.

You have a utopian view in *Mermaid* that is beyond technology. But is it ever possible to use technology for positive ends?

I tried to look beyond mass, centralized, cancerous technology. There's no such thing as humanness without technology (which simply means humanly created and transmitted—and therefore reworkable—language, tools, and social forms). I argued for a planned, world-cherishing technology. When you're working on a small scale, you're aware of the consequences of any change you make in the natural environment. If there's an empty space in your garden, you won't plant a tree without thinking about other plants being killed by the shade that tree casts.

Technological change is now much, much too rapid and reckless. But that we should create to some degree the environment in which we live is inevitable because that seems to be how our bodies evolved. Without the creation of tools we wouldn't be on our hind legs and walking; we wouldn't have these brains. Even our self-creation as a species, at our beginnings, might be described as reckless. But since we were forming ourselves so very slowly, there was no way we could know that we were doing so. By now, though, our situation is that we're doing it horribly fast! We *must* learn to consider consequences before taking steps that could further alter the natural surroundings and further threaten the integrity of the Earth's life-web. Now that we're so powerful we have to be very careful. This doesn't mean we should not do *anything;* it means that we should be aware of our power, and take responsibility for what we do.

Isn't there a danger in your way of thinking about evolution? Might not people on the other side say, "Well, we have these gender arrangements and they have obviously affected the differences in the two sexes." Couldn't the other side argue that because women were perhaps prevented from exercising their brains as much as men that therefore they developed in the evolutionary scheme as inferior to men?

The evidence of what women can do contradicts that. In most of human history, we haven't been able to afford idle women. Women do all sorts of work, under most human conditions, that require intelligence, initiative, ingenuity, strength. Think of the creative economic responsibilities women have carried in the earliest human groups, hunting and gathering people: they garden, forage, and fish; they weave, they make fishnets, they make clay pots. I see no reason at all to assume that women weren't just as active in the invention of tools as men.

Before you were talking about women's different style in solving problems, of their having a different kind of lan-

guage, of being less confrontative. One question that concerns us as critics of literature is how this difference can affect the reading of literature, the criticism of literature, and also, the writing of literature. Should men and women cultivate different styles? The French have a concept of an *écriture féminine,* that is, a feminine style of writing. They don't distinguish between the terms *female* and *feminine,* which gives rise to certain problems for us. But many of them do say that because women's experience of the body is so different from men's, this would of course affect the way they write, and they feel that these differences should be cultivated purposely. In contrast, in this country, there is a tendency to want to eliminate those differences and to say women can do whatever men can do.

Why not just let it go the way it wants to?

Pluralism, variety. Is that what you are saying?

What I am saying is that if living in a female body will in itself, quite apart from social arrangements, affect the way a person speaks and thinks, then let it happen. Don't force it on a person. What's been happening so far is that it has been forced on us. We've been *taught* to speak differently, think differently. For instance, we are depended upon to use certain intuitive capacities that I believe men also have, but are not encouraged to develop. We are freer than men are, for instance, to say, "My feeling about this is"—that is, to integrate feeling, quite consciously, with thought. Maybe men, if allowed to, could do it as well as we can. And certainly we can think logically, in a linear way, as well as men can.

I think it's too soon to say that men and women have characteristic styles of thought and self-expression that stem from their bodily structure or neural endowment, because we haven't yet liberated the bodily structure or neural endowment from a whole set of conventions and social rules that limit what men can do and what women can do.

But I think our conclusions can be very different depending on whether we start with the assumption that men and

women, women and men, can feel the same way, think the same way, or if we start with the assumption, as some of the French do, that there are differences and why avoid them? Let's cultivate them.

It's too soon to cultivate them because we don't know yet that they inevitably exist.

Their argument is that women's bodies are much more dependent on cycles than are men's bodies and therefore this is going to affect the rhythm of language, the style of language, the imagery.

Let it, let it! If it will, it will. But right now, there are constraints. We don't know what will happen if people are really free. And these preconceptions about what kind of thinking a certain kind of body can do are forms of coercion. I don't like them.

What's ironic is that some feminists seem to be falling into the same form of thinking as the very men that have been attacked by other feminists. For example, Erik Erikson has been attacked for his concept of women's inner space. But psychologist Donna Bassin feels that internal imagery is very important in women's poetry.

If it's description, that's fine. If it's prescription, it's dangerous.

You make a very interesting point in *Mermaid* about wanting to magicalize the male body. This is very different from the most pervasive feminist position, which is antimythology. Many feminists denounce the mythological treatment of the female body. But you're saying, "Let's treat both sexes in this animal poetic way."

I was writing out of my own experience. I didn't think of it as a great intellectual point. I was saying that it's possible to experience the male body as a magical thing.

It's a very important point. So many studies have spoken about the deemphasis of the male body in the female perspective, for example, those of John Money and Anka Erhardt. French psychoanalysts talk more about the impor-

tance of touch and closeness for women and have much less emphasis on the visual, but you're willing to accept the visual as well as the tactile as being important.

Well, it's true that women's proximity senses seem more developed and are more prominent in sex: smell, touch. It could be because of the particular experience that they have at the beginning, of being held by members of their own gender and being expected to take on this nurturing relation to other bodies. My guess is men would develop some of these proximity sensitivities also if allowed to do so.

I think the deemphasis of the visual for women also has to do with the male fear of being compared. If there is penis envy, it probably exists more among men than among women. Men fear being looked at and being found wanting. There is a certain defensiveness on their part.

You mean that it's hard for men to be evaluated by women as animals. But it seems as if men can overcome that in a homosexual encounter. When they have an opportunity to be appreciated as creatures by other men, they certainly rise to it. So why shouldn't they rise to it when they are appreciated by women?

Do you think that homosexuality is abnormal?

In fact, what I said in *Mermaid* is that conventional *hetero*sexual arrangements are pathological and reflect the presence of distorting conditions in childhood. I was trying to describe our present heterosexual arrangements as a sickness.

But is heterosexuality a sickness?

We don't really know what "normal" sexuality would be like under less distorting conditions. I assume it would include a lot of homosexuality, since feeling an attraction to other bodies and knowing that we can use this feeling for purposes quite apart from reproduction, we're likely, if socially and emotionally unconstricted, to do so. It seems to me that what's perverse is excluding homosexuality and other variations of the erotic impulse.

What other variations?

The only one that I can think of offhand that I would say is wrong, is the seduction of children. Because they're helpless. And that difference in power between people seems to be ineradicable: I don't know how you can make a world in which children would be as powerful as adults. You have to protect the weak. But except for that, I think anything whatsoever that people want to do with their bodies that's mutually enjoyable is all right.

What about animals?

What's the matter with animals?

If you're talking about protection, can we be sure that the animals would choose to be partners of humans?

I agree that coercive behavior to animals is wrong. But you can tell when an animal consents. Even if you're just stroking your cat, you know when the cat has to be held forcibly and when it comes over to you wanting to be stroked.

You speak of our current heterosexual arrangements as a sickness. We have some questions about the implications of your theory of new gender arrangements. For example, if children were reared equally by fathers and mothers, wouldn't there be a great ambivalence toward both sexes — double problems?

This reminds me of a talk I was invited to give to some traditional psychoanalysts. One impressive old man thundered at me, "What you're suggesting means that there wouldn't be a mother and a father. There would be two mothers. Where would the father be?" And what he meant was, who would rescue the child from the mother? And who would be the refuge from the mother?

Well, how did you answer that?

I don't think that a mother should be a person from whom we need a refuge. After all, the mother is a human being; it's the child who sees her as this teaming wilderness of semihuman qualities. This is something we have to outgrow. And with the father there to represent benign, clean humanity, it hasn't been necessary for us to outgrow it. Without the father there in that capacity—with all the adults around being people toward whom we have these complex, magical feelings—we'll be forced to learn what the truth is: that that other person who was taking care of us when we were young is just like us. That we too are mysterious, irrational, teeming with contradictions; that every human being is; that there is one part of every human being with which you can reliably communicate and another part which is a wilderness.

Isn't there a danger that equal parenting would increase patriarchal power? Traditionally, one of women's only powers has been the power over the children, not that this is a power that we want to perpetuate, but wouldn't this change in gender arrangements, under less than ideal conditions, give more power to the patriarchy?

What you're saying is that during the period of transition the weaker party can't afford to give up any of the power that it has until other aspects of the power relations begin to change. I agree. So it's a problem of transition. While men have this enormous economic and social and sexual power, it is important for women to hold on to the power they do have. I don't know what to say about this except that it has to be kept in mind.

What about the problem of the double standard of aging?

The fascination of an older person has to do with that person's authority, worldly power, wisdom: maturity in every sense. And older women can have that appeal for younger men, too. The problem is that economic and worldly power and sophistication are more likely, under present conditions, to reside in the older male than in the older female. Many women have nothing that men want except the transitory charm of youth. But that charm is also transitory in men. For many purposes, an aging woman would choose a young man if she could: for example, women's sexual prowess tends to last longer than men's. A young woman who turns to an older man is often making a big sexual sacrifice. This is another one of these transition questions.

Another question about the implications of changing gender arrangements. Doesn't our bondage to our mothers stem
less from the fact that they have reared us than the fact that
they have carried us, as Julia Kristeva says? Should we ever
come to this system of equal child rearing, wouldn't the
resentments still remain because of the fact that it is the
mother's body in which we resided to begin with? The
mother is still going to have much more power over the
imagination than the father.

You also emphasize the importance of breastfeeding. Well,
unless we inject men hormonally, they're not going to be
able to breastfeed, and wouldn't that, too, give the mother
much more power than the father?

That question is in the same category as the question of how can
women ever be men's equal in social and worldly power when
they're physically smaller and weaker on the average: even if we
develop our muscular abilities more than we do now, we still
won't compete with men in bodily strength. So how can we carry
equal worldly authority? It's the same question that you're asking
about how men can carry parental significance when their bodies
are incapable of containing a child.

I think it's a matter of compensatory impulses. I had a calendar
picture on my wall for a long time—it finally crumbled up—of a
man holding a baby: the baby was feeling the hair on the man's
chest, and the man was smelling the baby's head. And it was as if
that man was yearning toward that child in a very special way
exactly because he couldn't feed it from his breasts and because it
hadn't come out of his body. There was a kind of longing across
physical distance. And the baby was finding what there was in
the male body that it could connect with, the hair on the chest. If
it weren't hair, it would be something else. The size of the male,
for instance, gives him a parental quality. Maybe if men were
more involved in early child care, then it would be the boy who
is the "little me" to the father and the girl who is this fascinating
little different person as the boy now is to the mother. We women
haven't really had that experience of being handled as infants by a
person of different gender who makes a passionate effort to bridge

the gender difference. These are two different forms of love of the baby.

What do you think of the possibility—and it probably will come to pass in the near future—of reproduction ex utero? Now this started out as a utopian or dystopian fantasy, depending on who was writing the book. Marge Piercy, for example, writes about it in a positive way and Huxley, of course, writes about it in a negative way. But wouldn't taking reproduction out of the body be a means of achieving equality between the sexes?

I don't think we need that kind of equality between the sexes. I think we should enjoy the bodies that we have. There's nothing about the bodies that we have that makes it impossible for us to be each other's friends. And there are so many other differences among people that we overcome. When I think of how extremely different some of my women friends are from me even though they have the same sexual equipment, I realize that they are much more different than some of my men friends. But that's what makes life interesting. So I don't see that difference between man and woman is a fact to be obliterated. I think it's a fact to be enjoyed like all the other wonderful differences among people, like the differences between adults and children, for example.

As for reproduction ex utero, it seems to me unnecessary and disrespectful of the body. I agree with you that it could very well happen. But it's one of the nightmare possibilities that make me glad I'm getting older.

I also think the biggest question about the future is whether there will be any. And we haven't talked about that at all. But that's been in a sense the main thing on my mind since Hiroshima days. What's most important about our gender arrangements is that they are a part of a craziness that's killing the Earth. If we could start to stop killing the Earth, that would in itself be a mobilization of concern for life. There would be a new atmosphere of generosity, courage, life-affirmation, wholly unlike the atmosphere we're now living in.

Well, do you see hope for homo sapiens or not? Do you think we will be able to effect a change that will save the world?

I don't know. I hope we will, and I think that if we do, it would be largely through the ethics that peace feminists embody. If even 20 percent of the world's women mobilized their female concern —and I say "female" because traditionally women are for the continuation of life—then through some kind of strike, sabotage, or unified action we could stop the economic system until, to begin with, disarmament agreements were arrived at, and then feasible plans for reversing our policy toward nature. Because there are *two* things we humans are doing: we're killing nature just through cancerous economic development and we're threatening to wipe it out suddenly through atomic war. And if women used one-fifth of their collective power, they could stop that. *And I'm not interested in a feminism in which this is not a central concern.*

Well, why isn't there a sufficient number?

That's what I'm writing about now: the deployment of mental energy and how it comes about that so little of it goes into this project of keeping life alive. Don't you sometimes have a feeling that, as Freud said, the whole thing is more trouble than it's worth? I think that's a feeling that we all have, and we never really test it out to see what its relative force is compared with our love for things. It's like the way we hate our parents. Do we hate them more than we love them? How do we know as long as all we're feeling, when we're angry, is our hate? And it's that way now with the life of the world itself. People have this feeling that they'd just as soon let the whole thing go to hell, and they never really bring it face to face with that other feeling, their wish for everything to go on, for the children, plants, and animals to flourish. There's a split in human sensibility, between hatred and eros, that doesn't get resolved.

We would like to ask you about the masquerade in adult life that both men and women participate in. What would life without masks be like?

I think that men and women collaborate to keep this destructive process going, and since women feel that men are in charge, they criticize them harmlessly, ineffectually. And men go on. I do think that the most important thing about contemporary feminism is the possibility that women, who have less of a stake in worldly success because they happen to be excluded from that success to a large degree, would mobilize themselves for peace and the preservation of the Earth.

I don't see much hope that men by themselves will ever take an effective peace initiative. So the massive nonviolent resistance that seems needed, now, will have to be initiated by women. I think that the only hope we have is in the unpredictability of Eros: the insurgent human impulse to nurture and celebrate life.

Freud was really trying at the end to provide a social philosophy that would take psychoanalytic thought to a general historical level. He was talking about normal psychopathology and how it manifested itself in history. Not the kind of trouble that people take to shrinks but the kind of trouble that makes them organize politics, business, and science in the way they do—that kind of pathology. I respect Norman Brown because he, like Freud, was writing out of a psychoanalytic perspective on history, writing in the hope that if the historical process becomes more self-insightful it will outgrow its malignancy. *I'm not interested in a feminist approach, or in a psychoanalytic approach, that is not focused, now, upon keeping earthly life alive. These three are inseparable concerns.*

Jessica Benjamin is a psychoanalyst, practicing in New York City. Before becoming an analyst, she studied social theory in Frankfurt and at New York University, where she received her Ph.D. She has been writing about feminism, psychoanalysis, and social theory for several years and is a fellow of the New York Institute for the Humanities.

SELECTED BIBLIOGRAPHY

The Bonds of Love. New York: Pantheon, 1988.

SIXTEEN

Jessica Benjamin

Upper Montclair, New Jersey, Winter 1987

Donna Bassin and Jessica Benjamin are young analysts who practice in New York City and live in New Jersey. It was a freezing
day in midwinter when we set out on icy roads in a little car to
interview them in Benjamin's house. Their two young sons were
there (Bassin also had a baby son at home in her husband's care),
but soon they went off with Benjamin's husband to do some
serious sledding while we sat ensconced in the sun-drenched study,
drinking coffee and eating cake. The interviews which follow
were originally part of a single interview and should be understood as in some way connected to each other. (Bassin and Benjamin often engage in fruitful theoretical exchanges.) However,
since much of Bassin's material didn't record well on the tape, she

rewrote part of it. We then decided that the two versions read very well separately.

Would you tell us why you became an analyst?

Well, actually, I think that I became a psychoanalyst because I wanted to try in some way to bridge the gap between personal life and political life. As I came to feminist consciousness, which was in the late sixties, my last year of college, I simultaneously came to my interest in psychoanalysis. When I discovered psychoanalysis, first as an intellectual theory, it appeared as a great "solution" to a problem I had not yet been able to articulate, the bridge that I had been looking for. Of course, I was discovering psychoanalysis not simply through Freud but through Marcuse and N. O. Brown. When I read *Eros and Civilization*, it was as if a big light went on and I said to myself, this is what I want to know about.

Now, it didn't occur to me at first to become a psychoanalyst. My first experience with psychoanalysis—a classical analysis which ended in an open fight over feminism and penis envy—was, if anything, discouraging. And I also was discouraged by the professional organizations of psychoanalysis and of psychology; at that point, given my radicalism, I didn't really see how I could study medicine or psychology.

So, in fact, I ended up studying social theory and writing my dissertation about psychoanalysis. But it was only during that period when I finally was in analysis with someone else that I gained a trust in the psychoanalytic process. Then I began to feel strongly that I was so engaged in the process that I wanted to understand it from the inside, and that psychoanalysis as a way of helping people to deal with the deepest levels of feeling was as important to me as psychoanalysis as an intellectual tradition.

At that point, having my Ph.D. in sociology and social theory, I decided to go back and get clinical training, which I did. While that obviously very much changed my posture toward psychoanalysis, my own analysis had already done so. It had already made me feel that there was this enormous gap between psychoanalysis as an intellectual theory and psychoanalysis as a clinical practice.

That doesn't mean that I repudiate the theory in favor of practice, because there are times when I feel that the clinical perspective is too narrow and blocks the kind of criticism and questioning we need—this is especially so in American psychoanalysis. But on the other hand, the clinical experience of knowing and being and interacting with other people and sharing these very deep and inaccessible experiences can't be confused with or equated with the conceptional study that takes place around the psychoanalysis in other fields—e.g., in literature or philosophy. I am very happy that I have the opportunity to do both, and to live with the disjunctions between them.

For most of us, our theoretical work derives not only from our analytic practice but also our own self-exploration. That is a continual source that feeds all the other streams and as feminist psychoanalysts I think we've been able to keep sight of that. Most of us, in our peer group, became analysts after having our own analysis. None of us said to ourselves, well, we're going to go to medical school to become psychoanalysts and help all those sick people out there.

Do you have reservations about the term *feminism* **the way certain French analysts do? How do you define it? How do you think that feminism has affected psychoanalysis, and how has psychoanalysis affected feminism? Is there a feminist psychoanalysis? What would it be like if there isn't?**

I have no problems whatsoever with the term *feminism*. I am not particularly affiliated with the philosophical perspective that has problems with the term. I have to say that for me feminism is a revolutionary and wonderful idea that we are seldom able to grasp in its entirety. In fact, the attempt to grasp it in its entirety is probably even dangerous in the sense that to try to fill up a utopian idea like that leads to its reduction. It leads to a tendency to universalize, to devalue and deny specific concrete historical experiences and contradictions. For example, feminism as a great idea can become filled up with the content that only women are the bearers of some historical truths, just as people once thought that the proletariat was bearer of the struggle for a just society.

Nonetheless, I see in feminism some of the force contained in other historical ideas, like class struggle, because it aspires to change the most fundamental social relation that we know, that between a man and a woman. For me one of the great values of psychoanalysis is to come to terms with feminism in a much more critical way, so as to be able—without denying the full force of this great idea—to be very wary of political moralism, the dangers of idealism.

For me, psychoanalysis is a way of coming to terms with that whole Jacobin, Bolshevist tradition of authoritarian idealism which persists in radical feminism in many ways and undermines the very ideals that we stand for.

We might also ask what feminism can do for psychoanalysis. I don't want to make it seem that psychoanalysis is the holy thing, the cure for all ills. Nor is there, in my view, such a thing as feminist psychoanalysis. I don't think that feminist psychoanalysis as a practice is intrinsically different from psychoanalysis. There are many versions of psychoanalysis. I don't think feminism is necessarily allied with a certain set of practices the way the people who claim that there is such a thing as feminist therapy suggest.

I do think there is such a thing as feminist psychoanalytic theory, that is, there is a way of reconstructing the psychoanalytic theory of gender and the psychoanalytic theory of sexuality that takes a feminist standpoint, which is different from the traditional Freudian or even some of the modified Freudian standpoints. And I think that's the task we are really concerned with and that's where we are sort of stuck, because we don't—in America—have very much impact on psychoanalysis as feminists. You know, compared to the impact of feminism in the academic disciplines, that in psychoanalysis has been very small.

My deepest pessimism is about whether within the field of psychoanalysis we're going to have an opportunity to effect some kind of transformation or whether instead the larger body of psychoanalysis is going to sail on, oblivious. And that would lead to missing a really great opportunity.

Why do you think there's so much resistance, considering that psychoanalysis as a discipline was receptive to women from the beginning, more so than any other field?

Psychoanalysis is always talking about what's good for the infant; but what about the mother's needs? What if the mother doesn't feel like doing all these things that psychoanalysis says are good for the infant? Perhaps a normal mother, what we would consider a healthy mother, wouldn't always feel like doing them.

The antagonism to feminism has a number of roots. I think on the one hand it reflects an infantocentric point of view, that psychoanalysts really still want mother locked up and being there for the child in the way that Dinnerstein talks about in *The Mermaid and the Minotaur*. And I think the other side of it is that there is this tremendous idealization of the father. Recently when Chasseguet-Smirgel was here, she gave this talk that said, outright, all the things that are stated only implicitly in her other papers. How it's the paternal law that brings the child to the truth, to the reality principle; that it was Freud's reconciliation with his father that really made him understand that you have to take responsibility for your own drives and for knowing the truth; and only by forgiving the father can we (unlike the Nazis) take responsibility for our murderous aggression. So it's really the father that saves us.

I said to her that it seemed to me that this was an extremely one-sided viewpoint, that only the father brings the child to the reality principle. What about all the child rearing that the mother does, in which she really is socializing the child? Why is the theory set up so that we have this "progressive" Oedipal father saving the child from this very archaic, pre-Oedipal, primitive mother? And so then she said, well, of course, I am not talking about reality, I am just talking about the unconscious with its image of the archaic mother.

Afterwards, Donna Bassin and I asked ourselves why she juxtaposes this highly structured Oedipal father with this very archaic pre-Oedipal mother? Where is the archaic father, on the one hand, and where is the highly structured Oedipal mother on the other hand?

She is juxtaposing two ego states that are really quite different; it's really the idea that there is a historic battle within the child between the two ego states, the pre-Oedipal ego state and the Oedipal one. And in her view, the Oedipal ego state is exclusively associated with the father and the pre-Oedipal with the mother. I think her reading reveals the underlying thought structure of psychoanalysis which is normally left implicit.

I think this structure was there in Freud, it's there in Juliet Mitchell's writings, it's there for all these people who claim that the father is going to spring the child from the dyadic trap. Therefore this idealized father has to be protected. He's all that stands between us and barbarism. That viewpoint, as Dinnerstein points out too, is a really deep belief. It permeates psychoanalytic thought so that when you challenge the idealized father, you really see irrationality.

When you point out that the Oedipal father does not recognize the mother and does not teach his son to recognize the mother, that is experienced as the gravest attack on "reality."

What is the psychoanalytic explanation for this privileging of the Oedipal father, do you think?

The problem that we're trying to understand is either why the father is idealized the way he is, or why the mother is feared in the way she is. And what is difficult is to actually capture the interaction between those two things.

I sometimes think that everything has been said that can be said right now about why the mother is feared. I'm not sure everything has been said about why the father is idealized. I mean, American psychoanalytic feminists have done a good job of talking about why the mother is feared. It may require more work to understand this whole process of idealization and why it takes such a hold in people's minds; why people love things that are destructive and so on.

You know, from the daughter's point of view, the father is a much more regressive figure; he is a pull toward the incestuous relationship. I think that we, as women analysts, will not find out as much about this as do male analysts with their women patients. A male analyst and female patient can constitute a regressive father-daughter relationship in which a kind of active mother becomes the principle of separation. I think that's many women's experience; in fact that's the experience of feminism. Regressive relationships with men involve too much primary fusion and identity loss, which women friends and feminism help us to grow out of.

And I can think of a situation in particular where a woman forming a very—I don't actually use the word *regressive* in a negative sense generally, but I will have to for lack of a better word—infantile, regressive sexual relationship with a man finds it both deeply satisfying and at the same time incapacitating, preventing her from assuming an active stand in that relationship. Even though the woman is very active and successful in the outside world, the relationship with the man is regressive (with both its satisfactions and its debilitating aspects). What happens, I suspect, in the traditional consulting room, is that such a relationship gets analyzed as a repetition of her early relationship to her *mother*. It's because of this sequential thinking, in which the mother is identified with regression.

But that sequence is not what is happening in the unconscious, in which everything gets mixed up, so an incestuous attachment to the father which occurs later than the mother-child bond will change the whole integration of earlier experience. It sort of "grabs up" all the earlier stuff.

Can you suggest an alternative symbolism to the phallocentric to represent women's sexuality and experience?

Representation is not the thing itself. You could have a whole series of mental structures that represent the same thing. In my view, the symbolic level of representation is always, shall we say, further away from the concrete experience than the nonsymbolic or the presymbolic, and my experience with infants and my own child's infancy really confirms this. We can postulate a presymbolic way of representing the world and remembering things, which is what American infancy researchers think.

As I see it, the presymbolic is not simply the negative or the flip side of the symbolic. It's just different. In symbolic representation there is this purely intrapsychic phenomenon, and when you're on this level of intrapsychic symbolic representation, you don't care that much about what really happens. That's why you have all these people who say things like, it doesn't really matter whether the father seduced the daughter. Of course, that freedom to not care about reality has been very important for allowing symbolic representation to emerge in the analytic process. Without that kind of freedom that was given by Freud's writings about psychoanalysis, people would not produce symbolic representations in the analytic work, and they wouldn't have the freedom to create things that didn't happen in order to convey the truth of what did or might have happened and which they *felt* happened.

But there is a level where it matters very much what happened, at least to the extent that you can discern it. For example, it can really make a difference when the person in analysis goes back and finds out something about what happened at a certain time. Then the whole thing just completely falls into place, and there's no way they could have found that out without the reality. Masud Khan, for example, tells about a woman going back and finding out about a car crash with her parents, and linking it to a recurrent fantasy.

It can be very important at certain moments for someone to know what the analyst really thought, or to gain contact with the reality of the analyst's attitude toward them. That doesn't mean that they need to know exactly what you were thinking, but there can be moments when it really is useful and does not cut off the person's freedom to find out what was really going on in a given interaction.

Now, orthodox psychoanalysis has constructed this as an either/ or situation. Either you believe in reality, like the interpersonal people do, or you believe in understanding mental representation. The interpersonal thinkers have done interesting infancy research because they are looking at what really goes on between mothers and infants, while the really interesting symbolic theory has been produced by the orthodox psychoanalysts.

In my view, there is no reason for these to be mutually exclusive perspectives, if we understand that they are at times disjunctive and at other times can alternate or work together. We have to understand the difference between the two approaches, but we do not have to choose. And that's why we can take a critical stance toward the father's seduction and at the same time treat it purely as a mental representation that we play with. But when someone is too hurt or paralyzed by an event, she can't represent it.

In any case the whole issue of juxtaposing mental representation of the symbolic kind versus mental representation of concrete reality is very important.

Might heterosexuality be the arena where different symbolic systems encounter each other?

If we think of the inner space as being in fact an intersubjective space, as Bassin suggests, that includes the space between the self and the other, then what happens in sexuality is a coming together of the two sorts of different modes, the intersubjective and the symbolic. The real freedom of the symbolic, for example, the sharing of the phallus, or other kinds of symbolic play going on in sex, is only possible in the context where the continuity between self and other breaks down the rigid conception of who has the inner space, who has the phallus, who has what. Creating this kind of continuity between self and other, between the genders, allows a certain liberation of the symbolic dimension, which need not always be caught up in this rigid stuff. There have been many artistic and literary conventions that have tried to explode those definitions. What we are saying is that what allows those definitions to be exploded, to become ethereal or gassy, to take off and float around and change their forms, is this intersubjective connection—with the kind of transitional space two people create.

Many analysts, André Green in particular, have talked about how the analytic situation creates a transitional space. The analyst aims at creating a transitional space so that the person can experience her or himself as being creative, rather than merely transformed by the analyst. This raises the question of how you create that space with different kinds of people, and whether that involves being passive or active, withholding or asserting, in short, questions of analytic technique. How do you create this space in which people's own sense of creativity can emerge, so that they don't feel themselves to be a passive object of the transformation? This may be experienced differently for men and women. Often, for men, the mother is active and the child passive. The reason that men are so afraid of passivity is that their two models are either the child with the active mother/breast or the child with the active father/phallus. They may be afraid of the castrator or of being sodomized or reduced to a passive object. That resistance really makes it very difficult for men to make use of the transitional space, which in turn leads to envy, to denigrating the experience of having inner space.

We wanted to ask you whether you changed your mind about your theory of love in Western culture as presented in your article "The Bonds of Love."
I'm always surprised that people ask me this question about how I account for masochism in men because it seems to me that in my article it's very clear that I'm not saying that women have to be masochistic. I'm saying that there's some reason why femininity is associated with masochism and that Freud himself described male masochism as being feminine.

I argue that the association of femininity with passivity, masculinity with activity, this complementarity that develops in the relationship of domination, arises from the opposition between assertion (or negation) and recognition. The sadist is the one who negates, the masochist is the one who recognizes—whether as an object, being that thing on which the sadist leaves his marks, or as a subject, being the one who responds to his actions, the one who in some way absorbs, contains, or mirrors his power.

In the dyadic relationship of submission, the negating aspect becomes associated with masculinity by virtue of the little boy's negating or disidentifying with the mother, saying, I'm not you, which is what the sadist says. And the female body is associated with the maternal, that which is done to by the male.

But I don't think that means that men can't identify themselves with the object. This identification with being the object who is going to in some way incorporate the power of the other through this passive form of identification, is very frequently the relationship of one man to another.

This relationship may also occur among women. One woman puts another in the place of the mother, the all-controlling and negative mother. For both men and women, domination means restoring life to what it was before the child separated. "You're the negative mother and I'm your passive little baby." The next step is, "I'm not the passive little baby; you are and I'll do unto you." That is where the classic relationship of domination and submission arises, in this second step.

The cultural identification of masculinity with sadism comes from this second step, of reversing the relation to the mother. The culture has moved that primary relationship into the negative of it, the reversal, as in I do to you what you did to me.

That brings us to another question. Don't men idealize women? I think the answer is men idealize women as objects, whereas women idealize men as subjects. Women, when they idealize men, seek a version of the desiring active subject with whom they unite by identification. And this can take two forms: a more slavish form in which the woman simply loves and hopes possibly to appropriate this ideal subject, or a more active form in which now she can be like him, his epigone, his handmaiden.

By contrast, men idealize women as the beautiful but unattainable object. The experience of losing one's sense of self as a desiring subject may also afflict men in relationships of idealization: when the man perceives the woman as this dangerous object of desire, the Siren, who is imbued with the power of desire. When this happens, it's not the man who is feeling desire toward the object, it's the object that is radiating desire. This can be seen as a kind of regression. Originally, the boy moves from the stage where "it is desirable" to "I desire it," according to Ernst Abelin. When the object is perceived as acutely and enticingly desirable, the man can lose his own sense of being the subject of desire pretty much as the woman can lose hers when she feels that the man is this terrifically powerful subject of desire. Yet the man is overwhelmed by an object while the woman is overwhelmed by a subject. The woman, in all past conventions, is never overwhelmed by an object/man. Behind this object/woman, that men find so overwhelmingly desirable, is also a subject/woman that they can't recognize, who might actually be less frightening.

I think he can recognize her if she is very far away. If he puts her up on a pedestal that he can never get to, he can

then see in her all kinds of things that he doesn't have and wants to achieve. When she gets close, forget it.

I have to say, I still think that she is a symbol, not a subject of desire. The desire belongs to the man; he is the subject of it, desiring this wisdom that she has.

If you want to locate where the subject of desire is in a given moment—even when the woman is justice and virtue and the man is yearning for this wonderful ideal, he is experiencing himself as the subject of desire. The other configuration of idealization is where the woman is an acutely desirable object and the man loses his senses to his own desire and has to get away, or he is made passive, he is made impotent, he can't really deal with her desirability.

All of this comes from splitting the self, just as it does when the little girl splits off her subjectivity and as it were gives it to the father. Idealization is an insufficiently understood process of splitting off the subjectivity in the self. And one reason that it is insufficiently understood is because of the psychoanalytic assumption that of course we can't be the other gender.

But what we can be in the most literal and concrete sense is not what psychoanalysis is supposed to be about. It's supposed also to be about what we can be in the more symbolic, metaphoric, and transitional sense. And in that sense we can be the other, and we can be both things. In that more abstract sense the problem is not so different for men and women.

Where things are different is in the cultural outcome. Once children have gone through the Oedipal stage, they become Oedipalized into gender polarity. Once that happens, you see the real difference between male and female idealization. What's striking is that here we are in this "postfeminist" era and with all the impact of feminism—widespread change in the notions of parenting, the tremendous integration of women in the workforce—the sexual objectification of women is more intense than it's ever been.

Sexual objectification is supposed to counteract the fear that is evoked by the more active female subjectivity that has been allowed out in the public world. Women must continually appear to say, "Don't worry, I'm a sex object." They have to be a certain kind of sex object when they go to work, a not too alluring sex object. Objectification figures quite differently in the image of men and women, for example, in advertising. So the classic model for idealization of men and women still falls into this subject-object relationship.

She certainly has to be alluring at night. Maybe not so much in the office, but look at all the fantasy dressing that goes on in the evening.

Yes, as soon as she is back with the man in her life, she's the sex object to him. Where does this leave us in regard to the question of difference? An idea that's very hard for some feminists to accept is that perhaps sexual tension is created through all of the rituals of difference. Sexual tension may be created through the sense of one person having the power and the other person not having the power, or one person having the power of the master-ful subject who can "play" this alluring object.

Many feminists were disturbed by the issue raised by the "sex-ual radicals," which was the argument that sex without power and role play was really boring, that the only way to recreate sexual tension was to play with (if not believe in) power differences in the subject-object relationship.

One response to this was often a moralizing and silly talk about sex and love that took us back to the fifties, the books on what makes a healthy marriage. But the issue itself is genuine—the question is what kind of differentiation or difference can create sexual tension, if it's not the subject-object difference? One criticism of my papers, for example, was "I don't think I'm interested in sexuality that is purified of reparation of trauma, envy of the other sex, desire to be rescued by the power of the other."

As a compromise position, let us say that the issue is what stance you take toward your participation in the cultural, hetero-sexual fantasy, or if not heterosexual, the ubiquitous power rela-tionships. Do you take a stance that is in some sense playful and in some way distinct from the fantasy? I don't know if it really solves our theoretical difficulty.

Going beyond by going through is very different from trying

to skip over and deny something. We cannot avoid being saturated with the fantasies that we are critical of, yet we might find the way to move beyond them, because without working through them, we cannot transcend them.

In psychoanalysis, people begin to have a fantasy, and at first they're very afraid even to enter into the fantasy. They feel overwhelmed by anxiety. They finally allow themselves to go into that fantasy world, to have that fantasy that they didn't feel able to have. Let us say it is a fantasy of submission. The person says, "This fantasy of submission will be annihilating. I will feel myself being annihilated," but she survives. The outcome of having the fantasy is then distinct from the imagined outcome. The analyst is saying you may have your fantasy; your fantasy is a part of you that you may now own. In that way someone else recognizes you as being more than just that fantasy, just as you will be recognized as being more than this bundle of anxiety or grief. The analyst maintains the knowledge that this is not going to be the end of you, contrary to the person's own anxiety that "If I let myself feel this grief or this fear, I'll never come out."

The analyst's presence signifies, "You are not just this." In some way that process is what we're aiming for on the more general level: to be liberating in that sense, to create moments of recognition that this fantasy or feeling exists but it is not the whole truth. We know how to do that and therefore aren't so afraid of things like domination and submission.

How do you account for national differences in the psychoanalytic treatment of gender?

I sometimes wonder if a reason that gender splitting is so intense in certain branches of the French theory is because in that society there is much less of what I would call a nongendered zone, much less of an area in which a person can just experience oneself as the person, not this male or this female, but just as a person. And I think there's really a sizable area in our lives, by comparison, where we just are not thinking of ourselves in terms of gender, as if gender were not symbolizing what we're doing.

Gender segregation is not just a social matter, for example, who's at home and who's working; it has to do with the subject-object aspect that's embodied in the culture, and with the mind-body split, the dominance of the Cartesian tradition. In the An-glo-Saxon world, you have an empirical tradition that tends to abrogate those dichotomies to a certain extent, for example, American interpersonal theory doesn't understand gender very well but does allow for gender equality in its assumption that boys and girls aren't that different.

Donna Bassin has said that "the feminist child is much more a reality child, not a fantasy child."

Yes! Feminist theory sees the child in very concrete terms, not as the phallus or the fantasy, but the child who is desired for itself, as a child with whom one can act out the maternal identification or reparation for failures in that identification. But in any case, that child is closer to reality than a child who is the feces or phallus.

To a certain extent, reality is more flexible in the United States, so therefore we believe in it a little more. That has both its positive and negative side in psychoanalysis. We deal more with the realities of the patient's life, but this may detract from some of the deeper free associative states, certain kinds of regressions; on the other hand, it may contribute to other kinds of regressions in which early emotional states can be relived.

I see a difference between American object-relational tendency and the classic Freudian tendency which I experienced in Ger-many. I think that we have much more affective exchange with our patients, which can limit the deep focus on one's inside that encourages free association, but encourages the felt experience of loss and grief, the emergence of pre-Oedipal issues. The Ameri-can orientation has the same strength as maternal identification theory, the strength of emphasizing the issues of loss and separa-tion.

In Chasseguet-Smirgel's volume on female sexuality, it's the anal mother that is talked about; and this is the mother that she talks about "beating back." I think in American theory the omni-potent mother is much less aggressively tinged. It's a less hostile image, it's less anal, it's less about intrusive control and more around the sense of, my mother ought to be the perfect all-giving, all-understanding person, my mother ought to be the one that accepts all of my aggression. Mother ought to be the one who is always going to be there for me. In France, I suspect, a more radical crystallization of gender structures has led to a much greater consciousness of them. The danger in maternal identification theories is a tendency to think as if women had no hostility, as if all you have to do is to be an empathic analyst.

Here we see two different starting points, each with a different problem. We start with a problem of fantasy of the perfect mother, as Chodorow calls it, whereas French theory starts with the fantasy of the all-engulfing, dangerous, archaic, and then anal mother. It's a view in which only the most extreme side of infancy is even mentioned. When you're actually mothering an infant, you just don't see all that much of that. What you see is an infant who seems truly able to get over a moment of distress and enjoy the moment of satisfaction. The baby who has problems is the baby who is left to cry so long that by the time mother comes she can't suck. That is our notion of pathology. But when all goes well, the few minutes that the baby had to cry before mother came and the baby got the good suck don't seem to be that annihilating. We certainly believe that those moments of distress or loneliness, if they don't persist too long, can be generative moments, whether we think of them in ego psychology terms or in a Winnicottian sense of transitional space that the baby can do something in. Later on, when there is symbolic representation, you get a symbolic condensation of experiences of helplessness, anxiety, and distress. That symbolic condensation goes something like this: I was lying alone in my crib for hours screaming and Mother never came. That fantasy is a symbolic condensation, which an infant is incapable of producing until much later; the problem is that infants who regularly have those experiences don't get to the point where they have symbolic condensations. They don't develop a story line, a narrative that connects present feeling to past experience; instead, they have inchoate experience. They are in that state of terror which is presymbolic and which therefore has no means of communicating and being understood.

So we tend to distinguish more sharply between what really

happened versus the symbolic, but this does not mean that we devalue the symbolic. When symbolic condensations are confused with reality—whether it's this idea of the archaic mother versus the Oedipal father or this idea of the primary helplessness of the infant—it distorts the more complex process of interaction.

Donna Bassin holds a master's in art therapy, a Ph.D. in clinical psychology, and is an advanced psychoanalytic candidate at the Institute of Psychoanalytic Training and Research in New York. She was formerly assistant professor of psychology and art therapy at Pratt Institute and director of art therapy at the State University of New York, Downstate Medical Center. She is now the editor of *PsychCritique: The International Journal of Critical Psychology and Psychoanalysis* and the mother of two sons.

BIBLIOGRAPHICAL NOTE

Dr. Bassin has published articles in the *International Review of Psycho-Analysis, Psychoanalytic Review,* and *Arts Psychotherapy* and is completing a book for Plenum Publishing Corporation on women, communication, and creativity. Also forthcoming is an anthology she is coediting, tentatively entitled *Representations of Motherhood.*

SEVENTEEN

Donna Bassin

Upper Montclair, New Jersey, Winter 1987

Well, first we wanted to ask you why you became an analyst.

In my case, why am I becoming an analyst is more accurate. I am in the process of completing my training at a classical institute. There are many little moments that have contributed to my decision and still reinforce it as I return to them in memories. I am the daughter of a liberal doctor and a traditional family-oriented mother. I spent my childhood under my father's instruction; he loved to teach. I also spent a lot of time in the kitchen with my mother, drawing pictures and trying to figure out how these worlds connected. I see my own life inside out, and my decision to become an analyst, as a series of oscillations from the identifications and counteridentifications with both my parents. In fact, my educational background through premed, sociology, art therapy, and psychology reflect this. So becoming an analyst was a little like finally getting the bath water temperature right in a house with old plumbing—a constant struggle to adjust the hot and cold. At times these adjustments felt like a bobsled ride. I was holding on for dear life, and at other times, more like snowshoeing, where I was just plodding along. Going back and forth between my parents, up the stairs to the bedroom where my mother resided, down the stairs to the basement where my father played with his science toys. Each had permanently installed themselves in a particular location. I was the courier transporting instrumental and expressive information to and fro. I am still doing that with my patients and in my attempt to bring psychoanalysis and feminism together in one room.

The death of my sister as a child was one of those not so little moments that reverberates through many of my activities. The effect of personal survival guilt greatly figured in my gravitation toward a reparative helping profession. Moving on with one's life, despite past pain and loss and in spite of tremendous guilt, was my largest obstacle and one that I see in many forms with the people I work with. The symbolic attempt to restore life, psychic life, through psychoanalysis is transparent in my case. And yet, I constantly feel the need to pay attention to my "healing and raising the dead" fantasies. But what really cemented my choice, and stopped me from bouncing around so much professionally and psychically, was my own analysis. It was there, through my analyst and the analytic environment, nurturing yet nudging, that I was finally able to get up from under all those seductive but dried-up remnants of my past. I found there, in myself, the active mother who lived outside of the bedroom. So that in my identification with my analyst and a desire to share what I learned from her, I began psychoanalytic training in a serious way.

I loved biographies as a child. I read them voraciously. I have always been fascinated by the development of people's life work in relationship to their personal history. I strongly believe in the effect that the personal has on one's own theoretical and professional aspirations. I think here is where feminist theory and psychoanalytic work found their greatest commonality for me. That is, the awareness of how our realities are infused with our own subjectivity. I use this to check my own thinking and I suspect there are many narratives to be found in human development.

Of course, there are also more conscious variables operating in my pursuit of a classic psychoanalytic education. In a recent issue of the *Journal of the American Psychoanalytic Association,* Kernberg argued that psychoanalysis was no longer a scientific theory subject to examination, but a firmly established doctrine, and that psychoanalysis used as an ideological weapon squelches creative thinking and scientific productivity. Now it took a Kernberg, with his hard-won credibility within the system, to say it and to have it accepted for publication in the mainstream psychoanalytic association. I think feminists need to strive for this analytic credibility if we are going to effect changes. I see one of my own goals, and this is very transparent in light of what I said about my personal history, as bringing some of the feminist contributions within the language that the analytic community has accepted and now shares. I say language, but not theory, because until we put out new theoretical alternatives to clinical observation, we will only see what has already been seen. You can't be too outside to be read. Now I know that there is a counterargument that insists we need to stay on the margins to critique; however, this has been problematic. Jessica Benjamin has made the point many times that many of the valuable feminist contributions don't get read or cited in psychoanalytic literature despite the influence they have had. The more radical thought gets filtered, I suppose, and the feminists get appropriated without due recognition. In spite of my ten years plus of clinical experience I am, as are other feminists in the psychoanalytic community, very young professionally from the institutional stance. Perhaps this is unduly optimistic, but I am hopeful that as we mature clinically, we will have more of an impact on the field.

Why do you think there's so much resistance to feminism, considering that psychoanalysis as a discipline was receptive to women from the beginning, more so than any other field?

I think the receptivity to women early in the psychoanalytic movement is an interesting story that needs to be told. However, we can't assume that the presence of women will generate a prowomen mentality. If you read the biographies of Lou Andreas-Salomé, Anna Freud, and Melanie Klein, for example, you realize that these were not your average women. To some degree they all renounced family life. All of them greatly admired Freud and in many ways they nurtured and protected him. I think Freud was quite aware that their contribution was necessary. They served as mother substitutes in the transference and allowed him to flesh out his work. However, none of the women, to my knowledge, received the "golden rings" he gave out. Many of the women around Freud and some men like Jones did attempt to revise his theory of female sexuality. If you go back to some of the early papers of our analytic ancestors, you find subtle attempts to delineate some of the work that is now getting explicitly stated. Ruth Mack Brunswick spoke of the importance of the girl's pre-Oedipal love and identification with the mother, but she did remain loyal to Freud's stress on libido and was careful to pay tribute to his work.

I believe in order to understand psychoanalysis' resistance to feminism we need to take into account the historical threats to psychoanalysis in general. Psychoanalysis had to survive the assimilation into American culture after World War II, the crisis over drug cures in the fifties, the pressure of community mental health in the seventies, and now the feminist critique of some of psychoanalysis' basic assumptions, such as penis envy, the penis-baby equation, the role of motherhood in so-called normal female development, and the inferiority of women's superego. Now certainly, most subgroups get punished in some form for breaking away from the bonds of identification in any culture, and feminism is no exception. It has been difficult enough for psychoanalysis to survive the external threats, let alone the internal dissidents. Those who have drifted too far astray, like Karen Horney, have in fact been excluded from mainstream psychoanalytic membership.

In order to move forward we need to identify the congruence and divergence in the current intellectual landscape and the obstacles in our way. First of all there is a broad range of theoretical positions and praxes within the domain of feminist theory, and I am not sure that psychoanalysis is currently as resistant to some of the developments within feminist theory as it has been. In fact, there are already many critiques in mainstream journals of what Freud admitted was an incomplete picture of female sexuality. I am not saying that this is enough or that we should be satisfied. In fact, some of the work aimed with this critique in mind, in actuality undercuts the direction we need to go in. I have read many articles that suggest, "Yes, we all know that penis envy is overdetermined, that it is a metaphor or a defensive position that has more to do with pathological envy in general, so enough already." This position is debilitating and disarming, because for the most part the original theory remains steadfast in mainstream thought and still has a very tight hold on clinical observations. Theoretical developments are still ahead of clinical behavior. This is true not only for the feminist critique but for other significant areas of change, such as infant research.

Psychoanalysis can only listen to psychoanalytic research, clinical data, or assertions by those in authority who use psychoanalytic constructs to critique the existing theory. I think as feminists we need to strive for this authority within psychoanalysis and to analyze the resistance to feminism, not just ignore it. I believe that psychoanalysis should also ask to what degree can and should feminism and psychoanalysis embrace. Psychoanalysis would argue that it deals with individual consciousness, that it is not a social critique, and that it is not concerned with social cause but social consequence. Of course, this position can become a rationalization to preserve the institution. As is the way of all social movements, the perpetuation of the institution becomes paramount to the goals of the movement.

We have come to the point as feminist psychoanalytic theorists where we must also look at our own contributions to the difficulties we are encountering within institutional psychoanalysis. We can look at the history of the feminist movement for some understanding of the psychoanalytic resistance. I suspect the word "feminist" is now highly charged and therefore is problematic in that way. I recently asked what I perceived as a relatively benign question at a psychoanalytic scientific meeting on fathers and daughters. I received in return a rather defensive response from one of the presenters. Afterwards, a friend, herself a feminist, told me I should have left the word "feminist" out of the question. That word, she said, is like throwing up the red flag.

In the beginning of the women's movement there was a total denigration of Freud's work about female sexuality. This pre-Mitchell reading of Freud, which denied the existence of the unconscious, made it easy and quite appropriate for psychoanalysis to dismiss feminism.

Within psychoanalytic circles, feminism has become equated with an ideological stance of anger and blame. Our individual histories and the development of feminist theory reveal this course. Now, I think, despite the simplicity that any attempted analysis of feminism implies, it is necessary for our own increased self-consciousness.

In my perspective, in the beginning, feminism sought objects of blame. The blame was sometimes levied at our mothers, as victims of patriarchal society, and at our fathers as perpetuators of this unyielding, unsharing authority. I think, as we come of age and have moved out of our positions as daughters, we have become more reflective on our own contribution to our enslavement, that is, more aware of the process of internalization and the idea that what has been transmitted sociologically is now lodged intrapsychically. In the process of separation and differentiation from Mother, in trying to get outside of her, or out from under her, we denied or disavowed her good aspects as well. This defensive separation process was similar to the little boy's defensive repudiation of his mother in his attempt to genderize himself as male. So that feminism, while a bonding of woman against male authority, was also a process of separation from Mother. Although we came together as women, our model for liberation and active striving seemed largely based on some ideal of male machismo.

I think with that consciousness we have now begun to forgive Mother and reclaim her. What settled out of all that was an attempt to take a look at male authority and deidealize it, a necessary step in that it provided the first psychic rupture for men as well as women. It allowed for a celebration of the feminine as the repressed aspect of both man and woman, as well as an investigation into what might constitute a primary femininity. The "writing of the feminine" was an important contribution to reowning lost parts of ourselves. In addition, this celebration led to important contributions, particularly in academic psychology, where Carol Gilligan, Evelyn Fox Keller, and others suggested that there were other ways of knowing, of social reasoning, and of doing science than the traditional patriarchal model. This increased awareness of how psychology had skewed interpretations of data based on male norms has left a significant mark. However, along the way, the suggestions that these ways of women are not only different from men's, but improved, became a new form of the very domination we were originally resisting. This attempt to beat back male power with higher monuments to woman gets easily analyzed in the psychoanalytic tradition. Lampl de Groot in fact argues that this attribute of superiority of radical feminists is built on a reaction formation to unconscious feelings of inferiority, or on residues of penis envy which rationalize social suppression of women's activities. In this very paper, she reminds the reader of her so-called prowomen credentials, stemming from her position in the original thirties debate over Freud's theory of female sexuality. In all fairness to the Lampl de Groots, I think she points to a thorny issue for psychoanalytic feminists. Her position is not uncommon within psychoanalytic circles and needs to be addressed within the theory. Of course, I don't accept her interpretation, which I feel is overreaching and ahistorical. It negates the social justifications for the feminist movement. From my experience in training seminars, I see candidates, particularly female ones, who are reluctant to speak out in favor of a feminist critique, fearful that this behavior will be seen as a form of transferential acting out. In fact, many are not sure that their disagreements with classical theory are not just that. As Kernberg said, and I think Lampl de Groot's interpretation can be seen in this vein, psychoanalysis has all the tools necessary to analyze as pathological all who disagree.

It is a simplistic reduction to explain all feminist disagreements and feminism as a social movement as a masculine protest. That is, our inability to accept a sexual position of passivity and the social ramifications that position implies can only be a function of pathology or refusal to resolve the Oedipal stage properly. The analytic response that the little girl must give up and repress her active striving because she doesn't have an organ of focused penetration elevates the anatomical penis over the entirety of our biology. During some point in my own analysis, when I was searching for the energy to complete some theoretical work, my analyst reminded me of the pleasure I had described in gnawing and nibbling on my crib bars. So here I am years later, still gnawing and chewing away on that which theoretically restrains me. On the other hand, any radical critique that excludes the Oedipal, the cornerstone of psychoanalytic theory, is too far away. It moves the fulcrum of the theory and throws psychoanalysis too much off balance.

I think these early polarized positions have now led to a new stage of thought. Perhaps we are beginning to return to the original goals of the feminist movement—back to a lifting of restriction of gender roles for both men and women. If not, we just continue to polarize gender, and doing so just perpetuates the splitting of male and female in ourselves and in society. I think the feminist critique with the most potential for enlightening psychoanalytic thought at this moment is the challenge to the assumption of the primacy of motherhood as an indication of normal adult development for women. Motherhood has been seen as both the vehicle and symbol that a little girl has become a woman. Psychoanalysis reads motherhood as the culmination of a narcissistic process, that is, as a reparation for a lost phallus. There are many who are now questioning whether motherhood is a necessary step for healthy female development. I suspect, as well, that we will find sufficient clinical evidence that supports the idea that motherhood or maternal desire, as evidenced by maternal desire in some lesbian women, may be a separate developmental line that is not tied to object choice or to narcissistic reparation of the lost penis.

There is one more point I would like to make. I suspect that although I have advocated for subversion within psychoanalysis, staying within the system to change it, it may in fact be necessary for feminist thought to stay outside of psychoanalysis in order to change it. If we see the oppression of women as a cultural illness or neurosis, then a group that stands apart from it has an opportunity to interpret the neurosis much in the same way the analyst stands outside the patient's transference neurosis. Analogously, to stand outside avoids the inevitable danger of cooptation. However, at the same time, it is important that the so-called outside group use a language that can be heard by psychoanalysis. The interpretations of this cultural neurosis may allow for a creation of a group freedom, analogous to the freedom found at the end of a successful analysis.

How do you account for the privileging of the Oedipal father over the mother, whether the pre-Oedipal or Oedipal, in traditional psychoanalytic thought?

The privileging of the Oedipal father is a symbolic configuration that has to do with the psychoanalytic belief in the supremacy of the phallus, not the real father, or the real everyday male. Clinically, I don't think anyone sees the male as more privileged than the female. Men struggle with fears of their expressive inner life, intimacy, feeling empty in spite of their accomplishments, and so on. This is an obvious statement, although, I think, not always remembered. We focus on the social reality of inequality. Freud assumed that penis envy and castration anxiety were bedrock in the psyche. The privileging of the phallus was an absolute given —a preexisting condition of human nature. It was there in the beginning, like God, and it created both men and women—men through their biology and women through their longing and eventual acceptance of the substitute penis, a baby. God, the father, points to our dependency relationship with our parents. The Oedipal father is a fantasy, a symbol of our childhood fears of our parents. He is the giant in our dreams and in our collective dream, the myth. These early stages of thought don't perish but exist side by side with later post-Oedipal developments. We need to acknowledge the pervasive presence of this father in his negative aspects as well. A patient of mine, a black female, had a dream that is relevant to this question. She dreamed that a white businessman was molesting her and preventing her from going home. Her associations to the dream led us both to conclude that the ideals of the white phallic corporate world, which she rejects consciously, are lodged deep inside of her, beating her up and preventing her from moving on. However, there is certainly much more to this Oedipal father than has thus far been theoretically articulated. Jessica Benjamin's latest work makes a significant contribution to understanding other aspects of this father. I think the privileging of the father is, in part, a reflection of a primitive belief in omnipotence that individually and collectively we haven't been able to let go of. As a culture, we haven't reached the point where we can totally reject the stage of thought that Freud called spiritism and resign ourselves to the necessities of nature and death. The Oedipal father, who reflects our idealization of order, control, and rationality and devalues carnality, is a defense against our ultimate hopelessness and helplessness in the face of our inevitable death. We can "pretend" through the privileging of the Oedipal father that we have surpassed the mystery of life and death.

Dorothy Dinnerstein made a similar point in *The Mermaid and the Minotaur*. It's very interesting.

To return from the world to the body, Jessica Benjamin has said that after her little boy took a bath with his girl-friend, he said not that he wanted a vagina, but that he had one. Do you think that there is any validity to the theory of penis envy?

Early in childhood, kids want everything. As Irene Fast has stated, young children are undifferentiated and over inclusive in their gender identity. When they discover the biological sex differences, each sex wants what the other has. It's a loss on the concrete level for both sexes to realize they can't have it both ways. However, a girl wanting a penis at age three doesn't necessarily mean she wants it at the expense of her own biological sex.

Would you tell us something about your paper "Woman's Images of Inner Space," which was published in *The International Journal of Psycho-Analysis*? For example, can the concept of inner space be as exciting a metaphor as that of

phallic activity? How does your theory differ from Erikson's theory of inner space? Isn't your theory another version of anatomy as destiny? Isn't there a danger that it will feed into the old stereotypes of men as active and women as passive?

I think that one of the difficulties some feminist theorists may have with the paper is that it is based on a body ego model. The problem with this model is that it can be read as a version of biological essentialism, thus implying that anatomy is destiny or that there are fixed attributes that limit or define behavior. I think it is a shame that we refrain from looking at woman's biology or anatomy because of the historical use of woman's body as a sign. It seems ironic that the very same theorists who are critical of the patriarchal celebration of the rational mind, to the exclusion of other aspects of the psyche, such as the effect of body representation, are looking to that very aspect, in the form of socialization, for feminism to realize its goals. Women have had few opportunities to utilize their bodies for their own use or to explore their bodies as a wellspring of their unique development. As long as woman's body remains unwritten, it will remain ambiguous and will only inspire desire and attributed meaning. This paper was written in 1981, at a time when I was recapturing my own female identifications and reconstituting my body in a different representation than as a leaky sieve. It was clearly written to the psychoanalytic community with the not-so-implicit request that we need alternative interpretative categories for female development in order to allow for a more concrete and detailed schematization of the representation of the female. I was not familiar with Cixous' work at the time, but my paper does have an affinity with some of the French theorists who were involved in a similar task of writing the feminine.

I suspect also that my choice of the term "inner space" to describe this metaphoric source of woman's subjectivity, and its association with Erikson's model, has been problematic. I meant it much more as a metaphor, an alternative symbolic structure and means of structuring. The Erikson model carries some implication that women should focus on their biological destiny for motherhood, so if we work using the body as a departure point, that means we have to accept that being female biologically means motherhood or maternal ways of being. That position would imply that lesbian behavior is pathological, but that is not at all what I was saying. I said clearly in the paper that this inner space goes beyond maternal reproductive functions. Perhaps I should have said that this inner space may include our symbolic maternal aspects but is in essence much more encompassing that that. I think the term *inner subjectivity* or even *inter-subjectivity* rather than *inner space* might have clarified my intent because ultimately my notion has to do with interaction between self and other.

Getting back to the necessity for exploring alternative ways to organize clinical experience, I can also say that my paper was an attempt to dilute the strength of traditional psychoanalytic interpretative categories of castration anxiety and penis envy. Traditionally, psychoanalytic theory has neglected to illuminate aspects of woman's development outside the assumed sequence of Freud's instinctual Oedipal narrative. The feminist movement has recalled our attention to the fact that this model of compensation is problematic and in fact that the Oedipal is not the big event, but rather one in a series of moments that contribute to our ultimate sexuality and gender identity. Femininity has always been signified as compensation after renunciation of the original masculine orientation. Motherhood as both the symbol and vehicle of mature female development is in essence then a narcissistic construction based on deprivation and loss. This assumption of male morphology or sexual phallic monism has to be deconstructed. Despite the biological evidence that the clitoris is not a male organ and the increased acknowledgment that the little girl is aware of the existence of her vagina, we haven't really illuminated alternative body ego representations that reflect this proactive rather than reactive female self. Within the original reading of female development, we have no symbols or carriers to articulate the origin or pathways of the development of subjectivity and agency other than the penis and phallic representations. The original model only allows for repression of active strivings and therefore provides no opportunity to conceptualize otherwise.

I know that there is a strong sentiment within feminist theory to argue for identification with a strong and active real mother. However, I think there is more to the picture than the girl's selfhood originating through identification, and the concept of the body ego is a powerful one for this exploration. I attempted to argue away from the point that there is one psychobiological course, that of the male. To me that was the cornerstone of the difficulty with a psychoanalytic theory of female development and had to be addressed within the biological model.

In my paper I used the work of some women poets to illustrate the existence of a schemata for relating to self and other, that is, to delineate the existence of particular categories for representing woman's bodily stance and the implications that has for a sense of agency, intentionality, and activity that are not based on lack or deprivation and are not carried through phallic representations. Traditional theory holds us back, for without articulation of possible alternatives, we can see nothing more. I also argued that these images can't only be seen as cultural artifacts, although I do believe that language and cultural images shape our bodily representations. However, in my view, these images originate in the early preverbal period of development in both the Freudian and Piagetian tradition. Piaget argued that the basis for symbolic images emerged in the interaction of external objects with bodily sensations. These schemata then serve as the foundation for how we know and understand self and other. For Freud, the ego in fact is first and foremost a bodily ego, that is, the core of our sense of self is based on our bodies' representation of inner and outer stimuli. It is formed in interaction between the infant's self-touching, sensitivity to inner and outer stimuli, and parental holding. This body ego that I am speaking about is responsible for a sense of boundary integrity which allows for our recognition of self as initiator of actions in the external world. We get to know both the world and ourselves through this mutual interrelationship. This sense of intentionality and instrumentality in turn contributes to the development of an active subjectivity, an interiorized self.

In this frame, penis envy can be viewed in part as a body ego patch for certain women, where the penis is necessary to complete a body ego which has not developed in an optimal manner. I am working on this notion right now. It suggests that there can be problems in body ego formation and that this can be seen as a faulty interaction somewhere between a particular infant and a particular parental environment. These difficulties in body ego formation will affect the separation–individuation process, which in turn will affect the possibility for developing and utilizing transitional phenomena. Within a Winnicottian perspective, transitional phenomena have to do with the way we inscribe culture with our own subjectivity and thus feel able both to create and bond with the things we produce. In other words, without a specific sense of agency, separation–individuation becomes problematic and there is less development of transitional phenomena.

Do men have their own inner space?

Well, again, I think I have to be careful in using the term *inner space,* but nevertheless, yes, men also have the capacities for this deep inner, generative, creative space. For some men, I imagine it comes through early identifications with Mother and the nonrepudiated bodily relationship with her. For both men and women, it can also emerge in a good psychoanalytic treatment. Unfortunately, for some men it is associated with passivity. These aspects of ourselves that provide for our inner subjectivity enable us metaphorically to leave or transcend the body. Optimally, this imaginative capacity, utilizing both the earliest gender-undifferentiated and gender-differentiated body ego representations, capacitates each biological sex to empathize with the other. These representations, I believe, exert a continual influence on our self/ other representations throughout development. I do not believe that the so-called higher functions such as rational thought supersede and eliminate our earlier capacities. For example, on a symbolic level, during the erotic intimacy of sexual intercourse the man possesses the woman's genitals and the woman possesses the man's genitals. As biological females or males, we can envision and articulate both our psychic male and female aspects. For Winnicott, this playing or shared playing is the basis for all meaningful experience. I am basically talking about using gender creatively like the dancer who uses gravity and space but is not tied to it. Whatever our biological sex, we can either comply, defy, or resonate with it.

Is women's inner space threatening to men?

Certainly, the fantasies of women's inner space are threatening to all of us—fantasies of oceanic bliss, death, and so on. Hindu goddesses, who represent the creativity from which all is generated, often look malevolent unless they are accompanied by a male consort. The feminine divinity is associated with destruction. Restraint occurs in conjugal union.

As a psychoanalytic feminist, do you see anything as valuable for women in traditional psychoanalysis?

What's so wonderful about the classical psychoanalytic treatment model, ideally, in its most original, radical conception, is its advocation of a nonauthoritarian and nonintrusive method. It can facilitate a true unfolding of the self. I am not talking about the particular theoretical ideas that concern the content of interpretation but about the form of the so-called analytic neutrality. The problem I have with some of the post-Freudian treatment models is what I see as a more phalliclike stance of the therapist who often inserts his own affective content into the patient. This does not allow for the development of an authentic inner space, whatever that might be for a particular patient. In the classical treatment model, the analyst registers feelings but is taught to contain the feelings within.

Now, one of the problems I struggle with in my own clinical practice has to do with my dual feminist and psychoanalytic orientation. That is, my feminist use of psychoanalytic theory and my psychoanalytic view of feminism are at times at odds with each other. For example, there are certain ways that a woman patient might articulate herself that I see as problematic for my political views. On the other hand, because of my political stance, I have been made more sensitive to material that I might not have seen.

I can give you a brief and therefore superficial example from both sides. I see some women who eventually seem to be extremely happy in their so-called supportive role in their husbands' lives. They seem extremely joyous in the sense of their maternal creativity, yet when they compare themselves to the ideal of the contemporary feminist they fail. On the other hand, I was seeing a very bright and successful woman who was feeling victimized by her husband's domination over her, particularly in financial matters. She walked into a session, owing me for two months of treatment and said, "Remind me to give you a check at the end of the session and, by the way, I don't remember how much I owe you." This could be read as an innocent remark, but it was extremely powerful in the context of her victimization. I pointed out to her that she was relying on me to take care of her financial responsibility and in doing so infantilized herself, making me the dominant authority over her. Well, she returned the next session and had begun to work out an equitable financial arrangement with her husband without the resistance she anticipated from him. So, at times, the feminist in me objects on some emotional level to what I see as the repetition of old gender roles and at other times, the analyst objects to blaming the oppressive husband. However, to look even more carefully, this is a false polarization. In fact, the supporting-role women were using themselves actively and creatively in what superficially looks like an old gender role, and my successful career woman was replaying an old dependency relationship with both her mother and father.

Muriel Dimen is a psychoanalyst in private practice in New York City and was formerly professor of anthropology at Lehman College, City University of New York. She received her Ph.D. in anthropology from Columbia University and her certificate in psychoanalysis from the New York University postdoctoral program in psychotherapy and psychoanalysis.

SELECTED BIBLIOGRAPHY

The Anthropological Imagination. New York: McGraw-Hill, 1977.
Surviving Sexual Contradictions: A Startling and Different Look at a Day in the Life of a Contemporary Professional Woman. New York: Macmillan, 1986.

EIGHTEEN

Muriel Dimen

New York, Winter 1986

Muriel Dimen lives and works in an old apartment house in Chelsea, an area of quiet charm and brownstone houses on tree-lined streets. We were greeted at the door by her eighteen-year-old cat in white fur boots. Guardian of the household, she scrutinized us from our heads down to our own boots and walked scornfully away. The three of us sat at a round table, a profusion of books, plants, papers around us, a computer at the side. The interview, which took place over cups of tea and cans of diet soda, was welcomed by Dimen as another means of exploration. She is always interested in process, in what Bakhtin calls *heteroglossia*—a term Dimen uses herself to describe her work; one senses a searching intelligence in constant quest for multiple truths.

At the end, we had the privilege of waking the cat, who had slept the entire time in the bedroom, where a display of earrings hung on one wall. We also entered the analytic enclave and admired the antique couch in this small but inviting space.

Why did you become a psychoanalyst?

The conditions under which I decided to become an analyst were dissatisfaction with my work as a teacher and satisfaction with the process in analysis. I started analysis in 1968, and it was a revelation to me. There were two major epiphanies in my adult life. One was the revelation of social science, which could make sense of the outer world. Psychoanalysis was the revelation that there was an inner world.

I was really disliking the conditions under which I was teaching. Something about it made me very uncomfortable and I was ready for something else. The only way I can understand what I dislike is this: when you're doing therapy or analysis, anything that happens is relevant to what you're talking about, to what you're doing there. When you're teaching, that's not the case. If I'm talking about matrilineal kinship, and the students are reading newspapers in the back of the room, or falling asleep or failing, I can't integrate that into the lecture. That's the only way I know how to put what's wrong. It's this disjunction in teaching between what you're doing and what you're saying. And when doing analysis, there's no problem of that sort. I feel integrated when I'm doing analysis and disintegrated when I'm teaching. I always felt that I had to leave a part of myself on the doorstep. When I went into the classroom, I always felt that I was aware of my skin whereas in doing analysis I'm not aware of that.

Do you have an explanation as to why most of your patients are women?

In addition to being responsible for all the emotional housework, women then do develop emotional difficulties that need to be taken care of. We could argue that the typical personality style required by capitalism is an obsessional one, a restrained and managerial style, but there is something wrong with that; it's a version of the paranoid and that in itself is a disorder. Given that, and given the expectations of women, women develop problems in terms of making choices about what they want to do. What I am really talking about is the theory that if you have a sick society you're going to have sick people. And if there are sicker parts of the society than others, then people who are in those parts are going to be sicker. That's another reason that women make up the bulk of people's practices.

When I say "sick" I'm not saying it in a pejorative way. I'm saying it for shock value. But one of the reasons I use the word "patient" rather than "client" is that I think the term "client" makes therapy a product that can be bought. And to say "patient" says that something is wrong. And that's true. We can't deny that.

You obviously are comfortable with the term *feminism*. In France, we found a lot of people who are not. They feel it's just another -*ism,* another way of controlling women within a patriarchal society. Do you have thoughts on the matter?
Certainly we can see from the way that society co-opts feminist issues that it becomes another -ism. Feminism becomes just another of many interest groups. It's ranked along with various rights groups and labor unions and petroleum interests and so on. It's no longer the radical challenge that it was initially, in 1965, in 1970. But even the success of such books as *The Dialectic of Sex* and *Sexual Politics,* which had a radical content, makes you wonder about what was happening even at that time, in terms of the normalization of feminism.

Black people objected later that women, especially white, middle-class women, were the beneficiaries of the civil rights movement, that the culture was only too glad to take up the cause of the frustrated middle-class housewife—of a deradicalized feminism—and forget that of the oppressed black people.

Then, too, feminism develops its own forms, its own political correctness, which then becomes a force for conformity among women. It develops its own normality and therefore it creates its own taboos.

But the reason feminism *is* radical is that it's about who woman is, what her identity is; her identity isn't contingent on being connected to a man. This is the most radical challenge. She is a separate being. She defines herself, which puts her outside of man and, I think, politically, it also puts her outside the state. The attempt of the state is to dominate us, to get us to comply and to sign over our rights to define ourselves. And, in that way, I think that feminism is in fact a tremendous challenge.

Feminism is part of the extrication of the individual from the family. This extrication is double-edged because, on the one hand, there's a tremendous amount of freedom, and on the other hand, you're completely exposed. You don't have anything to protect you.

What would a truly feminist psychoanalysis be like?

There's a problem in the term *feminist psychoanalysis*. What's feminist heart surgery? On the one hand, feminist surgery, feminist medicine might be something in which the total context of illness is taken into account; that is, the feminist physician might include as part of her or his practice, the goal of making economic life less stressful so people would have fewer heart attacks.

On the other hand, I don't know that that's feminist, particularly. Certainly women's role is to think about connections, to think about context, to be holistic, so you might say that's feminist; but there are also other social movements that have that kind of philosophy.

In terms of the question about what is different in feminist psychoanalysis, certainly, the object-relations theorists and the self psychologists are talking in a way that, as Jessica Benjamin has said, represents a convergence with feminist thinking. The emphasis these days is on the analyst being empathic with the patient. The work of Kohut is most explicit about it among Americans. Then the object-relations theory in England, with its emphasis on what is going on in the quality of relatedness between the patient and the analyst is something that you could say has been influenced by feminism. You might even say it is feminist. On the other hand, it's also true that it was generated from within psychoanalysis as well.

Well then, has psychoanalysis affected feminism?

I think that the influence on feminism is easier to see than the other direction. That influence has given rise to what we might call psychoanalytic feminism, which is a term I'm far more comfortable with [than feminist psychoanalysis]. Psychoanalytic feminism, I think, had two sources. One is from feminism and one is from women's experiences. Feminists are now impatient with leftist theories that were used to try to explain the position of women. And that impatience is with the economism of leftist theories, the reduction of all experience to material conditions, to put it very simply.

Now, the reason that those kinds of theories don't work, in general, is that the lives we lead are not simply epiphenomena of the system of production; in particular, with regard to women, the theories don't work, and feminism grew impatient because women in our society share symbolic space with sexuality and subjectivity. This is something I'm quoting from Joan Cox. And in consequence, subjectivity, the intrapsychic, the unconscious, the nonmaterial symbolic become part of our experience and relevant to ourselves in our definition of who we are, and become inextricably part of our role and our activities in society.

If you have theories that are economistic and reductionistic, you can't explain what women do, and you can't explain what women's experience is. And you also eliminate what can be seen from the vantage point of women. Sexism is simultaneously an ideological/psychological system and a political/economic system. Because of the symbolic place that women occupy, it's crucial in the case of women and in the case of feminism to take care of that fact, because women's work is often psychological work.

There's a particular lack in the economistic theories having to do with personalized subjectivity, interpersonal relations, women's emotional housekeeping. And I think that psychoanalysis was there as a theory that could be used to begin to explain some of these things. At the same time, a lot of feminists were in therapy. In terms of their actual experience, psychoanalysis was having a very important influence on them; certainly it was for me. I started in 1968 and it wasn't easy actually to start in analysis at that time because there was a lot of ideological criticism. But in my personal life, I just built a little wall, and I kept doing feminist activity and kept doing my analysis because I knew I needed this kind of investigation. And I always felt—and I've said this in print—that what I got out of analysis would have been impossible had I not been a feminist activist, had I not been in CR [consciousness-raising] groups and reading and thinking about it, that the two mutually complemented each other. I think that many roads led to where I am. Psychoanalysis, when one is an analysis, does not take place in a vacuum. You always have another life that you're leading, and there are many things that help as well as hinder what's going on in the analytic process. And it may very well be that other kinds of things are productive for analysis.

I could see that from the patriarchal point of view, you might say that analysis is the only way. "There's only one route and you must listen to me because I'm God the Father," if you want to use that kind of language. "I know the answer, I have the Word." And I don't know if it's feminist or if it's anarchist, but from a political perspective I know there is no *the Word*. There are multiple words. In the opening scene of my book, the woman's walking down the street and then you have all the voices that go on in her head, all her responses to the street hassler. Someone said to me of that scene that what was interesting to her was the heteroglossia.

She meant that there is no single subject, but many glosses, many voices. That may be a feminist take on it. For me, there are many routes and analysis is not the only one. One doesn't have to preserve analysis as the orthodox, the one way to get better. Furthermore, one's improvement doesn't happen only in the session. One lives, one creates, one makes history in a sense, and you bring it back to the session and then you name it. You have put yourself forward by doing it, by acting, and then you talk about it, and that takes you forward, wherever you want to go, in another way. Perhaps that is feminist. It doesn't work just by going in there and talking about it.

Who would you say have been the biggest influences on you?

Winnicott comes to mind as most important and it probably has to do with the way he writes. He writes with this correctness and force, a simplicity; it's very powerful what he says. And what he writes about is very grounded in what's happening in a session. Maybe that's feminist also in terms of being connected with the immediacy of the experience.

What I was thinking about this morning is who is in a position to break new ground. Are we in the best position to break new ground as women who don't adopt the "traditional perspectives" because we are on a totally other territory? On the other hand, if we're on totally other territory, what we're doing is not going to be recognized by those in the traditional mainstream.

Now, you could say that we are using Harold Bloom's model of creative misreading. My analyst used to talk about the creative misreading by junior analysts of senior analysts of the previous generation. That's how change takes place and new ideas develop, and Bloom puts it in the context of the Oedipal struggle.

But women analysts are not in a position to engage in the same way in that particular Oedipal struggle. So, we are on other ground. What women do on totally other ground is to come up with something that seems weird, but, in retrospect, might be truly radical.

Does there have to be an Oedipal struggle for women who are arriving at new ideas? Maybe they don't go through the same rebellion that Bloom sees. Perhaps the influence is different between mother and daughter.

The idea which you suggest, that the influence on women might be from mother to daughter, actually scares me. Maybe this is the reason I didn't go to a female analyst. First of all, there are problems of differentiation and separation, but the problem of going beyond your mother seems to me the most dreadfully painful problem. We have the myth of Oedipus which will help the little boys, but to go beyond your mother, to be disloyal to her, to be stronger than her, to be better than her, the hurt that you would be inflicting seems so enormous.

There is no doubt in my mind that one of the most powerful things in the relationship between mother and daughter is the mother's envy of the daughter, and not only because she's more attractive and can get to Daddy, although perhaps that's at the root of it. Certainly in a society like ours where there have been greater and greater possibilities for each succeeding generation, including for women—though it's a little closing down now in a general way for the society—the sense of loss and anger that the mother must feel for the daughter is enormous. The daughter to the degree that she is entangled with her mother and loves her won't want to go beyond that.

Isn't it worse if she goes beyond her father? It's interesting to see the pattern of the famous father who encourages the daughter, who then has the freedom to go ahead and gain her own identity. You have a Freud, and then you have Anna Freud. But wouldn't the pain be even greater to go beyond the father?

That would be the terror of stepping outside and being alone, but I think that the sorrow in the daughter going beyond the mother is greater.

The mother's body is different for the male child and the female child. What effect on their later artistic creativity does this have? You work with artists. How do you see the differences, if you see differences, in relation to the pre-Oedipal mother?

I don't know if I can answer the question about art, but in terms of males and females on the issues of pre-Oedipal and Oedipal, in the session, what I find with women patients is that pre-Oedipal issues are in the foreground much more. With male patients, what I find is that it is simultaneously Oedipal and pre-Oedipal, that you're dealing with both.

In working with male patients, we have layers of Oedipal and pre-Oedipal material in the transference, and they come up in the same session. It's not as though you were working with the patient longitudinally and first you would deal with the pre-Oedipal and then with the Oedipal. At any moment, the two periods of time, the two clusters of problems come up, and they

can be expressed in the same language or at least in relation to the
same conscious difficulties.

**When you say that men very often bring up Oedipal and
pre-Oedipal material at the same time, doesn't this perhaps
suggest that men can fuse different areas of experiences,
different stages of development, better than women can?**

I think that these things are fused because of patriarchy, and the
reason that they are fused is because of men's relationship to
women. When the little boy turns away from his mother because
Mother belongs to Father, he does so on the promise that he's
going to get another one. If he becomes a heterosexual adult man,
he's supposed to get her again in whatever form, at many times.
Being a heterosexual adult male means that Oedipal and pre-
Oedipal are fused. He sexualizes the early mother. When he's got
a woman, he's got Mommy. That would be a social explanation
for why that is so.

**In a nonpatriarchal society, would the ideal situation for
women be one of bisexuality?**

What I think, in fact, is that it has been. Women, in many
cultures, have a subculture with other women. Women together
have many social institutions. In some societies it's the women in
the extended family: the in-laws, the mother-in-law, the daugh-
ter-in-law. And in other societies, it's all the married women of
the community belonging together. In still other societies, for
example among some American Indians, women have official
groups like quilting gatherings, which give mutual aid and which
serve to bring the women together.

The significance of this was brought home to me when I was
doing my field work in Greece, and I realized the way in which
women really help each other out even in the cities. I went once
to a party in the city and most of the men were in one room and
most of the women were in another. And these women whom I
did not know were sitting on a couch together, all bunched
together, and they invited me to sit with them. They put their
arms around me, they patted me. It was very comfortable, it was

very soothing. The same thing happened to me when I was on a very brief visit to Senegal, in West Africa. While the men were conducting their ceremony, the women were all sitting in a room together, and a couple of them were sitting on beds and chairs, and everybody was comfortable and cozy. It is a very sensual experience and makes you feel very good.

And this is in answer to the question about bisexuality. I think that in many cultures women have had a lot of affective as well as instrumental connection with each other which has been provided institutionally, and some of this may have been sexual, erotic, genital as well. I don't know. In urban American culture, with expansion, women didn't have that experience. They didn't have the kind of social institutions that permitted it. Feminism, I think, recreates the social institutions in mass twentieth-century society. It gives the legitimation for women to get some of the benefits of being with each other, some kind of mutuality as well as erotic experience.

Now, this is a very great advance, but in terms of our earlier question, it is a way in which feminism becomes co-opted as another institution in the society rather than something that's really radical.

What would be best is multisexuality, that we go wherever our proclivities take us, but in terms of institutions, like marriage, I think your question was provoked by the question of what happens with men and heterosexual marriage. Men get a woman who unconsciously to them is a mother. What do heterosexual women get? We get a man whom we ask to be a mother, and he tries to be like one.

But the question you're asking about bisexuality also has to do with the question of social institutions. If we should be bisexual, should we have some social institutions besides marriage?

There are certain questions about women that traditional psychoanalysis has ignored, such as menstruation, which you write about, defloration—we hate that term, but what are we going to substitute?—menopause. Now, conceivably, a feminist psychoanalysis would treat those subjects

and certainly feminist analysts must deal with them in their practice.

Let me take defloration, because that struck me the most. There are two ways to think about it. One is as part of the life cycle and another is as the question of "loss of virginity" and what that is. Now, if you're doing traditional analysis and you're a man and you're thinking about a male as the patient, what is the significance of loss of virginity? It is a big moment. Father takes son to the whorehouse and son loses his virginity, or he goes with the boys to prostitutes, just taking the old model. And it has this ritualistic, bodily aspect to it.

If you're thinking about a woman as your patient and the social significance of loss of virginity for women, then it seems to me, loss of virginity would certainly bring up issues of separation, issues of competition with Mother, the beginning of sexual activity, possibility of reproduction, becoming the mother, becoming your own mother, replacing your mother, doing her job better than she could. Loss of virginity is a very different issue for women than men, at least because of how experience is socially organized.

A century ago to deflower a virgin was to become her master, to possess. And it was also mystification of the experience.

Freud writes about this and says this initiation ensures that the woman will be tied to the man because she's had an experience nobody else can give her. So why are men running away from that today?

Because they don't feel like masters. In terms of the version of the father's power, they feel like they're not that kind of man. That's too intimidating a position for them to appropriate.

What about the biological effect? For some women, there is very little change in the body, for the hymen may have already been broken and there may be very little blood if any, while for others, there is much more significance.

The notion of the difference between a virgin and nonvirgin may not accord with experience. Little girls put their hands in their vaginas; some girls lose their hymens, either from masturbation or from riding horses, being tumbled, whatever. Sexual experience is a continuum and little children have sexual experiences with themselves or with other people.

My proclivity is to ask: what is the significance of the biological effect? I don't know how we start in the middle of biology. Questions about biology always have to do with the meaningfulness of biology. What you were implying, I think, is that the biological changes in women are much more visible than those in men: menstruation, defloration, the loss of menstruation with menopause. Therefore in analysis that starts from the position of women, from where women are, we'd have to take those into account.

On the other hand, there is nothing more visible than a man's erection, which is not taken into account by traditional analysis. It's the phallus, always the erect penis that's really assumed in traditional analysis. But Monique Schneider has developed a theory about the phallus being a sign of power whereas the penis is connected with the biological, where it loses all organization. In the sexual act, erection is problematic. The penis is vulnerable, only sometimes performing, while the phallus always performs.

The theory is one great wish fulfillment, that it always be erect, performing, and in charge.

And yet there have been men who have recognized the vulnerability. St. Augustine said it was the punishment for the fall that men would no longer be in charge of the penis, that it would have an independent will. So the phallocentric theory is a great fantasy.

You could look at it that way. There's never a moment of weakness. There's never a moment of neediness, there's never a moment of loss of control. It's like the image of the infant who's been scared and gets picked up by his mother and then is totally triumphant, having forgotten about the moment of being scared to death until he was picked up.

So the phallus then takes the place of that early mother. But you said earlier that men no longer want to be masters. Does this mean we are on the road to equality? Or does this mean that men want to be slaves now in relationships? Is there going to be a reversal of male/female patterns?

I was just thinking today that I really do believe that history is on our side and that we are progressing toward equality, and I mean, equality for everybody, in terms of classes as well as men and women. But it's not going to happen in our generation. On the other hand, that men want to be slaves, well, it might be that there's more permission to experience the wish to be subordinate, or to be dominated. I don't know how to perceive it. It's very confusing right now.

Why do you think there is such an emphasis on intimacy today? Is there a history to intimacy? Will it die?

How we actually got there concerns the state making people lonely. I can't say the power structure creates the longing for intimacy, but it makes use of and generates the cultural idea of intimacy, so that when you're stripped away from your family, and you're pared down, just you, the individual, I think there's going to be something compensatory.

Now I'm not sure that in other cultures you have the notion of intimacy that we have as the ideal mode of living for adults. Asking whether something like intimacy and the longings that it satisfies are cross-cultural always brings up the question of whether there are in all human beings and "human nature," longings for recognition and mutuality.

Some of these longings may in other cultures be met by institutions, friendship institutions. I think psychoanalysis may have a role to play in creating the idea of intimacy, of two adults being together and recognizing each other and sharing this very deep and cultivated experience of subjectivity.

I don't think the analytic setting provides intimacy, but it may have something to do with creating the wish and the social institution of intimacy, because it's true that the analyst doesn't share himself or herself in the same way that the patient does, and you are not as available to the patient as you are asking the patient to be to you. You're not vulnerable in the same kinds of ways. And also, the possibility of intimacy is limited by the frame of time and money. But sometimes I feel that it creates a wish for intimacy, certainly in the patient, and the expectation that this moment of sharing and recognition can be recreated with another person outside there, if only you could get the right person. And one of the problems is that this wish may often be created by male analysts in female patients. I think some of those guys really help you to create this utopian illusion of adult intimacy, and they do it in a way that's self-indulgent on their part.

I think that's very interesting, as if the whole mythology of romantic love is being kept alive by traditional analysts. There is this pedestal of intimacy here that's unreachable. And I was thinking before, as you were talking, that there's something sick about this notion of intimacy, as if it's taking the place of nineteenth-century nostalgia, except that now it's a nostalgia for the future, if you can term it that. And I think that's the essence of romantic love. The mere fact that there is the prohibition of a sexual relationship between patient and analyst puts that analyst into the position of object on the pedestal, the unreachable, and so anyone else has to be an approximation, can't be as good. It's trying to get Daddy again, the second time. But notions of intimacy may be different with female analyst and female heterosexual patient.

The sexual orientation may influence the hopes for intimacy or what is generated. It may be different with a lesbian analyst and lesbian patients, heterosexual analyst and lesbian patients, any of those permutations.

How did you decide to write your book *Surviving Sexual Contradictions?*

What it seemed to me that I could do in this work was to address both questions that have been bothering me all my life, and problems concerning feminism and the left. How do you answer the economistic arguments, which have a great force? How do you say that our theories must take into account the psychological, the unconscious, the symbolic, without going over to the idealist? How do we get beyond the silly conflict between the materialist and the idealist? And I thought, here's the way to do that. Here's a book that represents personal, ordinary, daily life experience, experience in which these divisions have no place; they're foolish. This is an experience that will refute the idea of single-cause explanations, that refutes reductionism.

So here I have a form interweaving a first-person narrative of a day in a woman's life with a psychoanalytic and social commentary on that day which challenges that, and then I have a form which enabled me to talk about the results of the challenge. Again, this form relates to what I was saying before about sexism being an ideological/psychological system and the political/economic system. It's simultaneously those two. And this form allows me to talk about both the social and psychological in the same breath. It permits me to put the theories together in any way I want to. I don't have to conform, and I don't have to give my reasons for it. One of the things I don't do, in most of the text, is discuss the intellectual heritage. I don't give a history of ideas. I don't say someone said this and someone said that. And I think that freed me.

We were going to ask you if the analytic part which follows the narrative, the experience, would have been different if you had been writing this book for a strictly academic audience. You're saying it's more what you wanted to do.

It was. But then I realized that in fact doing that freed me from the conventions. And in freeing me from the conventions, it freed me from the hold of ideas because the formal conventions give to ideas their dichotomization. The things you are allowed to say, the things you are not allowed to say, those I think are all part of the same roots as the formality.

Is this an example of *écriture féminine?*

I don't know. Of course, I have my uneasiness about calling something "feminine" because I think it recreates the traditional.

The French don't distinguish between feminine and female. That's what gets them into some difficulties for us, because when they use the term *féminine*, it sounds like the old, traditional sense of being feminine, but that's not what they mean.

Well, I would think that *féminine* means *other*. It's in the sense of otherness, female experience.

When they speak about literature, they are speaking about very original writing, which you cannot classify, which associates the feminine with more unity, with something you could not express before, and with being more affected by the cycles of the body.

I think I have in fact converged with some of those writers who are describing themselves as practicing *écriture féminine*. From a totally different position I have come to it. In fact, what excites me is to think that I have done that. On the other hand, because I'm an anthropologist, I'm critical of ideas such as saying, I write under the influence of the cycles of the body, or that it comes more from the body.

Somehow the way they put it, it's as though they're saying the body is outside culture and therefore completely original whereas for me, even the notion of saying we write from the body is a cultural notion. I think that kind of analysis suffers the same flaw, from the same causes, as the Lacanian notion of the phallus as being transcultural, as being in the unconscious prior to culture. It's the same flaw of universalizing something that is in fact a cultural phenomenon.

To say that we write from the body is original in the sense that it is coming from the terrain of the other. I think that *l'écriture féminine* is taking women's experience as culturally constructed very radically and is following its implications to this extreme conclusion. But that is not women's experience as a biological being because woman as a biological being is always constructed on cultural ground. I'm saying that none of us can get outside that. There's no place to stand outside that. Whenever we think we are, we are standing within. The culture has cleared a new ground in a way; there's some other way of talking. But we can never step outside it.

Now, this is an extreme point of view from an anthropologist, but I really believe in that, and I think it's very dangerous not to say that because when we do, we begin to think that we have the answer, which is what I think a lot of Lacanians do. They have God's truth on their side.

It may be that an alternative symbolic system isn't going to work either. Again, it's a fantasy.

It's not that it is a fantasy; it is real and it's extremely important, but its reality is that it's not the final or underlying truth. It's never outside itself.

It seems to us that you have gotten beyond binary opposition and that in contrast to that polarization of subjects and objects, your book seems to assume a third party, the integrator, and we were wondering if you agree with that.

I'm interested to hear what you have to say about that.

Well, the reader in effect becomes the integrator, who combines the subjective experience and the analysis and puts them together because there is no way that a writer can do that. A book is not a musical composition, where you can have several instruments playing at once or several themes sounding at once. You have to present words in a linear fashion. And then it's up to the reader to fuse together the parts.

It's very exciting for me to hear that because I think my work isn't complete until somebody reads it. I don't know what it's like to be the reader who hasn't written; that's a completely different experience from mine. And it's important to me to know what that effect is. There is an unknown for me in that, so that the third voice might be the reader's, although the third voice isn't the final voice. When you're reading it, there is something going on in your head that's integrating it, pulling it together, and then something is going to happen from your experience. If it has been effective, then it will affect something that you'll write, or a conversation that you have or something that you do and then that's a fourth voice, if you want to put it that way, or something else has been created. And that, if you will, is feminist. The notion of that ongoingness, the sense that this is not my final product, you do something with it and you share that with someone else, and the drawing-on effect is unbroken. Yes, there is this book, this product, but this book is part of an ongoing project.

Perhaps this is the difference between Harold Bloom's theory of misreading and Oedipal rebellion and feminist writing. Maybe feminist empowerment means that you think in terms of what this book will enable us to do; you don't expect others to fight against it. What your writing can do is to achieve this positive interrelatedness that you have just been describing. Maybe that's the feminist quality.

On the other hand, I would be critical of that because I'm a little bit suspicious of it in myself—

Is it too "goodie goodie"?

Yes. And relating to what I was saying before, about the pain of going beyond the mother, I sometimes think that my feminism is a little bit, yes, goodie goodie. Oh yes, I want all women to have a really good time and to have a lot of power, and that might be just a reaction formation to the rage, the desire to kill her and stand on her body and take my Daddy, or maybe stand on *his* body. I think feminism, American feminism or European feminism, may be influenced by all of that niceness of CR groups and listening to each other and everybody having their say and so on, while we may want to kill each other.

True. Well, that's democratic equality.

Yes. That's right. And along with that argument, in my saying that the reader is the third party and there's a dialogue going on, maybe I'm trying to prevent somebody from really taking issue. But I don't think I am. I am just not mentioning the possibility of someone really taking issue. And I am also not standing up and saying, "This is different, you sons of bitches, I know how to do it. You don't know what you're doing and these are the reasons."

You know that's one of the conventions. My predecessors were wrong. I'm right.

Well, I have not chosen that way and I am not comfortable with it and I just think I am not good at it, but on the one hand there's something progressive about that and on the other hand there may be something that I am fleeing from, the competitiveness of that model or the aggression that's in that model, and so I take my swipes in another way. And I do. You know, if you read the book in an informed way, you can see what I'm doing but I'll not say that I'm doing it. How do you have an honest argument without wanting to murder somebody? If you have a real difference of opinion or real disagreement in a society based on cutthroat competition and based on power hierarchies, can you have a disagreement without wanting to murder? Does assertion have to turn to aggression? To destructiveness?

I think that's the cultural construction of aggression in our society, that anything that has to do with assertiveness, with difference, with differentiation, is transformed into destructiveness.

But it's also because we assume that all difference implies inequality, that there is no difference without a hierarchy in our conception, difference meaning one's better, one's stronger, one's bigger than the other. And if we can get away from that, and I don't know if we can, then we might be able to have a difference of opinion without the murderous impulse.

That's what I write about in the last part, the conclusion of the book. I suppose the question is then what does happen to murderous impulses? They're murdered. I don't want to sanitize the psyche and say that those are all social creations. In other societies, the murderous impulses are often exorcised by ritual.

Is the psychoanalytic process the new ritual which prevents us from—

—acting out our murderous impulses?

Particularly against the State?

Certainly that could be, although I also believe it's liberating. In fact, psychoanalysis was liberating for me, as I said before, in conjunction with feminism.

What do you see as necessary for the true—whatever that means—liberation of women?

Sexual freedom, the difference being difference and not power hierarchy.

How are we ever going to get to that point?

I don't know.

Why do you think that so many people in this country want to get rid of the notion of gender whereas in France most theorists we spoke to said you cannot get rid of gender. If you do, you are going to have psychosis.

What I think is that there is a fusion of the notion of gender and the difference between genders and the difference between self and other. What leads to psychosis is the confusion of the difference of self and other. That is to say, that there is no other; there is no recognition of the other's otherness.

In psychoanalytic theory, the inability to differentiate, let us say, male from female, is read as inability to differentiate between self and others. And I suppose in the culture as a whole, if psychoanalysis would represent cultural thought, that differentiation between self and other is coded as the differentiation between male and female and not recognizing the difference between male and female, and I suppose therefore the right of Daddy to Mommy becomes the nonrecognition of the difference between self and other.

If you could have self and other as categories which were not gendered, then I think there would be no problem in getting rid of gender, but as long as gender is the means by which we differentiate self and other, then, of course, it would be dangerous to get rid of it.

Why is it that the French are so much more resistant? Do they see something we don't see? Or are you saying that their concept is somewhat different?

What you're asking me is a different question. Why are they more resistant? Well, they may be more steeped in psychoanalytic theory than the rest of us. They really do believe the theory. For them the theory is the accurate description of what basic human nature is. They believe it; they don't have a stance outside it. Americans may not have studied it that carefully, but there also has been American brashness of not necessarily believing the orthodoxy. I think that if you don't take the theory as a description of what must be, if you take the theory as a cultural construction of human nature, then you can say, well, maybe human nature isn't one in which gender is necessarily oppositional between male and female. Maybe human nature is something else. Maybe gender could be multiple. Maybe the critical difference is not between male and female, either in society or in the psyche, but between self and other. What we do in our culture is to collapse that difference between self and other and between male and female. We fuse the categories.

Maybe if we think of the categories as being separate, gender is one issue, self-other is another issue. As long as the person recognizes the difference between self and other, then you don't have psychosis. Maybe there doesn't have to be that cardinal differentiation between male and female, either in psyche or in culture. And the reason that I can say that, and maybe Kristeva and Chasseguet-Smirgel can't say it, is that they believe that psychoanalytic theory is a true description of human nature. And I am saying that any theory we have is a cultural description. It's not necessarily the truth. We don't, in fact, see through to the background. I think that one of the weirdest things about Lacanian theory is that on the one hand it seems to be giving recognition to the cultural fact of things, and on the other, it takes itself as the arbiter. It takes itself as the voice of truth, saying there is no subject speaking outside of language. Well, if that's true, then the very person saying that is speaking within language, but I think they fall into that trap. They are not speaking outside of language either.

So everything that they're saying, everything that's in Freudian classical theory, in the Lacanian corpus, is within culture. If you recognize that, then you don't have to believe that what it's saying is God's truth, or biological truth. There are some other possibilities. That would be the answer to why they are so worried about the elimination of gender.

Diana Trilling, distinguished literary and social critic, was fiction editor of *The Nation* from 1941–1949. A recipient of a Guggenheim Award and Rockefeller and National Endowment for the Humanities grants, Mrs. Trilling is also a fellow of the American Academy of Arts and Sciences. In addition to authoring the books listed below, she is editor of the twelve-volume *Uniform Edition of the Works of Lionel Trilling,* her late husband.

SELECTED BIBLIOGRAPHY

The Viking Portable D.H. Lawrence. New York: Viking, 1947.
Claremont Essays. New York: Harcourt Brace and World, 1964.
We Must March My Darlings. New York: Harcourt Brace Jovanovich, 1977.
Reviewing the Forties. New York: Harcourt Brace Jovanovich, 1978.
Mrs. Harris: The Death of the Scarsdale Diet Doctor. New York: Harcourt Brace Jovanovich, 1981.

NINETEEN

Diana Trilling

New York, Spring 1987

Diana Trilling lives in a comfortable apartment house near Columbia University. The windows of her spacious living room
overlook a quiet street, which gave the name to her best-known
volume of essays. Everything seemed to be in readiness for this
interview. As we sank into comfortable arm chairs, we felt immersed in a universe of disciplined freedom and order. All was
arranged with charm, taste, and discretion. We were taken by
Mrs. Trilling's aliveness, vivacity, and humor—her discussion of
the most serious matters is punctuated with laughter—and the
incisive way in which she connects matters of the intellect with
the experience of life. The orderly writing desk, in the middle of

the living room, though in no way obtrusive, seemed to beckon her back to work.

We wanted to ask you if you consider yourself a feminist.

Not in the sense, I think, in which the word is used by the people in the women's liberation movement. In a more old-fashioned sense, yes. I think that the present-day investigations of psychological parity between the sexes are in essence very important, but I have been alienated by the sexual hostility with which they have been charged. I don't like the sexual competitiveness; I don't think that the war between the sexes needs encouragement, so I prefer to stay with the old-fashioned public problems that still need attention: the problems of equal rights for women, equal opportunity, equal pay, that sort of thing. I don't like the relation of the sexes as it is defined by women's liberation.

How would you describe that relation?

Well, it seems to me that women's liberation expects that it can legislate the emotional relations of men and women, and I don't believe that can be done. The emotional relations of the sexes will of course change according to all sorts of things that are going on in a culture, including the way that women are treated in the marketplace or the way they are treated legally, but for a movement to try to govern or direct the personal relations of the sexes is a very destructive thing, because our emotional relations whether within the same sex or between the sexes are very delicate. They have to be achieved by individuals in terms of their own needs and their imagination of the needs of others.

Do you think that psychoanalysis has changed the emotional relationship between the sexes?

It's an interesting question. I really don't know what psychoanalysis is doing today but I do know that in some degree it is having to be responsive to changes in the situation of women. No psychoanalysts today could possibly say what an analyst said to me twenty-five or thirty years ago. I'm talking about a very gifted woman analyst and a wonderful person, Dr. Marianne Kris. I was complaining about my husband not doing the few things he was supposed to do around the house; or not that he didn't do them but that he did them carelessly or tried to put them off—and one of my examples was that he forgot to put out the garbage at night; I always had to keep reminding him. Dr. Kris interrupted me and said, "That's not what a man is supposed to do. That's the work of the woman." Even at that time I was upset that she could say a thing like that, but I was also worried that perhaps I was asking more of my husband than I should. You must remember that I was in a very positive transference relation to her and that she was affirming the attitudes of my upbringing—my father never did anything around the house except turn the garden hose on the dog on hot summer evenings. I very much doubt that any analyst would speak that way to a woman today.

What's interesting is that Margaret Mead used to say that taking out the garbage was men's work, the reason being that you have to go outside, and anything on the outside is men's work.

What about city people who live in apartment houses? I live in an apartment house: outside is outside the back door. Or if you're fortunate enough to live in a house with an incinerator, outside is down the hall. Mead's formulation has some point to it, but it's too narrow and has undesirable implications. Isn't she suggesting that not only heavy but uncomfortable work should be done by men and that women are too delicate for the unpleasant tasks? What about farm wives: are they not supposed to go to the barn? But you know, I myself still have ideas like that, and I certainly had them when I was younger. I often find myself thinking that something is man's work or something is woman's work. Yet in my marriage I also had a contradictory desire, to spare my husband anything that might be heavy or disagreeable for him. I remember doing things that were really quite crazy, like wanting to carry a suitcase instead of letting him carry it. When we were first married we had a Hardman & Peck baby grand piano. It was very small, but it was not something you pick up in one hand. Yet several times, when it had to be lifted to straighten the rug, I tried to put my own shoulders under it. Obviously I couldn't budge it but that was my impulse—I didn't want my husband to get a hernia; I'd have preferred getting it myself.

This has reference to what I was saying earlier about sexual competitiveness. I don't like even the competitiveness of the marketplace but surely it has no place in the home. For me, it is more important to protect another person or be concerned for the welfare of another person, especially someone you love, than to be concerned for your own welfare. All my close women friends feel that way: their first concern is their husbands, or their husbands and children. That is another view entirely, as you can see, from saying, "I'll do this and you'll do that; we'll draw up a contract so that everything is shared fairly." I guess that to a certain degree I'm in favor of being unfair to myself—so long as my husband is similarly impelled to be unfair to himself. There may be some basic masochism in this attitude but that doesn't particularly bother me. It doesn't have to be excessive. In my marriage I made it plain from the start that if my husband took advantage of my willingness to do the housework I would respond to it very badly indeed. I was willing to make the beds because I did it better than he did and because I wanted to free him as much as possible, but if he assumed that I did it because it was my job as a woman, I'd stop at once.

In a way, you may have partly answered one of our questions which is, do you think that gender should be eliminated? Should the roles that have traditionally been played by men and women be ended and arrangements worked out in individual cases whereby the people who do things best do them, regardless of sex?

Yes, I do think that. Margaret Mead proposed that idea in her book *Male and Female.* If the male does better embroidery than the woman, then he should be allowed to embroider and if the woman is a better harvester of the crops, she should harvest the crops. But you know, that's very theoretical. It really doesn't carry us very far into the problem of the relation of the sexes because the fact is that the culture is always operative in our lives and the assumptions of large numbers of people are operative. If the culture assumes that the person who is doing the embroidery is doing something female, that is going to be thought a female occupation and perhaps inferior for that reason. Mead herself said that there was no society that had ever been studied that didn't regard the work done by its men as the superior work: if the women do the fighting and hunting and the men take care of the children, the care of children is the superior activity of that society. If that's accurate, it's quite a stopper. What does it say to us?

That's our question to you.

I suppose it's saying something about biology and the importance of erections. Women in all societies instinctively know that there's a connection between the value men put on themselves and their ability to have erections. The sexual pleasure of women depends on the way men feel about themselves.

So the state of erection is a very vulnerable one?

Very vulnerable. Do you think I am being too simple? If what Mead reports as an anthropologist is true, that every known culture believes that the work done by its men is superior work, there must be some biological reason why men have always to be made to feel superior. And what is the biological distinction other than that?

Well, there's one other distinction that some people have grasped at, and that is the relationship to the mother, the fact that the male child has a different body from the mother's and therefore is more threatened by the mother's body than is the little girl who, after all, will grow up to be a mother herself in most instances.

Threatened by the woman's body? I'm afraid I don't understand that.

Well, the relationship to the mother, the all-powerful mother of one's infancy, seems to be more threatening for the male child than the female child who, after all, can become a mother herself. Because the little boy, the infant, is in a position of vulnerability to the mother, one might argue that the male always has the desire to do to her what she did

to him, that is, to assert the power over the woman that he felt was asserted over him as a child.

What is the source of that feeling of vulnerability in the little male in relation to the mother?

The penis.

In what way? What is going to happen to his penis?

The little boy fears that his penis will not be of sufficient size to satisfy the mother—

Do you mean the actual Oedipal fantasy of replacing the father and the little boy's fear that he can't do it adequately?

Yes. In a sense, I'm now agreeing with your theory that it is the need for erection that would cause the male desire to be superior in every sphere of life and to create institutions to fulfill that desire.

Well, I don't think that's implausible if you accept, as I do, the notion of the Oedipal relation.

What about the pre-Oedipal relationship? In the pre-Oedipal relationship the little boy may identify with the mother and think of himself as female.

And lost in the mother's personality. That would be a menace. The pre-Oedipal state almost seems to be a more fertile field of exploration here than the Oedipal.

So, men are afraid of women, right?

There's certainly no question about that! Their pre-Oedipal condition might even explain the preference of men for the company of other men. You might suppose that men would prefer the society of women because it reproduced the situation in which they were cared for by the nurturing mother. But that's rarely the case. Perhaps men prefer the company of other men because that's the company of the superior sex. And nobody's going to hurt them.

What are men afraid of in women?

I find myself troubled by generalizing or by talking, as it were, theoretically. If you don't mind, I'll try to answer you more personally: just my private opinions.

Most people are afraid of *not* generalizing.
In my experience what men are afraid of in women is that the women may be smarter than they. They're not only worried about intelligence, they're worried about any manifestation of superiority. Yet this isn't the way that they usually feel about other men. Most men are very respectful of other members of their own sex, very delicate and even deferential in their dealings with them. It's very rare that a man, even a very nice man, is intellectually deferential to a woman, and I think that's because it represents a threat to his masculinity. What it comes down to is that any challenge of a man's superiority by a woman is a challenge to his sexual superiority and thus to the reliability of his sexual performance.

Are you saying then that men cannot really perform with any reliability unless women are always in awe of them the way the cichlid fish has to have the female fish in awe, supposedly? Aren't you implying then that there really is no chance for equality of the sexes?
I really don't think there is. I look around at some of the young married couples I know and what I see is a kind of reversal of sexual roles, but I don't know what happens in the bedroom with these young people.

They do have children.
They manage, yes. But it's something I wonder about.

Perhaps they don't feel it's necessary to have that feeling of male dominance.
Perhaps. When I was doing those interviews at Radcliffe in 1971, I discovered to my amazement that the young men and women frequently went to bed together without having intercourse. They would just lie next to each other; there wasn't even a sheet between them—I asked about this in some detail. Well, to me this

was unimaginable. But they seemed to think it was rather obscene of me to be so surprised.

Did that come from a surfeit of sex? Were they getting enough sex from other sources?

No, I don't think so.

You've indicated that you see the relationship between the sexes changing today. In what ways do you think it's changing for the worse? Where do you think it's changing for the better?

Well, I certainly don't see any virtue in women getting into what we always so contemptuously called the rat race: going to business school, getting into corporate law and management, going down to Wall Street intent on earning their first million before they're thirty and their second million before they're thirty-one. I must know a half dozen charming and intelligent young women who work sixteen hours a day, doing the very things that we used to worry about men doing in our culture. Have they really achieved some goal that has been denied them? Is this what liberation means, being free to be slaves to money making? They're achieving the goal of parity, that's sure, but on the worst possible basis. And they're helping to destroy the values they once undertook to preserve against the money-making values.

Women used to marry money. Now that's no longer considered admirable. Well, what should women want?

Are you asking me that old question of Freud's: what do women want? I hate that question of his; how he asked it. Why didn't he ask, what do *people* want? Of course, he would have said he knew what men wanted: they wanted a life in culture. But isn't that precisely what women want, too, but have been denied? Isn't that what feminism is properly about: the right of women to have an equal claim with men on a life in culture? Once that right has been established, we then confront the question of what the culture should be. That is a question apart from gender.

But isn't there a contradiction between that and what you just said a moment ago, about young women today want-

ing to be in the rat race and do the things that we used to
deplore when men did them? Was that what Freud was
talking about when he spoke of man's life in culture?

No, Freud didn't quite mean that, did he? I think he meant the
life that establishes our assumptions, our ideals, our contribution
to the future and our link with the past. I suppose that to some
extent the life of business must be included in that too. But we
make distinctions between a worthy life in culture and a nonwor-
thy life in culture. I think that, yes, women have just as much
right as men to live an unworthy life. But it should not be
thought a triumph.

Well, there is a form of feminism, sometimes called cultural
feminism, that very much deplores this entrance into the
rat race. It transvaluates the traditional feelings and activities of women and says that they are better than those of
men—for example, embroidery and quilt making are better than making money. And there is another form of feminism that says, let's forget about this dualism altogether.
Men shouldn't enter the rat race and neither should women;
there should be some kind of attempt to transcend the usual
values and rid ourselves of the polarization of the sexes, to
look at what's best in the traditional behavior of both men
and women and try to make a fusion of the two.

This is ideally to be desired. If you think of women as creating a
haven of peace in the home, it's a very pleasant idea and I can't
see why any woman shouldn't love it. Except that if a woman
has imagination and talent, the creation of a home may not be a
sufficient occupation for her life. Take two different types of
female mind, Jane Austen's and George Eliot's. Both had the ideal
of serenity and domestic peace and respected a woman's contribution to its creation. Yet suppose they had been restricted only
to that? Eliot had to publish under a male name. Surely that's not
very desirable.

You see, I really have rather unpleasant thoughts about some
aspects of this subject. I don't think that most things that most
people do have to be done. An awful lot of disagreeable things

have to be done to make it possible for the things that are worthwhile to be done, but I don't think that what most women are
doing now is any better than what their grandmothers were doing
—or as good. They put themselves to all sorts of arduous activities that really don't add up to enough to warrant the amount of
anxiety that went into their accomplishment and the hard work
that's involved in sustaining it. Do these women get more gratification out of their lives than their grandmothers did? I just don't
know. I hate this kind of discussion really because everything
carries within it its own contradiction. Everything. My mother
and my mother-in-law used to say how lucky I was to be of my
generation and able to do things outside the sphere of domestic-
ity, and certainly if anybody denied me the right to my career as
they were denied the right to careers I'd be pretty miserable,
especially now that I'm alone and of my age. I can't imagine how
I'd sustain life at my age without work. So who am I to say that
women should not be able to do any kind of work that they want
to do? Who am I to bring in the criterion of worthiness: it's all
right for them to be writers but they shouldn't be on Wall Street?
That's absurd and presumptuous. Still, it seems to me that there's
something very wonderful about just sitting and knitting or doing
the family mending in front of the fireplace. But not in front of
the television set. So you see, what I'm talking about is another
time and culture, isn't it? A world of fireplaces, not of television
sets.

What was it like being part of a writing couple?

That is very complicated indeed. It was very nice—and I'll go on
from there. What you must ask me is, "Suppose I had been the
more successful writer, what would it have been like to be part of
a writing couple?" That's the bottom-line question. My husband
was the more distinguished, he was the more celebrated, the more
looked up to of the pair of us, and it was very nice that he could
respect what I did and think that I was quite good. I was no
challenge to him. But had I been, would he have been this supportive of me? It's easy to be gracious when you are in that
position, isn't it? And then there's the question of whether I did
the best and most of which I was capable or whether consciously

or unconsciously I held back because I was a woman and, as a woman, wanted to be in my husband's shadow. After all, everybody comments on how much more work I've done since Lionel died than I did before. Of course, that's partly explained by the fact that since he died there's nothing else to do. But I doubt that that's the whole story.

Lionel felt that I was very much underappreciated as a writer because I was his wife. I think that's true—people don't like the idea of two writers in the same family. When I began to write, our friends didn't want me to use my married name. They thought I ought to write under my maiden name. It was Lionel who wanted me to write under his name.

Why did he want that?

He said that was the name I was known by socially and he saw no reason to change it. He also was sure that I would write well and he would be proud of me. I think he was right in feeling that the suggestion that I use my maiden name derived from our friends' fear that I would detract from his reputation. He had more confidence in me—

And in him?

And in himself. But he would say, "It's not only that you use my name as a writer but we're such a *couple*. Who else in the writing community is such a couple? Does Mary McCarthy have a husband in tow to whom she defers? Hannah Arendt has her husband tied to a bedpost—no one ever sees him."

What about the Sartre-Beauvoir relationship? Of course they weren't married.

The most interesting thing in that relationship is the deference in her connection with Sartre. I was listening to a documentary about her on television the other night, an interview. She was incredibly stupid, especially about politics. Very glib, very sure of herself and of her position in the history of modern French culture, but so far as politics are concerned really a simpleton. Sartre was of course little better. But whenever his name was mentioned a new note of respect entered her remarks. I don't mean piously but quite unself-consciously. I was quite struck by it. When she spoke of him she spoke as an old-fashioned wife would speak. I don't know how well served she was in her personal life by their not being married, but in her public life she was very well served indeed. The official aspect of marriage does matter.

Would you say something more about that, about the official aspect of marriage?

The marriage ceremony is a way of announcing that you are entering adult society and accepting its duties and responsibilities. It is a social contract and you have to suffer the social consequences. That's entirely different from living together as lovers.

Is the fact that so many young people choose not to marry a sign that they refuse responsibility? Does it indicate a greater narcissim? Are we living in a more narcissistic age?

I have no question in my mind about that. We live in an extremely narcissistic age.

What has caused it? Has psychoanalysis contributed to it?

I think psychoanalysis has contributed to it but perhaps not as psychoanalysis really is or should be but as it has been misinterpreted. But it's not alone as a contributing cause; there are many other factors. The fact that the world has become increasingly difficult to understand and control makes for greater withdrawal into one's own self and into the family group. And within the family group there is therefore more sheltering against the world than there used to be.

But wouldn't that strengthen marriage?

I think it very much strengthens marriage. Where marriage exists with any seriousness among the young, it's very strong.

And it's coming back stronger.

Exactly. For instance, the young think we were a terrible generation because we were able even to contemplate the possibility of being unfaithful to each other in marriage. They're shocked that we even formulated the possibility.

What is the place of infidelity in marriage?
Well, I'm talking as an old lady so I have all kinds of freedom. I think that monogamy is against nature; I've always thought that. On the other hand, unfaithfulness is also in its own way against nature, jealousy being a part of nature. Sexual possessiveness is a strong force in nature and if you're indiscreet and your infidelity becomes known to your spouse, it gives great pain, enough to destroy the marriage. It therefore has to be handled with the greatest caution or perhaps even resisted, refused. But certainly, if not refused, then infidelity must be handled with the greatest discretion. Is that possible? Rarely, so there's a great deal of frustration in most marriages. People of course have different needs and also exist on different levels of self-awareness. Many people find it difficult even to admit that their minds stray. Do you remember that famous interview with poor Jimmy Carter in which he finally admitted that he had had lust in his heart? A religious man, but honest to the end, he had to pull this out of himself.

What do you think of the reaction to Gary Hart?* How do you explain what happened?
Oh, that's something else.

Would you speak about it?
I'm outraged by the hypocrisy of the newspapers in pretending to be the guardians of our morals when all they really care about is selling more papers. Even if they were guarding our morals, who are they, the journalists, to decide what is or isn't a proper mode of conduct? Or a proper mode of politics, for that matter? The authority of journalists in the present-day world is one of the most frightening things we have to cope with. They're worse

*Gary Hart, former U.S. democratic senator, temporarily withdrew from the presidential race in the spring of 1987 after disclosures on his personal life by the press.

than ministers with the right they take to themselves to shape our opinions and our morality. But the story of Gary Hart is something else again, quite independent of the press—I'd like to write about him, if I could find a place to do it briefly. The important point about Hart is that he was brought up in the Nazarene church, a very fundamentalist sect, and that he was not only raised in this faith but intended for its ministry. He preached in the Nazarene church when he was only an adolescent. Then he rebelled against his repressive upbringing, and how did he express this rebellion except through sex: it's the most ready means by which people of rebellious spirit break with the conventions in which they were reared. But his rebellion was only conscious. Unconsciously he was apparently still bound by his rearing; he was in great emotional conflict. So he told the reporters to tail him when he was with a woman who wasn't his wife. In other words, he wanted to be caught and punished for violating the precepts of his rearing. People talk about his self-destructiveness. I don't think he is motivated by simple self-destructiveness but by the need to be caught in his sins and punished for them. That's moving and sad but it's also a pretty dangerous pattern of behavior in someone who seeks the office of president of the United States. Ought the voters to know about it? Indeed yes, because heaven knows what else he might be led to do in self-punishment. In other words, the newspapers did us a service but not one for which they deserve much credit, because this wasn't their purpose in spying on Hart and even today they don't understand what really was going on. No one seems to understand that. We weren't at risk from his adultery, we've had many adulterous presidents, only from his unconscious need to put himself in jeopardy and then be caught and punished for it.

You're speaking of the vindication of one's early upbringing. Now assume that this is going to be the case for many, many people, not just Gary Hart. Women in general have been brought up not to enter the public world, certainly not to enter as political figures. What's going to happen when they do enter in increasing numbers? Is that early upbringing, that repressed aspect of the self, going to return

in ways that we are not sure of? That's one question. And second, is the entrance of women into public life, such as it has been, or specifically into political life, going to be a kind of taking over of the father's role and thus bad for children? This is related to the question of whether we can eliminate gender. Should women enter into political life? What will be the consequences? Will their early conditioning return to haunt them in ways that may be self-destructive?

Well, let's take that last part first. I think there's a generational confusion there, because if they had come out of my generation, they might indeed be likely to get into trouble. Perhaps even coming out of your generation, there could be trouble. But if you're thinking about younger people, they've already been conditioned differently. The cultural revolution of the sixties is almost twenty-five years old. We've already trained a new generation which won't be carrying the same burdens of the past.

But that answers only one part of your question. About women entering politics: the political past of course belongs to men. I've been watching the television programs on the writing of the Constitution: one is reminded that there wasn't a woman at the Constitutional Convention; there's no female signatory to the American Constitution. Politics belonged wholly to men. I nevertheless believe that you can eliminate gender in politics better than you can eliminate it in the sphere of family relations or emotional relations. We've seen that with Indira Ghandi and now with Mrs. Thatcher. Politics is a sphere in which women can function very well.

If men would let them.

I don't think that Mrs. Thatcher is being worried about as a woman, is she?

You haven't been watching English television.

No, I haven't been back in England for some years.

They show her in the satires with a man's chest, all hairy—

Do they really? I didn't know that.

They're pretty bad on Reagan too.

I suppose they've mocked their male opponents by putting them in panties, making pantywaists of them. No, I don't think we have particularly to worry about women in politics the way we do about men and women in their domestic relations. I'm worried about things that I haven't mentioned, such as the fact that we are making any deference to the needs of another human being somehow represent a lack of proper regard for oneself. We're beginning to act as if concern for other individuals or yielding to their preferences is a kind of weakness.

We're not supposed to want to please.

That's right. And if you take away these things from people, life becomes really awful.

It takes away the grace. You were speaking earlier about Marianne Kris and psychoanalysis. I wonder if you would talk about the experience of being in analysis with a woman. Did you ever have experience of a male analyst?

Yes, I had both.

Does the gender of your analyst make a difference?

Well, I was very reluctant to be analyzed by a woman.

Why?

I'd tell you if I knew but I really don't know why. It was very interesting. The person I was consulting—a male analyst—about whom I should go to had a list of people and when I went down the list and came to a woman's name I said, "I don't want a woman." He said, "Why? Is it so much worse to be seduced by a woman than by a man?" I didn't know a thing about analysis at that time. Looking back on it, I think this was an outrageous thing to say to someone in that situation. What it did to me was to make me defensive so I said, "Very well, I'll go to a woman."

Will you tell us who this was who was advising you?

Dr. Bertram Lewin. He was a very distinguished analyst, a president of the Psychoanalytic Institute.

What he said sounds like a typical male joke, the kind of thing my chairman would say, a little sexual innuendo.

My choice of that particular female analyst was disastrous. But if you don't mind I'd rather not dwell on that here—I'm writing about it in my book.

So you are not sure why you didn't want to go to a woman analyst?

To this day I'm not. But I think it was because I supposed that men have better trained minds than women. I still harbor that prejudice, I'm ashamed to admit. I didn't want to go to a woman doctor in any department, it wasn't just analysis. Today I still have some resistance to women doctors, except not to women analysts; I retain some reserve or worry. It's my age and upbringing.

Why do you think that women analysts are sometimes better? Some people say it has to do with women's training in nurturing.

There isn't any nurturing involved in psychoanalysis, or there shouldn't be. But I really don't want to go too much into this here. I'm seriously critical of psychoanalytical practice on the ground that it is directive when it has no right to be. It is always protesting that it doesn't interfere in people's lives, but it does interfere in people's lives. Analysts allow themselves to be parental advisers when they have no right to give the least bit of advice. A psychoanalyst is no more qualified to advise you in your life than Dan Rather is to advise you in your political choices; perhaps even less. The analyst has a technique by which to draw out the meanings of free associations and dreams in order to bring the patient's unconscious motivations under conscious control. If he would stay with that technique he would not be open to the criticism that I am making.

And besides what you just said, what else do you see as the limitations of psychoanalysis?

You mustn't treat what I just said so lightly. It's a very serious criticism I'm making. By and large, analysis as it is practiced even by members of the New York Psychoanalytic Institute is a distinctly other thing than analysis as I think it should be practiced. You can't be better trained than you are at the Institute. You're kept at it for years and years and you're supervised and controlled and watched over. But that doesn't remedy the situation of which I'm speaking.

Why do you think it took this direction? Is it a new religion?

I've known people who use it as if it were. I've heard of someone whose analyst performed his burial service. For many people the analyst has become the sacred authority in our culture.

The new priests.

I haven't yet heard of them performing marriage services. Of course, patients themselves ask for this kind of treatment. People want actually to be guided and counseled. They want their analysts to function as parents, only wiser and more benevolent than their own parents were. You constantly hear people speak of what their analysts said about this or that as if this were the ultimate certified truth. But what difference does it make what the analyst says, other than as it bears on the unconscious life of the patient? If Gary Hart were in analysis, what would be important would be the uncovering of his *motive* in involving himself in adulterous situations and then getting himself caught. Who cares about the analyst's view of adultery in itself? That's simply another individual opinion.

Do you see other limitations of psychoanalysis? Do you think it has harmed the culture?

Oh my, has it harmed the culture!

How?

One of its most harmful consequences has been to make parents afraid of their children, afraid to exercise the ordinary authority and responsibility of parenthood for fear their children won't love them. There have been many recent efforts to counteract this fear but I don't know how successful they have been. It originally derived, I think, from a misunderstanding of Freud, but in the general culture the idea still prevails that neurosis is simply the result of failed love on the part of parents or of repressive parental authority and that therefore the thing to do is to give a child love unbounded by rules. The analytic profession has a great deal to answer for in not having undertaken to deal more energetically with this grave misunderstanding of Freudian doctrine. They've allowed all kinds of wrong ideas to be disseminated in the culture. You may have seen a review I wrote recently in the *New York Times* of a book about Marilyn Monroe, in which I tried to deal with the failure of the analysts to acquaint the public with the fact that there are many different kinds of emotional disorder and that analysis is practicable in very few of them. Many people cannot be analyzed and there are many mental illnesses that are not available to analysis. Marilyn Monroe couldn't be analyzed for her personality disorder. She was a patient of Dr. Kris but she was in supportive therapy, not in analysis. No one instructs the public in these important distinctions. People think every kind of therapy is analysis.

Isn't this one of the reasons, though, why so-called psycho-analysis has taken a more directive approach? If somebody like Marilyn Monroe is not able to be helped by analysis, wouldn't any doctor she went to want to help her in any way possible, including being directive?

Absolutely. But that's supportive therapy; as I say, that's not analysis. Of course, you may be implying, and properly, that what we are now more and more confronted with in the clinic are personality disorders that are not suitable for analysis, rather than the old-fashioned hysterical neurosis for which psychoanalysis was created. They invite interference in the life of the patient.

We brought up the question of the difference between being analyzed by a man or a woman, but we didn't pursue it. Could we talk about it now?

Well, I've had quite a few analysts—three of them died while I was in treatment, one after the other. Two of my doctors were women, the rest were men. I don't think I can talk usefully about the gender difference because in all my years of treatment I don't think I ever had what I would consider a truly proper analysis. I now think I know what an analysis should be, but this is after a long lifetime of pondering the matter. I didn't have it. I'm not saying that I didn't have great analytic help. Certainly I did. But it was in large part incidental. Or in some part, it was the result of my own ability to use analytical method once I had caught on to what it was or should be. I regret this very much and I think it's going to make shocking news in my book. So it's very hard for me to answer your question about male and female analysts. I wasn't properly analyzed by anybody, so how can I speak usefully about the differences between being in treatment with a man or a woman? By the way, I don't think I know anybody who has had a truly serious orthodox analysis. I don't think it's practiced. It wasn't practiced by Freud.

That's for sure. From the questions we have asked analysts, it would seem that most of their patients are women. Why do you think that is?

Is that so? I didn't know that. Well, it's easier, I suppose, for women to admit that they need help than it is for men. Also, women have the time more easily available, or they did until recently. I never realized that there were more women in analysis than men because in my experience it was the opposite. I've known more men in analysis than women. Among the literary people I know that's surely the case.

I'm not sure we're using the term *analysis* very strictly. We may be talking about women in therapy, and if you're talking about strict analysis that involves three or four times a week—

Five times a week—

I would agree that there are probably more men in that. Do you think that feminism has influenced psychoanalysis?

I think that people feel more suspicious of psychoanalysis since feminism and that they don't look to it as they once did. They mistrust Freud, for one thing. Feminism attacked Freud, legitimately. After all, Freud did think of women as second-class citizens. I think feminism has reduced the attraction of analysis for women.

There is an attempt now to see the importance of psycho-analysis for women and to try to fuse feminism and psycho-analysis. In fact, there's a current of thought that's called psychoanalytic feminism. We would like to speak about a feminist psychoanalysis, but that's a little different and a little harder. But a number of people now are talking about psychoanalytic feminism because they feel that social the-ory alone, economistic theory, does not really explain the position of women sufficiently, and so there are feminist critics who are turning to psychoanalysis in combination with social theory to try to explain why women are where they are.

Yes, of course. That's the nature of our discussion today, isn't it? I was talking about feminism in psychoanalytic terms when I spoke of the biological problems in the relation of the sexes. I meant the psychobiological problems.

But when you said you weren't a feminist when it comes to psychological parity, doesn't that suggest keeping psycho-analysis out of the realm of changing the relationship of the sexes?

No, no. Psychoanalytic theory can help us to understand the relation of the sexes but analysis in practice hasn't anything to do with changing the relations. We come back to the strict limita-tions I put on the psychoanalytical therapy. Psychoanalysis may have something to do with changing the way a particular patient feels about herself as a woman in relation to men or the way that a man feels about himself in relation to women, but to come to the treatment of a patient with either a feminist or antifeminist bias is completely unacceptable. I don't think that it has anything to do with the proper practice of psychoanalysis. Now if you're talking about psychoanalytically derived or related therapies, it's a different thing. But then I think most such therapies are illegiti-mate.

You are against therapy in general?

Well, let's put it this way: I'd be against any therapy that undertook to tell somebody how to act as a woman in society. That's not the function of treatment.

So you would say that terms such as "feminist psychoanalysis" are a total misnomer—

Not a misnomer—

A contradiction—

No, not a contradiction. Invalid. I don't understand therapy in that way at all. Therapy is an attempt to reduce the conflicts within the individual psyche and it must proceed, so far as this is humanly possible, without preconception of how the individual is to come out. It has the specific purpose of bringing into consciousness the conflicts of which the patient is unconscious. Then it is up to the patient to decide how he or she wants to live in the world. Show the patient where his or her conflicts lie and bring them under the management of the ego. When they are in the realm of consciousness, the work of the therapist is finished. The patient's own ego is in charge.

It's value-free?

Absolutely.

You really think it can be?

Of course not but—

But insofar as possible, it should aim at being value-free.

It's as ridiculous to say that analysis can finally be value-free as to say that it can be class-free. It's obviously based in traditional society and in the middle class. How can it not be? I attack analysts with their class location but they just get mad at me; they don't want to deal with these problems. But look, would they accept anybody in the Psychoanalytic Institute who never bathed or shaved or who went around with his pants torn and filthy? I'm not saying they should, I'm just pointing out the values that they take for granted. They're middle-class values. Are you worried?

I'm always worried. Not properly analyzed. But there's one more question I want to ask about psychoanalysis before I go back to the writer. Maybe this is outside psychoanalysis but I want to ask whether you think analysis is a science.

Of course it's not; it can't pretend to be. Poor Freud, there he was a neurologist in late nineteenth-century Vienna, with science the big thing; he had to find some kind of scientific shelter for his wicked new ideas. But analysis doesn't at all meet the requirements of science and for anybody to try to persuade us that it does is very foolish. Why does it have to be a science?

Is it an art?

No. Just—

It's a phallus.

No, not a phallus. It's an exercise. For some people it's an ideology but it's not that either, or shouldn't be. By the way, if we're talking about feminism, one of the reasons that I resist calling myself a feminist is that it inducts, invites, seduces me into ideology, and that's something I want always to stay away from. Many of your questions about psychoanalysis and its relation to feminism indicate that feminism has the force of an ideology for you.

I'm using the term *feminism* chiefly as an abbreviation. What would you suggest in its place?

Isn't it better simply to talk about the role of women?

Or the condition of women? The position of women?

There's such a thing as the human condition and there's such a thing as the female condition.

Sometimes they go together.

They go together when we allow them to. You see, anything that reduces our humanity is bad. Anything that extends our humanity is good.

But there are many people who would argue that feminism extends the humanity not only of women but of men.

And they may be right; it takes time to know. But in the meanwhile the less ideological it is, the more good it does. Ideology is absolute and constricting.

We've met considerable resistance even to the term "feminism" among the people we've spoken to. It often rouses negative associations.

I don't know. I'd rather call myself a feminist than liberated.

What's wrong with *liberation?* It's another bugaboo term.

For me, it's unacceptable only by its association with the leaders of the movement. I mean, how can I associate myself even remotely with a movement one of whose outstanding leaders, Gloria Steinem, said that it didn't matter whether or not Ginny Foat was guilty of murder, given her socially useful years in the movement. This is a very extreme position to be led to by one's concern for the mistreatment of one's sex: anything goes so long as you're a team player!

Probably any liberation movement is going to be guilty of that kind of extremity.

Because they're making a revolution?

Yes, when you make a revolution—

—you scramble eggs. I know.

So let's go back to the subject of writing. How does the culture view the woman writer today? Or don't you think that it looks at writers and asks any question that has to do with gender? Are we no longer looking at a writer and saying, Oh, she's a woman and so we have certain expectations?

I think we still expect that a woman will write more delicately, more sensitively, more personally, more emotionally, more penetratingly than men, without so much intellectual force, without so much cogency of idea, without as much assertion of an overt kind. I think that that expectation in some way still exists.

Obviously you don't think that there is any truth to this?

I don't think there is any truth to it. I don't think that women are more gifted in insight than men; I don't think they are any more penetrating or more sensitive. I think that men are crazier than women. I've experienced much more obsessiveness in men than in women. Compared to men, women strike me as being reasonable creatures.

Is that psychological or biological?

I think it's psychobiological. It refers once more to those pre-Oedipal and Oedipal things that trouble boys so much more than girls. For whatever reason, girls deal with their Oedipal and pre-Oedipal situations, especially their Oedipal responses, better than boys do. Certainly they don't go around with those mad fantasies about men that men, intelligent men, seem to have about women. Men are absolutely weird about the things that women do which offend them. If you're traveling with a man in a car, you can't give him a direction without his taking it as an attack on his masculinity. I don't know any woman who would be offended by being told, turn here. But I know scarcely any man who wouldn't be offended by it. That's not sane. Men don't readily offer direction to other men either because of this masculine delicacy. It's crazy. I once drove eighty miles out of my way because the man who was driving didn't want to take direction from me. Take a novel like *Lolita*—that's a story of obsession. If there's enough talent, you can make a work of art out of male obsession. Proust is an even better example. But in terms of living with such people, it's impossible. They're mad.

I wonder if this is tied up with biology too—which brings me to a question on Lacan. According to Lacan and his followers, very often the well-groomed woman or the beautiful young girl is the phallus itself or symbolizes the phallus itself. Do you find any truth in this and do you think that women reify men in the same way?

I just don't know what Lacan means by that. In what way is the desirable woman symbolic of the phallus? I really don't follow that.

The always-erect penis. It took me a while before I was finally convinced that there was something to it, but now I am. And if it's the case, you can see why men don't want to be given direction by this creature. It would be another threat to the phallus.

Does it mean that there's another phallus that's more erect than theirs? Something like that?

It implies that the penis is not erect enough if the woman has to say something. Then the man is not perfect.

I just don't know how to think that way, so I can't comment. Even where I understand him I don't take Lacan seriously.

What about the new reproductive technologies? Have you any thoughts on the Mary Beth Whitehead case? What do you think of surrogate mothers? Specifically, what consequences do you think that there are for the woman who bears the child and for the child itself?

I have a very simple response to Mary Beth Whitehead: she made a contract and she should be held to it. I don't at all trust her sudden feelings of motherly need. She doesn't impress me as a reliable person. As for the general idea of these reproductive techniques, I find them appalling. I'm scared to death by them and they are among the developments in our society that make me glad I'm an old lady. I look with horror to a future of human engineering. We can scarcely manage the given of life without being asked to make choices of the sort that are forced on us by these techniques. My mind shuts down at the prospect. I say to myself, suppose I couldn't have had a child. Could I conceivably have hired someone else to bear a child for me? No, I could not. The world is full of babies who cry out for adoption. If you need a baby, take care of a baby who needs you.

We would like to ask you some questions about the older woman.

Well, that's at least something that I know more about.

Why is it that psychoanalysis has ignored menopause? Or should it perhaps be ignored? Another question is, how are we going to change the double standard in aging, is it possible to change it?

I'm outraged by the fact that men have the advantage that they have over women in terms of aging when they're so much more delicate in terms of the real biological process than we are. We're tough as hell compared to men, sexually.

So what are we going to do about it?

We're enduring creatures; they're very fragile sexual creatures.

Maybe that's what they are afraid of also.

But that's what they've got it set up for, all on their side. As I've said and written, a man can be held together with pieces of adhesive tape but his wife has only to die and women will want to marry him the next day.

Then it's women's fault.

It's women needing to have a man in our society. They don't feel complete without it.

What do they want? The penis?

It's such a nonperforming instrument, I don't know why they want it. But it gives them a better table in a restaurant.

That's true. Although the restaurant situation has improved.

Enormously. I get quite good tables nowadays.

You know, if the tables get too good, women won't be after men at all.

Maybe that's the answer: women have to deal with the *maître d's* of the world.

Do women like men?

It's a question. Do women like women?

I'm beginning to think that they like them more.

Do you think that women like women more than they do men? I'll now admit something I've never spoken about before: I've never had a visit just with a woman friend in which I've been entirely comfortable. So I'm a very odd character to approach with all these questions.

But you're comfortable with men.

Oh, yes. Now, is this my suppressed homosexuality? If so, it didn't come out in analysis. It should have got cured.

Would you say you're a male-identified woman, that awful term?

I don't know what that term means. Does it mean a woman who identifies with men?

That's right. What makes you uncomfortable with women?

I don't know. I don't feel that I can talk as truthfully with women as I can with men. I have to retract more of myself.

Are you afraid of hurting them? It has to do with the relationship with the mother.

Maybe. Of course, I don't feel that I talk very truthfully with men either. The only person I've ever talked really truthfully with was Lionel. I feel that I have to hold back.

Is it because you're smarter—

Fiercer.

Fiercer. I see.

It's very hard for me to handle something in myself—I don't know what it is; maybe it's aggression.

We have a question about desire. We were wondering what sexual desire is.

In old age or at any time?

It would be interesting if there are differences.
Look, it's a really extraordinary thing to live with sexual desire
past the age of its being accommodated.

**Which for the modern woman is age thirty. A lot of them
are celibate out there.**
I've heard that. It's not to be believed. But the fact is that I can't
even make a sexual joke anymore because of my age. It's thought
to be inappropriate; it makes people uncomfortable. People are
embarrassed if I make some kind of vivid sexual reference.

**What about men of your age? Are they permitted to speak
sexually?**
Not easily.

**What if they have a much younger woman at their side? Is
it acceptable then?**
That helps. You see, what I am talking about is the fact that a
whole part of my actuality, my reality, is denied me. It's somehow shameful that sexuality continues to exist right into one's
oldest old age. It's not even thought to be a proper subject of
conversation. How long society will hold this view, I don't know.
Remember that I'm old enough to recall that when Edward VIII
gave up the British throne for Mrs. Simpson, she was in her early
forties—forty-one, forty-two, something like that—and at that
time it was thought to be almost shameful for a man to desire a
woman that age. You wouldn't remember that there was a great
best-seller somewhere along in that period, *Life Begins at Forty,*
whose very title made it a revolutionary document. Life *begins* at
forty? Life was supposed to be over at forty. I remember a scene
with my mother when I was a very little girl and she was in her
mid-thirties—this was early in the century. We children were
playing in the snow with our sleds and she was dying to get on a
sled herself. She looked all around to be sure that the neighbors
weren't watching and then she let the maid quickly pull her
around the yard. Imagine being under that kind of constraint in

your mid-thirties! So maybe the things we've been talking about will change too.

You're a person of such intellectual courage, why do you find it difficult to talk about these matters? Or is it simply your sensitivity to what other people are thinking?

Obviously, I don't have the courage to lay myself open to mockery. Disagreement and challenge, yes, but not mockery. That's what I'm afraid of. I have friends my age but we don't talk about these things even with one another.

These are women friends?

I'm talking about women.

Maybe they're afraid of mockery too.

That's right. Even with close friends, other women, they don't want to be thought silly or inappropriate. We'll go so far, maybe, as to ask each other if what we are wearing is too young for our age—that degree of intimate talk is permitted to close women friends—but that's about as far as we go in acknowledging that this is a problem area, how to appear in the world at our age.

What about the new celibacy?

Of the young?

Studies have been done that indicate that an educated woman past the age of—one study says thirty-one, another says thirty-five—who isn't married has about as much chance of getting married as of being killed by a terrorist. In fact, I think the chances of being killed by a terrorist are greater. And never mind marriage, now, the fear of AIDS is introducing a new chastity.

It's of course also more of an inducement to marriage.

Talk about the sexual revolution. Some revolution!

At eighty—eighty-one, actually—I'm supposed to be preparing to die. That's what I'm supposed to be doing. That's what the culture expects me to be doing.

No. There are certain things our culture allows the older woman. I think it allows you to write.

It *allows* me to write. With amazement, it permits it. Sometimes I even have the sense that in permitting me still to write it is humoring me. The constant attitude is: "You're still writing? How extraordinary!" By the way, to return to the treatment of women in our society: I went to a new ophthalmologist the other day. Since he didn't know me and I thought it was important for him to be aware of my particular need for vision I told him that I was a writer. He didn't say anything at the moment but a little later he asked, "Do you write with another writer of the same name?" I said, "Do you mean, do I write with Lionel Trilling?" He said, "Yes." I said, "That was my husband," and I didn't go into it any further. Think of it! Do you write with another writer of the same name? If a man named Porter came in, would he say, "Do you write with a woman named Katherine Anne Porter?" Not for a minute!

The woman is the phallus of the man.

I have to think about that, I really don't understand it.

Index